Dance of the

Sleepwalkers

Dance of the Sleepwalkers:

The Dance Marathon Fad

Frank M. Calabria

Bowling Green Sate University Popular Press
Bowling Green, OH 43403

Popular Entertainment and Leisure Series
Ray B. Browne and Michael T. Marsden, General Editors

Copyright © 1993 by Bowling Green State University Popular Press

Library of Congress Catalogue Card No.: 92-73976

ISNB: 0-87972-569-9 Clothbound
       0-87972-570-2 Paperback

Cover design by Gary Dumm

To my wife

Angela

and children

Carl, Mark, Alissa, Mayela

Acknowledgments

Among those who have contributed guidance and encouragement for this study, I would single out one colleague and friend, Robert Browne, whose interdisciplinary bent in research informed the approach and scope of this study. George Eells, author and entertainment editor, gave me invaluable help in contacting informants and furnishing supplementary "insider" information related to dance endurance shows.

I owe a special debt to the following colleagues and friends who have been generous enough to have read my manuscript, in whole or in part, and offered insights and suggestions: Mary Lynn, Jill Sweet, Frank Gado, Robert Sharlet, Sharon Gmelch, Peter Heinegg, Linda Patrik, Malcolm Willison, Nancy Thornton, Renato Bobone and Rev. Charles Slap.

I drew heavily upon the resources of the Divisions of Dance, of Drama, and of Music, The New York Library of the Performing Arts, Lincoln Center. I would also like to acknowledge the assistance of the librarians of Union College ever willing to trace and obtain information through interlibrary loan.

I am grateful to Union College which supported this research through two research grants. Special thanks are due Janet Crosby, from Chartoff-Winkler Productions Ltd., for sending me numerous photos of dance endurance contests collected in preparation for making the film, *They Shoot Horses, Don't They?*
I am greatly indebted to Susan Schafarezek, who assisted me with the article, "The Dance Marathon Craze," which identified the key themes elaborated upon in this study. My deepest thanks go to Margaret Wadehra, Director of the Writing Center of Union College. Her careful reading of the text in its several revisions encouraged me to strive for clarity and directness in communication.

Grateful acknowledgment is given for permission to quote from the following:
"Dance Marathons 'For No Good Reason'," Carol Martin, *The Drama Review*, Vol. 31.1, 1987, MIT Press, 55 Haywood Street, Cambridge, MA 02142.

"Interview with Betty Herndon Meyer," "Interview with George Eells," and "Interview with Richard Elliot," Carol Martin, *New Observations*, 142 Green Street, New York, NY 10012.

"The Hollow Men," from *The Collected Poems of T.S. Eliot, 1909-1935*. Harcourt Brace & Col., 1250 Sixth Ave., Santiago, CA 92101.

"The Life of Joan Crawford," by Edward Field, published in *Mirror of Man: Readings in Sociology and Literature*. Ed. Jane Dabaghaian. Little Brown & Co., 34 Beacon St., Boston, MA 02128.

"The Bard in the Depression: Texas Style," D. Whisenhunt, *Journal of Popular Culture*, Bowling Green State University, Bowling Green, OH 43403.

Contents

Introduction

The 1920s conjure up vivid images: the Charleston, hot jazz bands, bootleg whiskey, the "flappers," Model T Fords, Al Capone, speakeasies and celebrities like Babe Ruth and Rudolf Valentino. An Age of play. During this era of boom and bust, Americans went on an emotional spree eagerly welcoming a rash of fads and crazes that included flag pole sitting and cross country bunion derbies. Among these fads and crazes, none was more fascinating or bizarre than marathon dancing.

Social psychologist Emory Bogardus, who made a study of fads over a 25-year period, found that most fads, such as Chinese checkers or party pajamas, had a life expectancy of less than one year. Although he lists marathon dancing among these prominent but superficial fads, the dance endurance contest lasted 30 years from 1923 to 1953 (307-308).

The dance marathons began as a craze but soon evolved into a money-making show business enterprise (Seltzer 220). As a commercial venture, couples—a male and female team—competed against other couples. Teams were required to remain in motion, on the dance floor, 45 minutes out of every hour, day and night. Additional physical demands were made upon contestants in the form of a variety of strenuous foot races. The team who lasted the longest won first prize, though there were many other ways of earning money during the course of the contest.

Some 20,000 contestants and supporting personnel directly participated in these sport/entertainment events. Brothers and sisters, fathers and daughters, mothers and sons, teenagers and near senior citizens competed. People from many walks of life, from East and West coasts, from various ethnic backgrounds including numerous American Indian couples all competed. Audiences, the majority women, totalled well into the millions (Eells 154).[1]

Though I grew up during the period when dance endurance contests played in locations not far from home, my first acquaintance with this sport/entertainment was seeing *Marathon '33*. This play describes June Havoc's experiences in a number of dance marathons; she was 14 years old when she entered her first contest. The full impact of the dance endurance contest came six years later, in December, 1969, when I saw the movie adaptation of McCoy's novel, *They Shoot Horses, Don't They?* This movie, faithful to McCoy's novel, depicts the dance marathon as an exploitative form of mass entertainment. The impact of this film upon me as well as on film critics and audiences was powerful.

1

2 Dance of the Sleepwalkers

I was fascinated by this movie and curious. I wondered what motivated American men and women to enter dance marathons and what appeal this entertainment had for audiences. How is it that this craze took hold in America and nowhere else and lasted three decades? Importantly, what does this unusual form of entertainment tell us about American culture during the 1920s and 1930s when the dance endurance contests were popular? In short, why dance marathons?

In gathering material for this study, I puzzled over what appeared to be a paradox. Dance marathons were in the American vein; they were obviously popular, having lasted some 30 years. Yet, this amusement also went against the American grain; there was an aura of something not quite right about it. Here are some facts.

By the mid-1930s, half the states of the Union were enforcing statutes against dance endurance contests, and many cities, in open states, barred dance marathons by local ordinances (Kaplan 27). George Eells, writer, entertainment editor and long-time student of dance endurance contests, found that publishers were loath to accept stories about dance endurance shows. American literary critics gave McCoy's novel, published in 1935, mixed reviews; one critic saw in McCoy's searing description of the dance marathons, shades of what Herman Melville once referred to as "the power of blackness in American culture." The screenrights to McCoy's novel, initially purchased by Charlie Chaplin, in 1936, changed hands 12 times before the movie was produced 33 years later (Pollack 133). June Havoc's play, backed by the prestigious American National Theatre Association, had a short run on Broadway. Finally, the notion that there was something not quite right about this form of amusement was confirmed when I learned that few, if any, dance endurance contests were run on the up and up.

Arnold Gingrich, in the first issue of *Esquire*, in 1933, after seeing his first dance marathon contest, referred to this exhibition as "The Poor Man's Night Club" (61). The dance endurance contest was the dog end of American show business, a bastard form of entertainment which borrowed from vaudeville, burlesque, night club acts and sport.

But Gingrich also coined a second metaphor for dance endurance shows: "The Innocent Jail." What may have prompted Gingrich's second figure of speech was the mode of operation of dance endurance shows: contestants were housed in one building for the duration of the show, which might last six weeks or many months. During this protracted period, couples were required to follow a strict regimen that seemed like serving a prison term. Nor was Gingrich alone in suggesting through imagery and metaphor that there was more to this form of amusement than appeared on the surface. Other literary allusions to dance endurance shows included "The Glory Walk," "The Palace of Wasted Footsteps," and ominously, "The Dance of Death." These images and their vivid associations, and the sensational publicity which dance endurance contests attracted, interested me as a psychologist, psychotherapist and long time teacher and student of social dance.

With the exception of the author's publication and that of Martin, the subject of the dance endurance contest has been largely neglected.[2] Historians and social critics of American popular culture have either dismissed the dance endurance contest as a lamentable expression of American mania during the turbulent 1920s or damned this form of entertainment as a dehumanizing spectacle accompanying the hard times of the Great Depression. Neither response begins to do justice to a singular form of show business which has a unique place in the annals of American entertainment, an amusement which has left an imprint on American consciousness to the present day.

I have approached the subject of the dance endurance craze from multiple points of view and have sought to integrate the insights of the social scientist with those of the literary and film artist and critic. Literary and cinematic descriptions of dance endurance contests have been interpreted from several perspectives of depth psychology in order to reveal the covert side of American culture projected through this form of amusement, those aspects which are frequently unacknowledged and often repressed.

Part I is a history of the dance endurance contest as it evolved from fad to show business. Part II describes how this show business operation was run. Part III reveals how walkathon shows were depicted in literary and cinematic documents and what meaning and significance can be given to these accounts when viewed through differing perspectives of psychological literary criticism. Part IV examines this expression of play as myth and symbol to further deepen and broaden our understanding of the dance endurance contest as popular amusement. Part V highlights persons and events which shaped the 1920s and 1930s and points up this important theme: that the dance marathons, though an aberration of play, were based on traits and values that were (and are) pervasive in American culture. Part VI suggests that the dance marathon contest as an expression of American sham was largely escapist entertainment, an amusement which reinforced the human predilection to sleepwalk, to live the life of the automaton, thereby restricting spontaneity and freedom.

This in-depth psychological study of the dance endurance contest, a quasi-legitimate show business enterprise and outlaw operation, illuminates what lies underground in dark corners of the American landscape where the collective shadow-side of the American psyche finds its covert habitation. My reason for telling this story of the dance endurance craze is contained in Jungian scholar James Hillman's view of history. Hillman writes: "In part, we turn to history, this depository of cultural memory, as a therapeutic exercise. We search for the myths within the facts, the archetypal patterns that can broaden and deepen connections in ourselves, offering our painfully raw experience a bed of culture" (xv).

Part I

I

✧

From Fad to Show Business

Chapter One
The Fad

The dancing pair that sought renown,
By holding out to tire each other down
Oliver Goldsmith, "The Deserted Village"

A cornucopia of fads may have prompted Westbrook Pegler to give the twenties the apt name, "The Era of Wonderful Nonsense." In the home, there were marathon hand-holding and husband-calling contests. Vincent Toro and Louise Heath were declared the winners of a kissing marathon, having held a kiss for 96 hours, 32 minutes, 3 seconds, allowing 5 minutes every hour for a break. Endurance competitions in milk drinking and meatball eating races were staged in the kitchen.

Outside the home, there were kite flying, chair rocking and flagpole sitting endurance competitions. In this latter event, Shipwreck Kelly once sat atop a flagpole of the Paramount Hotel in New York for 13 days, 13 hours and 13 minutes in zero-degree weather and sleeting rain (Sann, 42). One man even tried a stint at uninterrupted piano playing. On a grand scale, C.C. "Cash & Carry" Phyle, a business entrepreneur, promoted a Bunion Derby, a 3,400 mile cross-country foot race from Los Angeles to New York (Sann, 47-56). In the aftermath of World War I, Americans sought quick and easy release in mass culture amusements.

Given the enormous popularity of social dancing during the tens and twenties, it was not strange that endurance dancing would capture the interest of the American public. Russell Nye gives us a vivid account of the world of ballroom dancing during these years highlighting the importance of Vernon and Irene Castle, the innovative ballroom team, in stimulating a "dance craze" during the pre-War years (Erenberg 146-175). Abel Green and Joe Laurie, Jr., in their massive compilation of American entertainment, *Show Biz: From Vaude to Video*, report that, "By 1927, dance halls and ballrooms were doing an amazing business from coast to coast with a family-type trade content to sit at ringside seats and in balconies to watch exhibition dancing, novelty bands and other entertainment" (230).

The dance endurance fad actually made its first appearance in America before the twenties. Green and Laurie note that it was Sid Grauman, an enterprising showman, who staged the first dance marathon contest in America, in 1910. There were two events held two weeks apart, the second contest terminating on the recommendation of physicians after 15 hours of non-stop dancing (36).

But at the turn of the century, the efforts of dance hall operators to interest

5

the public in endurance dancing met with only limited success. Americans before World War I seemed more interested in innovative dances done with spontaneity rather than repetitive shuffling to establish an endurance mark. This spirit of innovation was present in the improvisational rendition of ragtime music, played by performers like King Oliver and Louie Armstrong, to the infectious movement of the Negro "ragged-time dance."

Ragtime music aroused hostile opposition in the early decades of the twentieth century, perhaps because of its direct appeal to the senses. As this music spread from the brothel and speakeasies in New Orleans to ballrooms and dance halls in Chicago and New York, it influenced the expression of social dancing. Booth Tarkington voiced the response of middle-class Americans to this influence by writing, "ragtime belonged to the underworld or where nature is extremely frank and rank" (Cable 341). Critics of marathon dancing voiced similar feelings once the fad took hold.

One reason why the dance endurance fad did take hold had to do with the popularity of social dancing, an activity for young and old. The growing acceptance of the cabaret as a place where patrons could more easily shed their inhibitions, vestiges of a bygone Victorian age, played an important role in the renaissance of public dancing during the years between 1912 and 1916 (Erenberg).

A more profound reason had to do with the climate of the times. The dance endurance fad took hold in the early twenties during a time when a sense of restless vitality permeated the air. It was as if viewing others in perpetual movement allowed spectators to vicariously release the collective anxieties and tensions of the turbulent decade following America's first global war (Merloo, 28).

Credit for initiating the dance endurance fad during the twenties goes not to an American but to two young dance teachers from Sunderland, England, Olie Finnerty and her partner, Edgar Van Ollefin, who set the original mark of seven hours, on February 18, 1923. Two months later, the announcement that Victor Hindmarch, a compatriot, had pushed the record for non-stop dancing to 25 hours was the stimulus which started a chain reaction in the United States.

The first American to respond to the challenge from England was Alma Cummings. This 32-year-old woman, a dance teacher at the Audubon Ballroom in New York City, exhausted a succession of six male partners, all younger than she, to remain in motion on the dance floor for 27 hours. The indefatigable Cummings ended this feat of endurance with a flourish by spinning to the middle of the floor in a whirlwind waltz to the cheers of several patrons who had stood vigil.

By her singular accomplishment Cummings had challenged three widely held myths of the day: the superiority of England, the primacy of youth, and the preeminence of male fortitude. A strict upbringing, first in a Roman Catholic convent and later in the Church of the Seventh Day Adventist, may have given her the fortitude to set an example which was soon followed by a parade of American zealots. This woman's triumph of body and spirit occurred in 1923 on April Fool's Day.

Meanwhile, in England, following a spate of dance endurance records, the Sunderland Magistrate emphatically refused to permit any more tests remarking, "It is an idiotic idea, verging on lunacy" (*N.Y. Times*, 11 April 1923, 3). In America, however, where novelty had an irresistible appeal, the idea caught on. Within a few weeks, the craze spread to big cities, from Philadelphia to Seattle, from Houston to Chicago. Contenders from a half dozen states eagerly vied to establish a new endurance record in dancing. These zealots set out to prove that what one American could do, another could do better, or at least longer.

The *New York Times*, on April 15, 1923, applauded the ambition of the brave and daring youngsters of the Empire State, alive with the spirit of civic pride, who were determined to regain the title set the previous day in Houston, Texas. Proud parents and boastful friends urged the contenders to do something that had not been done in the world before. Social clubs competed against local fraternities in this worthy endeavor.

In the light of continued supremacy by women, Russell Brady, an Irishman, set out to prove that any "real man" could defeat any woman in an endurance contest. The battle of the sexes fueled the fad. As an instance of male chauvinism, Brady's comment was an idle boast; female contestants had the greater stamina.

Melodrama, which was to become the staple ingredient of dance endurance events in the years ahead, made an early appearance in an incident which took place at the Audubon Ballroom less than a month after Alma Cummings had set the first American record. Eight young dancers, five men and three women, already in motion for 28 hours and 50 minutes, were alerted by the ballroom manager to an imminent police raid. The law enforcement officers, without having an exact precedent to guide them, were ready to invoke an old statute pertaining to six-day bicycle races which made it illegal for any contestant to continue in a race or contest longer than 12 hours during any 24-hour period.

The latest contenders for the marathon crown, with the help of parents and friends, planned an escape with all the earmarks of an episode from the current movie serial, *The Perils of Pauline*. At midnight, the eight contestants left the Audubon Ballroom and entered a large moving van which transported them to a dock in New York harbor. Still dancing, they moved out of the van onto a ferry which took them across the Hudson River to New Jersey where a second van awaited them.

The contestants continued shuffling their feet in the moving ballroom until they reached the Pekin Dance Hall in Fort Lee, New Jersey. When they arrived, the forewarned police forced the dancers to move on. A new destination was selected, East Port Chester, Connecticut. Here, the local police were somewhat more hospitable and allowed Vera Sheppard, the sole remaining contestant, to extend the record of 69 hours before they invoked a Sunday blue law.

The next day, Sheppard returned to the Aububon Ballroom, ten pounds lighter, having danced in three states, two dance halls and one private parlor, four times in a moving van and once in a ferry boat, to receive the news that her record had already been topped by a Cleveland girl, June Curry, who had lasted

90 hours and ten minutes (*Literary Digest* 44).

The editors of *The Literary Digest*, after listing the string of dance endurance records, compared this latest manifestation of American dementia to prisoners harnessed to a treadmill. At worst, the unfortunate victims of that punishment of earlier times had had to tread no more than six hours a day with intervals of rest. How was one to explain human beings in modern times voluntarily seeking punishment even harsher than the treadmill? Without finding a satisfactory explanation, the editors concluded: "They certainly earn their grotesque glory and the small purse that goes with it, and fortunately there are enough hospitals and asylums in the country to take good care of them" (5 May 1923, 44). Sporadic reports of contestants in need of medical attention after leaving a contest goaded civic authorities of a half dozen states to check the contagion of this latest form of St. Vitus Dance. *The New York Times* reported on April 16, 1923, that Mayor Curly of Boston had banned "dance races" as public nuisances and degrading to health and morals.

In an age given to tabloid sensationalism, the morbid effects of participating in endurance contests were often exaggerated; recovery from exhaustion usually followed a good night's rest. Still, the Surgeon General in Washington, D.C. warned that such excesses might bring about an acute dilation of the heart and sudden death. Such an outcome might have been the cause of death of 27-year-old Ward Morehouse, who collapsed on the floor of the country club where he had been dancing with a partner continuously for 87 hours.

Other warnings issued forth. A Chicago judge pointed to the moral dangers in such tests of sheer animal endurance which he felt were identical to bullfights and cockfights in attracting the morbid curiosity seeker. In the lawless years ahead, a similar hue and cry was to be raised to which those in positions of authority responded with equivocation, especially when suitably rewarded for maintaining a judicial, if not judicious silence.

Legal action directed at prohibiting endurance contests in Massachusetts prompted the *Boston Transcript* to editorialize:

To a certain level of intelligence, there is apparently amusement in watching a young man or a young woman going through the steps of modern dance, hour after hour, while musicians and partners work in relays, and pauses are made from time to time that the dancer may change shoes whose soles have disappeared for shoes that are whole. But it is not wholesome amusement. These contests are likely to cause over-exertion on the part of many who are poorly equipped for trials of endurance. Long distance dancing does not come within the scope of those tests of skill and strength that serve a useful purpose. It is a good thing that the craze will here receive no official sanction (qtd. in *Literary Digest*, 5 May 1923, 43).

The city fathers who inveighed against this latest manifestation of rhythmic mania might have received some measure of solace in the record of William Kemp, an actor and contemporary of Shakespeare, who executed a lively Morris dance in the spring of 1499. Kemp, immortalized in a popular song, "Kemp's

Jig," covered a distance of 100 miles, more or less, from London to Norwich over a nine day period (*N.Y. Times*, 6 May 1923, 1).

Could a chronicler of those times have predicted that 424 years later, history would repeat itself in America during an era called, "The Age of Play"? For it did, minor differences notwithstanding, in the terpsichorean feat of Mary "Hercules" Promitis and her partner, Joey Reynolds, veteran marathon dancers, who covered a distance of 64 miles in 36 hours and 50 minutes, travelling from the Boston Post Road, in Bridgeport, Connecticut, to Times Square, New York City (*N.Y. Times*, 7 Aug. 1923, 2).

Chapter Two
The Dance Marathons

Show business entrepreneurs, ever alert to promoting new forms of entertainment, responded to the sudden interest in setting dance endurance records. How to capitalize on this fad? Show operators were aware that there was a potential audience in the family trade, content to watch exhibition dancing. The challenge was how to make the endurance contest more entertaining.

There were some difficulties. Initially, dance marathons were unvarying spectacles, with scores of nondescript teams, indifferently attired, some even barefooted, circling monotonously around the dance floor until contestants dropped from sheer exhaustion. The transition from fad to business venture would be hard to glamorize.

A reporter for the *New York World* described the following scene at one contest:

A dingy hall is littered with worn slippers, cigarette stubs, newspapers and soup cans; reeking with the odor of stale coffee, tobacco smoke, chewing gum and smelling salts. Girls in worn bathrobes, dingy white stockings, their arms hanging over their partners' shoulders, dragging aching feet in one short agonizing step after another. (qtd. in *Literary Digest* 5 May 1923, 4).

Al Howard, a self-styled historian of dance endurance shows, remembers the early days, "...seeing the game when it was a three-day 'walk-thru,' without seats or training quarters, and with private managers instead of professional trainers" (*The Billboard* 31 Aug. 1935, 25). Despite such unpleasant working conditions, there was an abundant supply of volunteers to ensure the tremendous financial success which endurance exhibitions enjoyed in the first two years of operation. Show entrepreneur Leo Seltzer estimates that by the end of the 1920s, dance marathons had played in nearly every American city (*The Billboard* 29 Dec. 1934, 220).

Dance marathon contests during its early phase could best be described as "pageants of fatigue." To add liveliness to these exhibitions, imaginative showmen began to incorporate any scheme, stunt, or gimmick, however crazy or bizarre, into the amorphous format of this latest form of show business. Leo Seltzer credits Al Painter for making one of the major alterations in the dance endurance business by combining marathon and vaudeville features in his show in Portland, Oregon (*The Billboard* 29 Dec. 1934, 220).

Painter and other live-wire promoters like "Duke" Hall, in California, could draw upon a loyal cadre of vaudeville troupers, now mostly unemployed, who were eager to perform their acts even at a dance marathon, a form of show business they held in low regard. These vaudevillians helped relieve the tedium of watching couples weaving their way laboriously across the floor over protracted periods of time. In addition, celebrities of stage, screen, and radio and local talent from nearby nightclubs and cabarets who came to watch the contest volunteered their services. Opening a dance marathon with well-known bands like Guy Lombardo and Little Jack Little drew especially large crowds.

In addition to vaudeville and big-band entertainment, easier rules and regulations were introduced. The duration of the dance marathon contest was extended which resulted in a larger gross at the box office. Before the Stock Market crash brought the 1920s to a halt, other innovations were introduced to make dance marathon contests more attractive to a wider public. Local businesses, breweries, soft water laundries and restaurants were encouraged to sponsor couples in the contest. Each team wore matching shirts and blouses identifying their sponsor, who gave the clothing and a small stipend. Since winning the grand prize was always a gamble, teams welcomed such support. Show promoters found a ready source of revenue in advertisements placed by tradespeople in *The Marathon News*. Local newspapers welcomed human interest stories about contestants in the show and gave dance marathon contests almost unlimited coverage. Publicity and advertising men were in a seller's market.

The Dance Derby of the Century, held in the summer of 1928 at Madison Square Garden in New York City, was one of the first dance marathon shows to be held on the East Coast. Although not the first dance marathon to reflect the marriage of endurance show and vaudeville, this contest was the best publicized. Jimmy Scott, one of the prize winners, describes the attention the media devoted to this show extravaganza:

Newspapers gave greater coverage to this event, probably, than to any previous entertainment attraction during my many years residence in New York City. Reporters and photographers were assigned running stories; trade papers and magazines ran special articles; for columnists it was a bonanza!…One tabloid, claiming to be opposed to continuance of The Derby, ran retouched photos and exaggerated stories with a horror angle, which, no doubt, created longer lines at the box office. (*Ballroom Dance Magazine* July 1951, 8)

Promoting this mammoth show was one of the most colorful press agents of the "Roaring Twenties," Milton J. Crandall. Pudgy, balding, sporting a straw hat, cane and diamond belt, the "Professor," one of the many names conferred by friends and enemies, had impressive credits as one of the more imaginative press agents in Hollywood. Crandall paired the dark temptress, Theda Bara, with a skeleton and revealed to bewildered reporters that it (the skeleton) was her one true love, and that "Not even the grave can separate them" (Sann 57).

Crandall invited Bossy Gillis, mayor of Newburyport, Massachusetts, billed as "The World Championship Mayor," to open the contest. Gillis performed this office by firing three shots into the air of the spacious Madison Square Garden arena. This signal was the cue for the house band to open with

"Sweet Sue, I Love You," as the 91 couples, poised and ready, broke away into a fast two-step. A gala mood pervaded the opening night with dancing couples attired in multi-colored outfits, the men sporting lavender blazers, tuxedos, flannel trousers, silk shirts and sombreros, the women, their hair bobbed, wearing short skirts, evening gowns and costumes of all styles.

A grand prize of $5,000, and a tour in vaudeville was an attractive inducement to a drove of couples who entered the dance marathon from a dozen foreign countries. Contest rules set by the show promoter reflected the changes that had taken place in dance endurance contests since Miss Cummings established the initial record five years earlier. In place of a non-commercial exhibition of dancing, without respite, with dancers using a succession of partners to establish a new record, the 1928 contest required couples to dance one hour and rest 15 minutes around the clock with no change of partners permitted. The 15-minute rest periods between hourly stints afforded contestants the opportunity to rest, eat at their own expense, use the public bathrooms and have their bodies attended to by an entourage of masseurs, hairdressers, barbers, manicurists and chiropodists. Family and friends sought to energize flagging spirits with gifts of flowers and prophetically, for those soon to leave the contest, bon voyage baskets. The progress of the contest was marked by the 91 peppermint-striped tents, which acted as shelter, being folded, one by one, as couples faded away into the night (Scott 20).

Crandall adopted the time honored format of vaudeville into his contest by introducing a variety of special events. There was the froth of three-minute "smile" popularity features. Mary Promitus, described in one newspaper account as "a tiny blonde who looked like she had just been sent home from a toy department," excelled in this event. Her admiring fans did admit that Mary had over-smiled in her first contest but had corrected herself and gone on to win the other four events handily. This performance was no mean feat, especially after having been confined with scores of other teams in mid-summer heat to basement quarters which had recently housed circus animals while a pre-scheduled boxing match was taking place in the arena above. There were, in addition, other features more noteworthy. Talented amateur and professional ballroom teams competed for prize money in waltz, foxtrot, and two-step contests. To add luster to the daily shows, celebrities like Jack Dempsey, Mae West and Texas Guinan were invited to share the spotlight.

The main attraction of the show continued to be the surviving contestants struggling to keep each other in an upright position after traveling forty miles a day. Teammates, when verbal exhortations failed, administered stronger measures to keep their partners alert. They slapped faces, punched jaws and kicked partners in the shins. Such acts were greeted with cheers from the "sporting element," spectators who wagered which teams would hold up longest under such abuse.

Some contestants experimented with more ingenious methods of encouraging a faltering partner. Mary Promitis tried a series of methods to keep her partner awake, first tickling him, then holding smelling salts to his nose, finally pressing an ice pack against the back of his neck. This last strategy proved successful though it resulted in a chase around the arena to the delight of an expectant audience. Incidentally, to live up to her nickname "Hercules," Mary had her feet pickled in brine and vinegar by her ex-pugilist fiance before entering the contest.

Physical exhaustion notwithstanding, contestants were faced with other sources of pressure. Charlie McMillan waved dollar bills in the air and whistled lugubrious tunes to discomfit his fellow competitors. These antics prompted *The New York Times*, to identify McMillan as a disciple of Professor John B. Watson, the psychologist, whose behavioral approach to psychology was in vogue during the 1920s (20 June 1928). McMillan's most ingenious strategy was practiced during the early morning hours when "the sap," as other contestants referred to him, continually shot pennies across the floor in hopes that other dancers, seeing these coins rolling about, would believe themselves to be going insane.

McMillan resorted to other tactics as well. He chose as his victim Marianne Jacques, who had claimed the title, "The Non-Stop Champion of the World." Noting her weeping, he jeered at her partner's efforts to revive her with smelling salts. "Dance you world champion...the rules are to dance at all times, ha, ha, ha! Dance you world champion" (*New York Times* 20 June 1928, 27). The beleaguered self-proclaimed champion did rally enough to prevent a fight between her partner and her tormentor. McMillan informed reporters: "I'm not winning with these," pointing to his feet; "I'm winning with this," pointing to his head. "I jeer at them when they feel bad and I say things that irritate them when they feel good. I've got their nerves all on edge. I'm driving them crazy. I upset 'em so that they can't eat or sleep and do it without laying a finger on them. Ha, ha, ha! Headwork is going to win this derby" (*New York Times* 20 June 1928, 27).

The contest wore on into the tenth day. Tension mounted and erupted in unpredictable behavior. When music over the giant amplifier was turned off during a rest period, contestants demanded that it be turned on since they could not live through three minutes of "reason destroying silence." More bizarre were the actions of hallucinating contestants. In these altered states, contestants held conversations with non-existent persons and acted out a variety of charades. One woman plucked imaginary flowers from her shoe tops or out of the air to pin to her partner's lapel. Another appeared to savor the leaves of potted plants which served as decorations around the arena. When one contestant rushed around the floor announcing that the show promoter had put poison in the coffee, several marathoners, in a dazed state, apparently believed him.

Patrons relished these antics. For the contestants, however, these episodes could have serious consequences. In one instance, which had all the earmarks of a Keystone Cop movie, Mortimer Jack broke away from his partner and raced out of the arena in pursuit of pickpockets he imagined had stolen large sums of money from his rest quarters. This action, which led to his disqualification, occurred on June 20, 1928, when the contest had been in progress for 211 hours and 30 minutes.

Health authorities reacted to this show enterprise with vacillation. Queried early in the contest, Harris, New York City Health Commissioner, remarked that there was no law preventing people from being foolish. A team of visiting physicians were amazed at the stamina of the 13 remaining couples after the contest had passed the 312-hour mark. One tabloid hailed the show as an ongoing experiment which would help science learn more about the potential ankle and toe strength of the nation as well as the minimum motive power with which the human brain could function. Dr. Edward Cowles, a psychiatrist, who visited the show after it passed the mark of 398 hours, voiced the opinion that contestants would suffer no ill effects from their long strain because they had become adjusted to it. "These people have begun to live according to a pattern of rest and movement which is as regular for them as their former mode of living once was" (*New York Times* 27 June 1928, 27).

Despite such medical assurance, suspicion lingered among some public officials that something was not quite right. When 28-year-old Fred Quinn collapsed some time after leaving the show and had to be rushed to the hospital in serious condition, New York City health authorities ordered the marathon halted. Accounts differ as to what happened next. One version reported that the promoter obtained a court stay but the stay was vacated and the city authorities prevailed; the other version was that there were dark hints to the effect that a dwindling gate had impelled the Professor to get a friendly newspaperman to go and steam up the Health Commissioner in the first place.

Crandall's summer pageant was reported in *The New York Times* under headlines which read: "Young Woman Who Can Smile For Three Minutes At A Time Is Now A Favorite In Derby." Another headline announced, "Night Club Habitues Show More Stamina Than Outdoor Man in Endurance Derby." *The New York Evening Graphic* took the occasion of this dance extravaganza to evangelize on the ravages of sin in the big city with this headline: "Dancers Enduring Torture, Going Mad, Lured by Society Gold." In contrast to this condemnation, staff reporter Heywood Broun in *Vanity Fair* identified himself as a member of the "Marathon Dancers Boosting Association," whose interest in the contest began after the first 300 or 400 hours (48).

Broun was fascinated by the spectacle of the marathon show, excited not by the contenders who slumped and quit, but by those who showed their "exultant strength" by continuing on in the contest. He regarded the twirling couples with admiration for battling against "the Sandman." For this reason if no other, he pronounced that Mr. Milton Crandall's dance marathon came close to being the most moral and uplifting exhibition in his experience (48).

The Madison Square Garden Dance Marathon, which *The New York Times* referred to as "New York's Great Summer Drama," closed after 19 days. From a gross of $121,000, Crandall claimed a salary of $25,000, a sum he added to his previous earnings in dance endurance contests of $65,000. The premature closing of this show netted each of the nine remaining teams $500 plus added prize money and stipends from sponsors. Not all contestants were content with this financial settlement. It was Mary Promitus who voiced the opinion of dissident couples: "A lot of pineapples we are dancing here and Crandall getting all the money. Next time, we don't enter without a guarantee of so much a day." Such a guarantee was secretly given in the years to follow with the advent of the walkathon show.

The success of his first Madison Square Garden show was a sufficient inducement for Crandall to open a repeat show the following year in the same arena. A number of attractions were added to recapture the attention of an audience now accustomed to dance endurance events. There was Shipwreck Kelly, "champion flag-pole sitter," perched on high, sitting stoically, disdainful of the couples circling below him (14). Dr. Alexander Meyer, "the prewar rocking chair sensation of Russia," a man of prodigious bulk, sat in a rocking chair on a platform, moving to and fro, with the constancy of a hyperactive child. He vowed, along with Art Hoffman, a twice-decorated infantry veteran of W.W.I who had chained himself to a steering wheel, to keep awake as long as the last dancing couple remained upright.

In addition to these side-show features, Crandall made changes in the rules and regulations of his new show. Conditions were made more strenuous for contestants by lengthening the one hour period on the dance floor to two hours while extending the 15-minute rest periods to 20 minutes. Three times daily, a red flag similar to one hoisted at bicycle races, announced contests which tested the skill of teams in a variety of ballroom dances. Judges, chosen from celebrities in the entertainment field, used a grade-point system to evaluate the winners. This arrangement more nearly merited the name "Dance Marathon" in combining both endurance and skill in ballroom dancing.

The "Second Dance Derby of the Century" came to an end after 23 days without internal or external pressure other than an unresponsive box office. Again, this show was a financial success and grossed a total of $121,000. Jimmy Prior and his partner, Jeanne King, outstanding ballroom dancers, out pointed the remaining eight couples and were awarded the grand prize of $2,500. Critics of the redoubtable professor accused him of being a "piker" for reducing by half the grand prize money in this second contest. Crandall had other critics as well whose criticism went beyond words. It was the fate of this bumptious promoter to meet an untimely end during the mid-thirties probably at the hands of underworld characters who expected him to share the profits. Whatever else might be said of this latter-day Barnum of the walkathon contest, Milton J. Crandall did run a legitimate show. There were few promoters who ran dance endurance contests during the years of the Great Depression who could honestly make this claim.

Dance marathons, like other forms of entertainment in the late 1920s, reflected the climate of racism in America. There were few contests in which black and white teams competed against each other. One of the few exceptions was the show which took place in June 1928 at the Manhattan Casino, a huge ballroom not far from Madison Square Garden. This contest, which opened with 80 couples, was notable for another reason. It was at this show that one of the most popular ballroom dances in America to this day was introduced. George "Shorty" Snowden, the "All-Time Champion Dancer" at the Savoy Ballroom in Harlem, created a new dance, called the "Lindy Hop," named after celebrity hero Charles Lindbergh. Snowden remembers doing a breakaway step, flinging his partner out while improvising a few solo steps. His energetic performance filled with improvisation, done to the fast tempo of Tiger Rag, had an electric effect on both audience and musicians. Snowden outclassed other contestants with this novel dance routine and later succeeded in winning one fourth of the $5,000 prize money (Stearns 315).

Though less publicized than the Madison Square Garden shows, another notable dance marathon took place in New York City. John Lazarro, a wealthy Italian, opened his "Dusky Derby" in Harlem on June 18, 1928. This dance marathon was unique in that both whites and blacks competed, a rare occurrence throughout the history of dance endurance contests. Edna Smith, a black woman with three children and three months' pregnant when she entered this contest, remembers dancing one hour and resting 15 minutes around the clock. Smith recalls winning waltz and two-step contests for $10 and $15 prize money. At the end of the contest, which was closed down by the police after 389 hours and 15 minutes, Smith and her partner, another black couple and a young Puerto Rican couple were the only remaining contestants left (*New York Times* 13 June 1928, 11:2).

The New York Times reporter who covered the story of the Lazarro show wrote: "The colored people excel in a great many things, but nothing is more natural and more instinctive with them, than dancing." However natural and instinctive dancing was to blacks, there were, few, if any, opportunities to test this "natural and instinctive ability" in endurance dancing. Racial discrimination, for once, worked in favor of the discriminated, since dance marathons had little to do with dancing, and, according to its critics, even less to do with wholesome entertainment.

Chapter Three
The Walkathons

The early 1930s saw significant changes in the operation of dance endurance contests. These changes were largely brought about by Leo Seltzer, the man whom Eells called "The Barnum of Walkathon Promoters." Seltzer had begun his career doing promotion in movie theatres. His first encounter with dance marathons was as a member of a board set up to censor this fad. But he was quick to register the popular response to it and opened his first show in 1930 in Aberdeen, along the rugged coast of Oregon. He characterized this location a "town of a thousand whore houses." From the employees of these establishments he was deluged with calls in response to his ad offering a first prize of $1,000 for the winning team (Interview).

Seltzer went on to open a show in Denver in the dead of winter. There he found the public unresponsive. He met this challenge by introducing a variety of novel walking and running events. At first, veteran promoters who heard of these innovations were resistant to what they regarded as radical ideas. But the Denver show clicked. The sport features testing contestants to the limits of endurance were incorporated into the contest. Seltzer followed this early success with a Kansas City show and proved conclusively that this new format was a winner (*The Billboard* 29 Dec. 1934, 220).

Seltzer, a taskmaster who sought to instill a "fear complex" in contestants, attempted to convince vocal critics of walkathon shows that the rigorous challenges to contestants which the new format introduced were, in fact, healthful, not harmful. He invited Dr. Martin Corrigan, renowned physician at the Denver Tubercular Hospital, to test the effects of walkathon shows on contestants. According to Seltzer, Corrigan found that eighty percent of the show contestants had ailments at the beginning of the contest which were cured as the show progressed. For example, leg swelling decreased due to the introduction of foot races. Further, Seltzer boasted that, despite the wear and tear, contestants actually gained weight. The enterprising entrepreneur, perhaps with tongue in cheek, suggested that anyone interested in making a million dollars could open a sanitarium based on the principles of walkathon shows.

The Billboard described the new format of the dance endurance contest under a variety of names: "Walkathons," "Dance Derbies," "Dance-a-thons," "Jitter-a-thons," "Walk-a-shows," and in their closing days, "Walk-a-derbies." The name changes reflected the substantial difference between the dance marathon and walkathon. Walkathons represented a unique combination of walking, vaudeville-cabaret and athletic acts. Nevertheless, the name walkathon accurately described what contestants did most of the time: walk.

Richard Kaplan, walkathon attorney, placed the walkathon show in an historical context. He noted in *The Billboard* that in 1879 a Chicago newspaper advertisement had announced the presentation of a walking contest to be held in Exposition Hall in that city. A new idea had been born, the outgrowth of the old marathon run and marathon walk. With the passing of the years, what changed in the present-day walkathon was not the sport, but the form of the presentation to the public (29 June 1935, 31).

The athletic acts grafted to the dance endurance contest had compelling names: Zombie Treadmills, Back-to-Back Struggles, Dynamite Sprints, Bombshell Derbies, Hurdles, Circle Hotshots, Heel & Toe Races, and Duck Waddles. By 1933, these strenuous athletic events, based on speed not on slow exhaustion, became the major draw. In addition to sport features, walkathon shows sought to sell entertainment by staging production numbers. Professional contestants, who came to dominate the field, had to act as well as run.

A bastard, sub-basement form of show business never to achieve a high status among other forms of entertainment media like vaudeville, nightclubs and the movies, sources from which it borrowed, walkathon shows did play to large audiences and attracted thousands of contestants during the first half of the 1930s. Walkathon shows flourished at the height of the Great Depression in America, a collapse of terrifying proportion, part of a world-wide cataclysm. The great economic machine failed. The unemployment rate jumped from 3.1 to 25.2 percent; 12 to 14 million of the total civilian labor force in America were out of work. In writing about the Great Depression, Bird observed, "The mood of the marathon was very similar to the aimless, endless movement of superfluous people around and around the country" (Bird 66). The dance marathon contests, like the Great Depression itself, emphasized the need to endure.

The years of the Great Depression were times of torment for many Americans; in place of patriotism, there was a sense of hopelessness. The specter of poverty and joblessness brought with it feelings of humiliation and despair especially to male breadwinners who blamed themselves and not the economic system for their plight. In the early 1930s, a good number of teams who competed in walkathon shows were unemployed. The need to survive was not the only urgent reason. Contestants often felt uprooted and unwanted, a lost generation. Joining a walkathon show was finding a home—of sorts.

Song titles captured the ambience of the 1930s. The lyrics to "Time On My Hands" might have been the theme song for the many unemployed. People had time but it was not what they wanted; they wanted to get a job; they wanted to get an education; they wanted to get married. What they did not want was to have time on their hands, waiting to get a job, waiting to get an education, waiting to get married.

Other lyrics were meant to act as a soothing palliative; "Wrap Your Troubles in Dreams and Dream Your Troubles Away," "On The Sunny Side of the Street," "Down The River of Golden Dreams," and "Over The Rainbow." James Rorty, who traveled 15,000 miles across the United States during the depression years, concluded that most Americans he came in contact with had an addiction for fantasy (xiii). Walkathons were a place for fantasy. If the world was crumbling, audiences could count on the walkathon show to be there, day after day, creating melodramas of struggle and romance, scenarios which aped those of the Hollywood film and its world of make believe. Woody Allen's 1985 movie, *The Purple Rose of Cairo*, reminds modern audiences of the powerful impact that Hollywood, the Dream Machine, had, as a form of escape, on the lives of many Americans during the 1930s.

The Lost Generation: A Portrait of American Youth Today, written by Maxine Davis in 1936, emphasized the same idea. The writer estimated that 20 million boys and girls were addicted to the movies. Hollywood, the mecca of the movies, was as much a state of mind as a physical location. In the Hollywood world of glamour, both adolescents and their elders could lose themselves in wish fulfillment. Walkathon shows mimicked, at a low level of sophistication, the promotional schemes of the Hollywood studio. Every walkathon show featured a Sweetheart Couple, the clone of Hollywood's current romantic team, Janet Gaynor and Charlie Farrell.

There was less money to go around during the Depression, and the entertainment field, like other business enterprises, suffered. The large vaudeville circuits which tried to hold on and not go the way of silent screens had to charge high admissions that the majority of patrons could not afford. Sports stadiums and fight arenas with large overheads, similarly forced to charge high admissions, were hardest hit. Not so walkathon shows, which supplied the demand for inexpensive continuous entertainment. An entrance fee of 15 cents for general admission and 25 cents for reserved seats was an attractive inducement as was the invitation to come early and stay as long as one pleased. Besides, going to the walkathons was something new and the "thing to do."

Walkathon contests opened in big cities and small towns across the United States, from New York to Los Angeles, from Maine to Florida. *The Billboard* listed in its endurance column between 1934 and 1938 the following marathon sites:

Asbury Park, New Jersey	Marion, Indiana
Spokane, Washington	Waterbury, Connecticut
Somers Point, New Jersey	North Platte, Nebraska
Lynchburg, Virginia	Tampa, Florida
Battle Creek, Michigan	Green Bay, Wisconsin
Detroit, Michigan	High Point, North Carolina
New York, New York	Frankfort, Kentucky
Chicago, Illinois	Wichita, Kansas
East Dubuque, Illinois	Birmingham, Alabama
Danville, Virginia	Great Falls, Montana
Ocean City, Maryland	Enid, Oklahoma
Minneapolis, Minnesota	Williamsport, Pennsylvania
Flint, Michigan	Charleston, South Carolina
Long Beach, California	Yankton, South Dakota
Miami, Florida	Washington, D.C.

Cleveland, Ohio	Huntington, West Virginia
Swawnee, Oklahoma	Portsmouth, Rhode Island
Knoxville, Tennessee	Cheyenne, Wyoming
Manitou, Colorado	Avon, Massachusetts
Macon, Georgia	Shreveport, Louisiana
Union City, Tennessee	Freeport, Illinois
Fort Smith, Arkansas	Corpus Christi, Texas

No doubt there were other shows not listed in *The Billboard*.

Big time shows playing to as many as 5,000 spectators were held in large arenas, armories in cities, pavilions at amusement parks, or under a big top if no other large space was available: places with names like Olympic Hall, Winter Gardens, Dreamland Park, Engineers Hall, Castle Arena. Small shows were run in auditoriums and former dance halls, even in factories, which might hold 200 to 300 spectators. If the dance endurance contest was held in a country town with little to do for amusement, and if the people there had little money to spend, the show was sure to do well.

In the early 1930s, Jack Curley, a sports entrepreneur, operated walkathon shows on a chain-store plan. He found this entertainment ideal for promoters, contestants and fans. The promoter made money because customers returned again and again to the same show. Contestants, even those who didn't win first, second, or third prize money, had cash thrown to them by the audience, and they were fed. The public enjoyed a variety of entertainment. "It's the softest thing I've ever struck. As a craze it beats midget golf hollow. There, my boy is the secret of success in the exhibition business. Never make your customer exert himself beyond paying at the gate and getting his seat" (*Collier* 23 July 1932, 27).

Walkathon shows which opened in resort areas attracted celebrities from stage, screen and radio. In the Second Annual Boardwalk Marathon Dance Contest, which opened with 101 couples in 1932, show promoters George Ruty and Zeke Youngblood could boast such notables in their "Parade of the Stars" as Raquel Torres, exotic Mexican movie star; Mae West, glamorous Broadway actress; James Hall, the silver screen's romantic hero; Nick Lucas, the "Crooning Troubador" of stage, radio and screen fame; Sally Rand, star of the burlesque circuit; and Gladys Glad of the Ziegfeld Follies, acclaimed the "most beautiful girl in the world." To add zest to the show, Ruty and Youngblood invited a "glittering array" of comics and clowns which included Olsen and Johnson, the "Hooligans of Hilarity"; Harry Langdon, noted screen comedian; and Jack Pearl, celebrated stage comedian. Among many other celebrities were Hal LeRoy, sensational Follies dancer; Mark Hellinger, noted New York columnist; and Mitzi Mayfair whose dancing the prior winter made her the toast of Broadway.

Youngblood opened his contests with the official dance marathon song, *Take Me To The Dance Marathon*, played in waltz tempo (Mathews Scrapbook). The chorus went as follows:

Down in that ring first prize money crowns the
    queen and king
On that dance floor you'll see sights you've
    never seen before
If it's midnight or it's morning, some are
    laughing, some are yawning
I don't care if the Depression is on,
    Take me to the Dance Marathon.

On the west coast, an equally impressive array of Hollywood stars contributed their services free: George "Snake Hips" Raft performed the Tango; Bill "Bojangles" Robinson did a tap dance; Eddie Cantor sang a song; the Marx Brothers clowned; and Mickey Rooney and Frankie Darrow acted as emcees.

The sobriquet "Poor Man's Night Club," coined by Arnold Gingrich in the first issue of *Esquire* in 1933, was apt. He characterized the walkathon contest as "a place where celebrity is immediate, stardom easy, and human dignity is very low" (61). Among its many attractions, walkathons invited spectators to dance to live music when contestants took their 11-minute break. The "dog end" of show business, a "make-do" operation, walkathon shows were entertaining. To the present day, the popular image of this amusement is that people went to walkathon shows primarily to see others suffer, "to see them die." More accurately, Americans flocked to walkathon shows to be entertained and to while away time.

The evolution of the dance contest from fad to walkathon was complete. This is not to say that walkathons as a show business media did not undergo change. Before 1933, walkathon contests were less cut and dried; they sold endurance and mirrored that quality needed to survive both in the show and in the world outside. After 1933, with a professional cadre which accounted for over 75 percent of participating contestants, the format became more structured. There were three kinds of acts: the walking act, which required contestants to continue in motion, on the dance floor, 45 minutes every hour, day and night, for the duration of the contest; the athletic acts, comprised of sprints and lap races featured every evening at show time; and the vaudeville-cabaret acts, which drew upon the resources of a hired staff of emcees and clowns supported by talented contestants with occasional talent from outside the show.

The regimen walkathon teams followed was exact. At the sound of a police siren, on the hour, contestants were to be in dance position ready to start moving on the dance floor; after 45 minutes, a second siren sounded; contestants had two minutes to leave the dance floor. The next 11 minutes could be used to sleep or rest, attend to personal needs, or find some form of recreation. Two minutes before the hour, a third siren sounded calling couples back to the dance floor to begin their next hourly stint.

This routine was followed day and night for the duration of the contest with few exceptions. A one-hour period was set for showers in the early morning; at show time, during matinee and evening performances, the schedule was altered to include a variety of athletic events. There were other times when contestants were not required to follow this strict schedule: when they were sick, preparing a special act, or having a tooth pulled. Leaving the dance floor for hygiene purposes took two minutes; only one such visitation an hour was permitted, and then only if accompanied by an attendant and with the floor judge's permission. Richard Elliot, who worked with promoter Hal Ross realistically estimated that contestants ended up sleeping four hours in rest quarters and supplemented this by sleeping on their feet as they moved around the dance floor (*New Observation* 4 April 1985, 7).

Contestants in walkathon shows were subject to a long list of regulations: showers were compulsory; fighting brought instant disqualification; there was no spitting; gum chewing was permitted only during show events at designated times; men were to be clean shaven; women were permitted to wear trousers only late at night; there was no smoking on the dance floor. Breaking rules brought penalty points which could result in disqualification.

The change in format in walkathon shows called for a new breed of professional contestant. Women and men who earned their livelihood by competing in walkathon shows had to be able to withstand the stress of nightly elimination races. That required considerable skill and stamina. In addition, they had to surmount the "normal" strain of the repetitive walking act. The number of couples opening a show might vary between 21 and 64 teams or more; most often, the number of starting couples was less than 50. The proportion of amateurs to professionals varied with each show. By 1933, professional contestants outnumbered the amateur teams by three to one.

In their ads in *The Billboard*, show promoters identified the necessary talents of this new breed of athletic entertainer: good feet, easily awakened, generally strong, and lots of will power. They counted on these seasoned professionals to carry the show once the local amateurs folded after two or three nights. Walter Grafsky was an example of this new breed. Grafsky had started his endurance career in 1928 when he ran 2,500 miles from California to New York in C.C. Pyle's Bunion Derby. Later, Grafsky danced 260 hours in a walkathon and won second prize (*The Billboard* 29 Sept. 1934, 25).

Professional marathoners with a flair for comedy, who could sing or dance the waltz, fox trot, lindy hop and tango, and who were good athletes became the celebrities of the walkathon circuit. Whether professionals or amateurs, contestants with a modicum of talent were encouraged to entertain audiences at show time and during the interminable walking acts. Walkathons were a great buy for the money. Where else could one see a live show, day and night, for 15 or 25 cents? Old vaudeville features and new cabaret acts spiced up the variety of athletic events in which two person, male-female teams competed against other teams, and females and males were pitted against their own sex. Walkathon shows combined sport with romance, something to suit everyone's taste.

Audiences changed during the course of the day and night; fans came and went as they pleased. At matinee shows, housewives and old ladies toting pillows to soften the hardness of the wooden planks during the long hours of sitting and waiting trooped in with small children. They brought picnic baskets and knitting to pass away the hours, munching, gossiping, giving words of advice to their favorite contestants and offering them small gifts. Within an arm's reach of these walkathon fans was an assortment of seedy-looking youngsters whom they could feel sorry for, men and women in need of nurturing and encouragement. Whatever mothering instinct was present in women came to the fore and was directed at these couples struggling to survive the hourly ordeals.

Later in the afternoon, when school let out, teenage daughters arrived to talk with their favorite couple, a man and woman not much older than themselves who spoke with a cultivated "tough" quality and sounded like Humphrey Bogart and Joan Blondell. These adolescent fans viewed the contestants as living a life of glamor and excitement.

The biggest crowds came in from 7 p.m. to 10 p.m. High society went slumming at walkathon shows in formal dress and attracted the attention of everyone else. Blue collar workers and trades people frequently attended, as did engaged couples who stopped over after seeing a movie. Show people, newspaper reporters, sports writers, magazine editors, film and movie directors from east and west coasts regularly attended walkathon shows. Though sophisticated about the world of show business, they were nevertheless fascinated by the nightly dramas which unfolded at the walkathon contest.

Late night shows attracted a very different audience, the sporting element. At evening shows, prostitutes and pimps, mobsters and tarts sat in the reserved seats at the edge of the dance floor. They drank openly from hip flasks while gambling on the outcome of the variety of sports events. To add to their amusement, these denizens of the underworld played pranks at the expense of show contestants. They howled with glee at the surprised and pained response of a contestant who picked up a coin they had heated and thrown on the dance floor. Promoters who catered to this clientele could expect trouble. Periodically, fights would break out and disrupt the show.

Not represented at walkathon shows were the middle class; it was rare to find doctors, lawyers, or teachers in the audience. Some women's organizations, in particular, took a militant stand against walkathon shows. They branded them as immoral, a threat to the spiritual fiber of those misguided enough to participate or be spectators.

Although the background of the audiences differed, their behaviors were similar. Fans were boisterous and volatile; they screamed and stamped their feet. They were rabidly partisan. Encouraged to identify with a favorite couple, they shouted warnings when it appeared that their team was in trouble. One woman, when her voice failed to carry, took off a shoe and banged it on the rail to alert her favorite team, seemingly in the death throes. Fans responded to the often amateurish performances with lusty enthusiasm. They shouted across to friends and yelled at contestants. They disagreed with floor judges about their rulings. They bet privately on their favorites and booed the villains. Show emcees made unabashed appeals to the emotions, stressing how important patron support was to the "kids" in the show. Walkathon fans gave both financial and psychological support. Show patrons were generous in contributing nickels, dimes, quarters and half dollars to supplement the modest resources of those who appeared to be less well off than themselves. Contestants did come to rely on encouragement from their fans to see them through the daily ordeals.

Someone watching a walkathon contest for the first time might waver between fascination and suspicion at the unusual events. Not so the true-believing fan who was unquestioning when his favorite team, repeatedly on the brink of disqualification, recovered miraculously from every impending crisis. The spectator turned skeptic might notice that in addition to this recurring event, there was evidence that required a further suspension of disbelief. How was it that the most exciting races took place at show time in the evening when the crowds flocked thickest? The skeptics stopped coming, but the walkathon fans, despite such "coincidences," faithfully returned night after night.

Critical to the success of any walkathon show was the master of ceremonies who kept the attention of audiences with a continual round of chatter and comic asides. Notable emcees in walkathon shows included Ted Brown (by the year 1934, he had been in over 70 shows) and "Pistol Pete" Wilson, Red Oleski, Joe Solar, Charlie Loeb, Jimmy Kelly, Phil Murphy, Dick Edwards, Billy Mack, Benny Leonard, Archie Gayer, Dud Nelson, King Brady, Moon Mullins, Red Carter, Eddy Snyder, Skipper Spiegel, Henry Polk, Chick Snyder, Al Lyman, Freddie Hall, Joe Purtell, Eddie Leonard, Monte Hall, Duke Brown and Rajah Bergman. Bergman's stage name, the "Rajah," came about from his taking this role in a "Harem" skit. Bergman had come from a family of show people, left high school at age 15, and gravitated to vaudeville where he was noticed by a walkathon promoter. *The Billboard* did a thumbnail sketch of the talented emcee and noted that he did not smoke; he did not use suggestive material; he was serious off stage; and he was packing in some of the largest audiences for Seltzer's Chicago Show (*The Billboard* 8 Dec 1934, 25).

The fact that walkathons continued around the clock made it necessary to fill much empty time, a responsibility which fell principally on the shoulders of the emcee and his staff of comics, clowns and stooges. A round of emcees played straight men to walkathon comics, clowns and celebrity contestants who carried on in the rowdy tradition of burlesque and vaudeville by telling jokes, taking pratfalls and performing skits.

Professional comedians, the "Mad Marathon Maniacs" who performed on stage but were not contestants, had among their ranks men with descriptive stage names like: "Squirrely" Bradly, "Pistol-Pete" Wilson, "Wiggles" Royce, Eddie "Shadow" Davis, Tony "Charley Chaplin" Lewis, Cliff "Offty-Goofty" Real, Jimmy "Snozzle" Kelly, "Rubber Legs" Martin, Freddie "Bozo" Lewis, "Pee Wee" Roony, Freddie "Bad Boy" Eaton, Clye "Stooge" Morse, "Ducky" Costello, "Gypsy" Carol, "Ready Money" Phillips, "Popeye" Knight, Kenny "Porkchops" Bird, "Big Bang" Bixie, "Cherry-Pie" Chowder, "Horseface" Gayer, Buddy "Dogface" Dyer, Jimmy "Wooden Leg" Johnson, Forrest "Sour Puss" Bailey, Johnny "Puddin Puss" Armbuster, Pierre "Dish Face" Nony, Carl "Sleepy" Bahke and Charles "Peachie" Cuthburt.

At a time when economic, social, and religious foundations were being shaken, it was comforting for walkathon fans to know that there was no ambiguity in the drama between good and evil in walkathon contests. The Trouble Maker team and the hard-hearted floor judge were the bad guys; the Sweetheart Couple were the good guys. To everyone's delight and no one's surprise, it was The Sweetheart Couple who invariably triumphed in the end despite what appeared sure victory for The Trouble Makers.

Show emcees worked closely with the floor judges and professional contestants who were the celebrities in the show. All three colluded in "working heat," or playing to the crowd to arouse a strong emotional response. "King Kong," "Dracula," "Frankenstein" and "Simon-Legree" were frequently used stage names for "heat" judges such as Joe Piccinelli, Jim Coffee, Earl Clark, Ernie Bernard, Dick Leyer, Larry Capo, Johnny Agrella and Maxie Cappo. When *The Billboard* asked people in the business who was the best "sour puss" floor judge, Jim "King Kong" Coffee was acknowledged a front runner for the title. His strict judging enabled him to retain his standing as one of the most hated judges in the field (*The Billboard* 12 Feb. 1938, 30).

Floor judges were colorful villains, men to be feared and respected. They instructed the emcee "to sell what you see." What emcees did report was the strict surveillance and punitive measures of the floor judges. No wonder a floor judge was often called "The Meanest Man in Town."

Important functions of the show emcee were to sell every contestant to the audience and to attract a sponsor for each team in the show. Emcees were most effective in gaining a following for contestants by combining "corn" and "con" in their sales pitch. (Just as male show promoters dominated walkathon enterprises, female emcees like June Harley, who proved to be a sensation in Harry E. Cowls Minnesota Show, were a rarity [*The Billboard* 20 Oct. 1934, 26].)

Questioned as to why people came to see the show, emcees were prone to answer: "People come to see someone worse off than themselves." Lachrymose appeals were made to audiences, the majority who were women, hard luck stories with which fans could identify and empathize. *The Irish Echo* printed the following description of a happening at the Second Annual Boardwalk Marathon Dance Contest:

...hundreds of early morning spectators were witnesses to a touching scene yesterday when Mrs. Jean Davis of Augusta, Ga., was compelled to drop out of the contest because of the illness of one of her children. Mrs. Davis has two youngsters and was trying to better provide for them. A generous purse was raised by her fellow contestants to which scores of fashionably dressed spectators contributed. (Mathews Scrapbook)

Fiction as often as fact, these stories, told with melodramatic flair, were interchangeable with scripts from daytime radio serials and the lonely-hearts column in the daily newspaper.

Not all stories needed embellishment. Patsy Salmon, who competed in walkathon contests and appeared as mistress of ceremonies in endurance shows in the early 1930s, had forsaken Broadway after a shattering romance.

Columnists Walter Winchell and Mark Hellinger referred to her as "The Girl of the Golden West," and the "small town girl who made good on Broadway." She was a headliner in smart night clubs who once appeared in the Zeigfield Follies and the Vanities and had earned a weekly salary of $2,500. Her report to the newspaper reporters ran as follows (Mathews Scrapbook):

I had my big chance and I muffed it. Sure I was in the big money but the promoter got most of it and the chap I fell in love with got the rest. You see we were engaged to be married and I thought he was wonderful but he figured I was just a small town girl. After that I gave up in disgust and left Broadway or Broadway just left me—it all means the same. But I'm not through yet, and you can tell the newspaper boys who have written so much about me that they'll be going back to the files for those clippings yet.

Clippings such as the above are fortunately preserved in Lawrence Mathews' invaluable scrapbooks. Mathews was a right- hand man to promoter Zeke Youngblood, and listed his jobs variously as medical supervisor, head trainer, masseur and mechanical technician. Unofficially, Mathews was friend and father-confessor. Ms. Salmon autographed one of her photos, "Here's to you Larry, the original Mr. Sunshine to many foot weary marathoners. Best wishes for health, wealth and happiness. Always." She signed the inscription: Patricia "Skippy" Salmon (Mathews Scrapbook).

Contests opened with a mass of bodies from a ready supply of amateur local volunteers. The backbone of every successful show, however, was scores of professional teams with devoted followings. A show advertised as a Contest of Champions attracted the elite contestants who tended to travel in the same circuit. Every show typecast contestants, "Innocent Little Nel," "The Seductress," "The Hillbilly," "The Jitterbug," "The Old Timers," and "The Clown." Two roles were given prominence in walkathon shows: "The Sweetheart Couple" and "The Trouble Makers." "The Sweetheart Couple" was represented by a female who looked and acted like Marilyn Monroe, a "Little Chick" with a loving heart; and her partner, a clean-cut, likable young man. "The Trouble Makers" were as stereotyped as their arch rivals; the female "heavy" was dark and full-bosomed; her partner acted tough.

The villains of the show, "The Trouble Makers," provided the dramatic highlights of every show. Chad Alviso, an olive-skinned, never-smiling woman of Mexican descent, was the quintessential female villain in the walkathon circuit. Nicknamed "The Gypsy," Alviso enraged walkathon fans with her underhanded tactics against her fair-haired rivals. In one show, it took eight policemen to get her to her dressing room after she had assaulted and victimized her adversary. Unrelenting in her persecution of her favored rival, Alviso colluded with the floor judge whose attention was always directed elsewhere during these perpetrated bouts of mayhem. Alviso played her role so well that she wisely avoided the perimeter of the ring of spectators for fear of being smashed over the head with a chair.

Norma Jaspers, one of Alviso's fair-haired rivals, reports that her archenemy was so convincing in playing the heavy that an enraged spectator, wildly screaming and waving his fists, fell right out of the balcony. Alviso and Jaspers immediately sought to divert the attention of the audience when this happened (Martin *The Drama Review* Spring 53). Audiences also played a part in instigating rivalry among contestants. Jaspers reports that in a 1939 Chicago show, Al Capone's sister handed her $25 to get into a fight with another contestant. Al Capone (always with his bodyguard) was an avid fan of walkathon shows. At the close of the contest, he extended a blanket invitation to the remaining teams at the Victory Ball to come to a party at his Palm Island Estate.

Louie Meredith, whose specialty was ballroom dancing, often teamed with the dangerous Alviso, however tough was too short to be a creditable villain. When he became a victim to his partner's rages, fans would shout advice to the put-upon Louie: "Don't give that black bitch nuttin'!" These two Trouble Makers were legitimately married at a walkathon wedding, one of their numerous nuptials with each other and with other contestants. Their competitors (and close friends) were Hughie Hendrickson, slim and suave, whose partner, Helen Caldwell, was a talented entertainer. "At one time," wrote George Eells, "by merely putting an ad in a Washington, D.C. newspaper—HUGHIE AND LOUIE ARE HERE—a promoter could be assured of a full house" (Eells *"Some 20,000"* 154).

Al "Mysterios" Howard, who started in the dance endurance business with Crandall in 1923, and had been a contestant, trainer, judge, head trainer, publicity man, ticket man, dope sheet writer, emcee, manager and promoter, announced in 1934 that there was a "definite aristocracy of the marathon game." Among the notable female professionals who competed in walkathon shows during the 1930s and 1940s were Ruthie Booth, always the most popular contestant; Patsy Gallagher, regarded as a "Young Martha Ray," the target of less talented professionals; Angie Oger, the idol of Polish fans; Ruthie Collins, who won every year at the Coliseum in Chicago; Ruthie Carrol, the Carole Lombard of the walkathon circuit, who accepted any dare and was idolized by fans. Helen Caldwell was a legendary performer. She sang, danced, ran well, wore lots of flashy costumes and was a comedian. Eells notes that when Caldwell turned solo, male professionals took the first opportunity to throw their partner over the rail.

Included among walkathon celebrities were the "Iron Horses," the indestructible west coast brother and sister team Joe and Mary Rock, and their east coast married competitors Joe and Margie Van Raam. Another perennial male favorite, besides Louie and Hughie, was Johnny Makar. His sense of drama brought cheers as a contestant but, in later years, jeers as a floor judge. Also notable was Earl Clark, an unbeatable speed demon as a contestant, and a showman at "working heat" as a floor judge. According to Eells, the only way Clark could be beaten in a foot race was by having a mediocre partner and competing against Helen Caldwell teamed with one of her usual partners, Louie or Hughie.

Another celebrity team was Al and Ruthie Smith, veterans of many walkathon shows. By 1933, the Smiths had competed in 17 contests, winning prize money in 15, and first prize three times. Ruthie Smith, once employed as a salesgirl, had participated in a skating marathon before winning first prize with her husband in a 26-mile dance derby; the Smiths covered this distance in seven minutes less time than the existing record. In addition to being good runners, the Smiths were talented, popular entertainers whose specialty was ballroom dancing. They were a natural choice for the role of "The Sweetheart Couple."

A walkathon "Hall of Fame," had there been one, would have honored three contestants. Kay Wise is given credit for winning the longest dance endurance contest without athletic features (treadmills or dynamite sprints), an event which lasted over nine months. This record breaking contest took place in White City, Chicago, in 1930-31. In 1934, at the Arcadia Gardens, Al Astro and Edna Gowacke set the longest record for a walkathon contest with treadmills and dynamite sprints; this contest promoted by Leo Seltzer lasted six months and 13 days (*The Billboard* 12 March 1938, 25). Both records exceed those reported in *The Guiness Book of World Records,* which credits Frankie Lane and Ruthie Smith with 3,480 hours, and Sann who credits June Havoc with 3,600 hours (5 months and 9 days).

The record for longest solo is claimed by Nobel "Kid" Chissell, who continued on his own for 468 hours. In the Wanatchee Show in Washington, in 1935, Chissell and Billie Boyd won after 1,492 hours; the final derby went nonstop for three hours and 20 minutes (*The Billboard* 7 Dec. 1935, 27). The energetic Chissell, one time U.S. Navy Middleweight Boxing Champion, supported his walkathon partners by having them stand on his feet as he moved around the dance floor. Chissell was a trainer in a Hollywood show in which writer Horace McCoy worked as a bouncer and served as a consultant for the film production of McCoy's novel *They Shoot Horses, Don't They?*

Chissell recalls the time when "Socks" McDonough, one of George "Bugs" Moran's Chicago gang, was shot over an argument in a card game in the Palm Garden, a building adjoining the walkathon arena. The Los Angeles police used this incident to close the show: their reason—the walkathon was a breeding ground for crime (*The Hollywood Independent* 28 Aug. 1969, 3). Between shows, Chissell, a Hollywood extra, worked at odd jobs, as did other professional contestants, to earn money until the next show. One of his jobs was being employed as a bodyguard for a manufacturer and political boss in Hammond, Indiana, across the line from Chicago. It was a time when rich and important people were held for ransom. While on duty, he was introduced to Vince and Louise who, he was later to learn, were "Machine Gun Jack McGern" and his famous moll, Louise Rolfe. The infamous pair were on the loose, barely ahead of the law (*Hollywood Studio Magazine* June 1970, 4A).

During the 1930s, dance endurance shows were low on the ladder of prestige though millions of Americans were avid supporters. Despite their questionable standing in the world of entertainment, walkathon shows served as a training ground for some contestants who were to later achieve acclaim in more prestigious forms of show business. June Havoc used her experience in seven dance endurance contests in the early 1930s as thematic material for her play *Marathon 33* which she adapted from her autobiography *Early Havoc.*

Havoc entered her first contest in 1933 when she was 14 years old. Her performance of the song "Ace in the Hole," a specialty number favored by gamblers and prostitutes, earned her a generous tip of $20.

Red Skelton was known as "The Midnight Maniac" in the walkathon circuit. Skelton found the walkathon stage a testing ground for original skits and gags written by his wife, Edna Stillwell, whom he married in a walkathon wedding in Kansas City. In 1938, Skelton, who made his debut with Ginger Rogers in the film "Having a Wonderful Time," was to become a national celebrity as clown and comic on radio, film and television.

Anita O'Day, jazz stylist, and crooner Frankie Laine, began their careers as singers in walkathon shows. O'Day, an avid fan of walkathons, won first prize in a Lindy Hop contest in one walkathon show and second prize in an amateur event, the Dynamite Sprint. Like Havoc, O'Day entered her first show in her early teens. O'Day, a stage name for her Irish name, Colton, remembers her screening before being accepted as a contestant: a physician took her blood pressure, listened to her heart and "checked for lice, crabs and other body vermin" (43).

O'Day recalls her distress when "Daddy" Fox, the show promoter of a 1931 walkathon held in Key West, Florida, ran off without paying any prize money. Stranded after having held out for 375 hours, O'Day, along with the staff and other contestants, were inventive in raffling a "real-live baby" to keep the show going. One newspaper reported the coming attractions: "Tomorrow night will be a real surprise night with the feature being the presentation of a real live white baby to some Key West family. This is done to ease the burden on a family that is overlarge" (41). This notice, though it stirred up women's clubs, church groups and the Humane Society, did work in the interest of the abandoned contestants. By 6 p.m. on the night of the raffle, fans were lined up halfway around the block. At show time, there was standing room only when a "real live baby" piglet was given away to the delight of fans.

In her next show, O'Day came in second, covering 4,656 miles in 2,328 hours, over a 97 day period (42). In still another show in 1936, she was runner-up to the first prize winner. O'Day recalls that when people asked her why she had become a contestant, she signed her photograph (as did others) with the cryptic: "For no good reason." She acknowledged that her response was one way of "putting fans on." She continued her musings: "We did it for money, for shelter and food. On its own level, too, the walkathon was a form of show business. Trendy thinkers bemoan the sadism of the crowd and the masochism of the contestants. But there was talent developed there" (43).

Frankie Laine, a contestant in a number of walkathon shows from 1931 to 1936, entered under his original name, Frank Lo Vecchio. His rendition of plaintive melodies during the Disqualification Ceremony, songs like "My Buddy," and "Oh, How I Miss You Tonight," were guaranteed to bring tears to the eyes of every spectator. Laine, "The Marathon Songbird," set an endurance record of 3,480 hours (20 weeks, four days) with his partner, Ruthie Smith, in a contest operated by George Ruty and Zeke Youngblood. This walkathon show, which began on May 27 and ended on Oct. 19, 1932, was held in Atlantic City at the Young's Million Dollar Pier. The arena had a seating capacity of 12 thousand.

Competing against Laine and Smith were Joie Ray and his partner Mary Fenton. Dan Parker, well-known sports columnist, traced the rise and decline of Joie Ray from his zenith as an Olympic star, "America's greatest miler," to a series of careers including professional running, marathon roller skating in a six-day stint in Madison Square Garden, and marathon snow-shoeing, a sporting event in which Ray trekked from Montreal to Quebec in the dead of winter.

The Ruty and Youngblood show opened with 101 couples and, according to their publicity, included champion contestants who originally came from Germany, Ireland and Canada. Despite the stiff competition, Laine and Ray were finalists. When Ruty and Youngblood were forced to close the show because their lease ran out, the contest was thrown into Non-Stop. The two remaining couples were no longer permitted to eat, sleep, leave the floor, or receive medical attention. At one point, Ray, who was 37 years old, rushed to the men's room and was immediately disqualified. His 19-year-old competitor magnanimously refused to win on a technicality and insisted that the contest continue. The ordeal did go on until the attending physician decided that the aging athlete might suffer permanent damage were the contest to continue. More than 3,500 persons, the majority of them women, witnessed the dramatic finale after staying up all night for the final grind.

Ray entered another Ruty-Youngblood show. Once again, the persevering athlete did not succeed in winning first prize. Ray's departure from this show prompted conflicting reports from two newspapers. *The Newark Star Eagle* reported on May 2 that Ray would sell his 850 medals to pay doctor bills for his 10-year-old daughter, Rosalie, the *New York World Telegram* reported that his daughter was not dying but was attending school. In the official Disqualification Ceremony, fans were unusually generous in the hail of coins they showered upon the departing Olympic athlete.

Laine was a magnet at the box office. For this reason, the "ragged-pants" dancer kept getting "patched up" by the training staff until he obtained the first prize (Chissell). The management estimated that there had been 1,500,000 paid admissions for this show and that contestants had picked up $50,000 in "floor money." Laine and his partner netted a total of $6,000. With this king's ransom, Laine returned to Chicago's Little Italy where his father was a barber supporting a family of nine on a weekly wage of $21 during the dark days of the Great Depression (*Los Angeles Times* 29 Nov. 1970, 22).

Laine competed in some eight shows and twice finished fifth, for which he received $250 each time. In one show promoted by Ruty and Youngblood, Laine remembers the finale. His rival, Frank Miller, 56 years old, a veteran of 16 contests and a grandfather with six children and 13 grandchildren, (partnered with 22-year-old Ruth Smith), edged Laine and his partner out after completing seven hours of dancing without rest, food, medical attention or permission to leave the floor. Publicity had it that Miller had contemplated suicide when he was 53 but entered the dance endurance field instead and went on to win 12 of his 16 marathons. Over the 56-day period, the contest, which ended with the struggle between Laine and Miller had been witnessed by 250,000 people. In this show, the indomitable Miller, earned $1,000 in prize money.

In a newspaper interview, Laine commented on his experiences in walkathon shows. "I must say I enjoyed it and had no complaints about my treatment...we had a lot of comraderie and I didn't regard the contest as exploitation" (Ripton 22). Laine, had he remained a professional contestant instead of moving on and up the ladder of show business, may have changed his opinion, particularly as walkathon shows became more competitive and more exploitative in later years.

Eells, a faithful observer of dance endurance contests, notes that walkathons provided a training ground for a number of performers like Laine. Comic Dick "Lord" Buckley, who ran into difficulty with the law for smoking marijuana (not an uncommon practice among staff and contestants who referred to it as "tea"), made an easy transition to the world of the night clubs. Rajah Bergman made good use of his experience as did comedians B.S. (Bullshit) Pully and H.S. (Horseshit) Gump. Other well known laugh-makers were "Pistol Pete" Wilson, Red Oleski, Joe Solar and Jimmy Kelly. Charlie Loeb, a member of the walkathon fraternity, had himself shipped in a box to a show for approximately one-fourth the regular fare. He arrived in the crate upside-down. Loeb's specialty was being "buried alive" in blocks of ice (*Hollywood Independent* 4 Sept. 1969, 3).

Walkathon shows were also influential in initiating or furthering the careers of others who were in walkathon shows: comedienne Cass Daley; stripteaser Lili St. Cyr; musician Frankie Little, featured with Spike Jones; radio comic Johnny Morgan; and game show host Randy Merriam; ballroom dancers Nellie Roberts and Bennie Rothman, who performed in the Olsen and Johnson show; comic Tiny Epperson, who was in Cole Porter's *Panama Hattie*; and Hollywood choreographer-director Charlie Curran. Nick Castle, another Hollywood choreographer, reminisced: "We didn't make as much money, but we had a helluva lot more fun" (*Hollywood Independent* 4 Sept. 1969, 43).

Walkathon contests reflected a promoter's style. Notoriously individualistic, promoters fashioned their shows by blending the walking, vaudeville-cabaret and athletic acts in a variety of ways. Often loners, each promoter had his own conception of how to run a walkathon contest.

Hal Ross, who opened his first dance marathon in Omaha in September 1928, promoted at least 59 contests in the United States, in Europe (France and Germany) and in Mexico. Ross viewed walkathon shows, properly run, as a "Family Man's Night Club." He urged promoters to approach the walkathon contest on a "high grade business basis." Ross cautioned against the menace of "Slicker-Type" and "Mr. Fly-By-Night" operators who, along with inexperienced beginners, were responsible for the walkathon business degenerating into a racket. Priding himself on running the dance endurance contest as a legitimate business, Ross collected letters from city officials attesting to this fact. In 1933, Ross claimed that in one year his shows drew one million paid admissions and played before audiences totalling six and a half million people (Mathews Scrapbook).

Ross earned a reputation as a hard taskmaster who ran the strictest shows in the endurance business. His contests terminated in six weeks and required that contestants pick their feet off the floor at all times even while eating at waist-high food tables. Paradoxically, Ross was suspected of being a genuine sadist for such practices, though in a field riddled with chicanery, Ross stood out as a model showman. In contradiction to this sternness in running a contest, Ross was an easy mark in responding to the real or fancied plight of professional marathoners not above mooching between and during shows.

The key to a show's success, Ross reminded fellow promoters, was timing: knowing when to turn on the heat, not too much, but just enough to build up new enthusiasm and keep patrons coming back. Ross added that, "Nearly 57 percent of our audiences are women and they won't stand for the rough stuff. These same women patrons like a few tears mixed in with the laughter." (*The Billboard* 25 Aug. 1934, 43). He further advised walkathon promoters to start selling contestants from the start of the show and keep them sold. He felt that within three weeks, every contestant should have a good following. Ross took out the following ad for a new show in *The Billboard,* June 22, 1935: "Midnight and Afternoon Emcees who can produce clean Blackouts and Bits—no smut. Also a No. 1 Straight Man who can and will sell contestants and show my way" (43).

"King" Brady, in contrast to Ross, ran walkathons which lasted three months, often longer. Contestants were allowed to rock back and forth during the walking act, a practice less taxing than the one enforced by Ross. However, Brady structured his show around gruelling athletic acts; each night, sprints and lap races were extended in duration and made increasingly taxing.

Brady, who entered the dance endurance field in the late 1920s and continued to have successful shows up into the late 1940s, worked as both a promoter and emcee. A master showman, he had an eighth grade education and a practical "seat-of-the-pants" approach to operating walkathon shows. Brady spiced his contest with burlesque and vaudeville skits performed by the Derby Stock Company made up of staff and professional contestants. "A Night In a Turkish Harem," "The Kourt Room Kaper," "The Hillbilly Wedding," and nightclub reviews, "Nite Life in Chicago," "Smoke Ring Follies," and "The School Daze Review," were the names of some of the exotic acts which he featured.

Brady, a risk-taker, experimented with the show format. He once ran a two-in-one show in which amateurs and professionals competed against their own kind; he opened one show with all amateur contestants and it worked. Brady's shows were a potpourri of acts and events. In a 1940 Chicago Walkathon, two female contestants wrestled in mud; the act proved popular and Fox Movietone filmed the event (*The Billboard* 17 Feb. 1940, 26).

Walkathon shows featured variety entertainment. Every night was a specialty night, with red-letter events, such as "Sadie Hawkins Day," "Topsy Turvey Night," "Amateur Night," "Movie Night" and "Carnival Night." On "Country Store Night," three-foot-high bags of groceries were welcomed prizes, especially in the dark days of the Depression when waiting on a bread line for the one meal of the day was not an unusual experience.

Brady attracted top walkathon contestants like Louie Meredith and Chad Alviso. These celebrity teams were favored with the most opportunities to earn money and had priority in receiving medical treatment. In one newspaper exposé, Brady was accused by a female amateur contestant of showing favoritism and worse. During the first week of the show, the uninitiated contestant welcomed sleeping on an army cot covered with white sheets. After the first week, however, the top sheet disappeared, then the bottom sheet, then the pillow case, then the pillow. Left only with a blanket, she wrapped herself in her robe. When her legs and ankles ached and her toes began bleeding, she became further disheartened after her requests for help from the training staff were delayed. She became totally disenchanted while receiving treatment when the floor judge, Dick Gough, who had planned to take some contestants out for a walk in Buffalo as a publicity stunt, told the trainer "Get that girl off the table and back on the floor right away." She returned to the dance floor with swollen ankles and legs (*Buffalo Evening News* 20 Jan. 1933, 1).

Brady took such negative publicity in stride and, in some instances, capitalized on it. In one of his shows, a squad of plain-clothesmen apprehended contestant Dale Cross, who was wanted for robbing more than a half dozen banks. Newspaper reports of the capture brought a sell-out crowd the following night. Eells, a frequent attender at Brady's shows, was surprised when Cross was arrested. "Gentlemanly Dale," who had entered only one contest in the late 1940s and had chosen to hide out on the floor of the walkathon arena, impressed everyone with his politeness and good manners.

To close a show, Brady threw his contest into Non-Stop. Contestants were denied rest; they were allowed a two-minute hygiene period every six hours; and they raced until one couple survived the ordeal. The winners were crowned "King" and "Queen" at "The Victory Ball." The winners received the first prize, $1,000; the second prize winners, $500; the third prize winners, $300; and the fourth prize winners, $100.

One highlight in every Brady show was a walkathon wedding. Whether real or mock (Brady would act as the minister when the gala event was replayed "mock" for the second show), this act joined a couple, most often the designated Sweetheart Couple, in wedlock, an occasion which drew a sell-out audience. Marsha Seligman, who wrote a book on marriage customs, classifies the walkathon wedding with other offbeat weddings: she lists weddings on water skis, horseback, roller skates and on a trapeze, marriages while skydiving and underwater, topless weddings and weddings in Forest Lawn Cemetery. Seligman describes a walkathon wedding in 1930 in which "couples had to keep continually in motion, walking nonstop from contest arena to marriage license bureau, back to arena where the minister walked backward while pronouncing the vows" (201).

Walkathon weddings were preceded by an engagement party and a wedding shower which took place earlier in the week. Professional marathoners remarried the same or different partners in subsequent shows, in new towns and cities, each time generously rewarded with gifts from admiring fans. O'Day writes: "I knew one handsome guy and a cute chick whose act was to enter the show separately, team up, fall in love, get engaged and have a public wedding. They did it in contest after contest, always collecting carloads of shower and wedding gifts" (37).

Brady was an early innovator in using daily radio broadcasts to advertise his walkathon shows. Acting as radio emcee, Brady "worked heat" by painting a vivid word picture of the mayhem in the fiercely contested sprint race between The Sweetheart Couple and The Trouble Makers. Brady also included in his broadcasts a running account of the antics of the comics and clowns in the show to persuade listeners that a good time was to be had by seeing the show live. A shrewd showman, Brady knew that listeners could become addictive patrons. He sought to appeal to patrons like Betty Freund's mother who was deeply involved with walkathon shows. Freund reports:

My mother was obsessed with them. They were broadcast from over the floor at least two times daily on the local radio station (KHQ). One was early in the morning and one was at noon. My mother always listened and had her favorite couple. I went one time and just remember it being sleazy and depressing. But my mother would take her lunch and stay all day. (Martin 52)

Brady was not the only emcee to exploit the power of radio. Jack Freeman received over 1,500 cards in one mail delivery at his hotel in High Point, North Carolina, in connection with a walkathon popularity contest he ran over Station WGY. Martin reports that in Winslow, Illinois, where they didn't have radio, the local telephone operator called 20 miles to the Freeport Walkathon management each morning and then rang her customers with the news about how Winslow's favorite couple was doing (Mathews Scrapbook).

As promoters, Ross and Brady had a lot of muscle in their shows and were highly visible. Some promoters like J.B. Steinel raised the capital to start a show and were rarely seen by contestants once the show began. When Brady worked as an emcee for Steinel, the promoter let Brady run things. Other promoters, like Ray "Pop" Dunlap, when partnered with Ross, controlled the money while Ross ran the show.

Each promoter had his favorite professional teams to get the show off to a good start. *The Billboard* served as a promoter's medium to establish contact with contestants and other show personnel. Under the column headed "Endurance Shows," Jack Steinel placed this announcement: "Have City license to operate. No collect wires or calls. No transportation unless I know you. Former employees and teams who have wardrobes and can take a fast show write" (*The Billboard* 12 Oct. 1935, 25). Hugh Talbott similarly advertised in *The Billboard*: "Must have good wardrobe, good reputation and be able to stand good treatment from a good operator, whose good shows have made good money for good kids" (*The Billboard* 26 Oct. 1935, 34).

Promoters experimented with different show formats to keep audience interest alive. They paced their contests. If box office receipts were good, they made less strenuous demands on the contestants so the contests would last longer. If box office receipts dropped, they speeded things up by introducing more events certain to eliminate contestants rapidly. Ray "Pop" Dunlap, after his shows reached the thousand-hour mark, ran the following program:

Monday: Zombie Treadmills (1 Hour Duration)
Tuesday: Figure-Eight Races (25 Laps)
Wednesday: Elimination Lap Races (Male Contestants)
Thursday: Dynamite Sprints
Friday: Heel and Toe Derbies
Saturday: Elimination Races (Female Contestants)
Sunday: The Argonne Forest

By the twelfth week, the 50 teams that started in the Dunlap contest were reduced to six couples and one solo. Contestants in the 1934 Revere Beach Show held in Maine, did 1,050 laps per day, or 13 and three quarter miles; each subsequent day, 50 laps were added.

The changes which had taken place in dance endurance contests from the early days were highlighted in the article in *The Billboard* entitled "Old Time Marathon Revived, Goes 107 Hours." In this event, which took place in Detroit in August 1935, contestants were required to dance rather than walk and there was a strict rule of three-minute rests in every hour. After 100 hours, two girls and three boys fought it out for seven hours to a draw (*The Billboard* 31 Aug. 1935, 30).

Big time show promoters like Leo Seltzer had highly specialized organizations with staff members experienced in the entertainment field. In 1933, Seltzer opened a show at the World's Fair in Chicago, billed as "The Race of Nations," with contestants representing 33 countries. Seltzer and his partner, Sid Cohen, operated several contests concurrently; they were businessmen to be reckoned with.

Seltzer is a study in contradictions. He acknowledged that he, along with other big-time promoters, were forced to pay off local politicians to open a contest and keep it open. (He referred to these public servants as "dignified gangsters.") But Seltzer denied carrying professional contestants on a weekly salary, a common if not universal practice. Seltzer was on the board of directors of the National Endurance Amusement Association, a watchdog organization set up to police practices in walkathon shows. However, in an interview with the author, he denied that such an organization ever existed, despite the prominent coverage that this landmark event received in *The Billboard*, a publication for which Seltzer had written articles.

Seltzer, always enterprising, left the dance endurance field in 1935 and started roller derbies. But he denied any relationship between his newest brain child and walkathon shows. In fact, both enterprises borrowed from each other. Walkathon operators adopted the practice of choreographing races, "jamming," to heighten the excitement of these athletic events. In turn, roller derby operators adapted the idea of The Sweetheart Couple against The Trouble Makers; Seltzer designated the former, the "Home-Town Team" and the latter, the "Visitors," although both teams were in his hire.

Spectators viewing the variety of elimination features advertised as bringing "thrills and chills from harrowing spills" seemed willing and ready to suspend disbelief. A similar response is reported at professional wrestling matches (Craven and Mosley 326-36). When star contestant Louie Meredith helped his archrival Hughie Hendrickson to his feet, after the latter had fallen during a fiercely competitive Dynamite Sprint, admiring fans applauded this selfless act. After the race was over, the good samaritan, whose gesture had been carefully planned, was greeted with showers of coins when he performed his specialty act. Louie and Hughie, personally good friends, had the last laugh, back stage, after arousing audiences to a state of uproar. When they appeared in separate shows, each sent the other congratulatory telegrams, their messages relayed to the audience by the emcee.

Every night athletic features were introduced to make the contest seem harder. To close a show, contests were thrown into Non-Stop. In order to break a tie, the two remaining couples ran for 30 minutes, rested three minutes, then ran another 20 minutes, stood motionless for five minutes, then ran with arms extended sideways for five minutes, etc., until one couple collapsed. The important thing was to put on a good show for the audience and to make it look believable. Staging sprints and derbies worked out with the precision of a choreographed dance took considerable planning and skill. The trips, spills and falls which were most dramatically staged and then followed by near miraculous recoveries were the ones which brought the most cheers from the audience. Few fans of walkathon shows seemed the wiser for these simulated heroics or the collusion making them possible. Even fewer cared. What mattered was the welcome respite a "click" show offered from the hard times.

Public reaction to walkathon shows was mixed. In a street interview conducted by the *New York Daily Mirror*, May 2, 1932, Frances Winarsky, a private secretary, said she did not approve of such contests because of the drain on human vitality which, in turn, brought out the worst in people in the form of jealousy and rivalry. Jeremiah Murphy, an electrical engineer, thought the contest a good idea if the contestants were physically able to handle the strain and if the contests were closely supervised. King Brown, a transportation engineer, responded to the inquiry by noting that the number of contests in progress vouched for their popularity; he felt that while not exactly a dignified way of earning a living, being in a walkathon was better than being on a bread line (Mathews Scrapbook).

Years after these interviews, Gig Young, in preparation for playing the role of the opportunistic emcee in the film *They Shoot Horses, Don't They?*, conducted his own survey. "I did talk to a lot of people who had attended them and not one of them could tell me why they went. I think they went because they could pay two bits and stay as long as they liked and leave feeling a little less miserable about their own lives. It was a cheap form of therapy during the depression" (Interview).

Ross, Brady, and Seltzer, and a dozen or so other top promoters dominated the walkathon field. They often worked with partners so that if the show was a flop, there was somebody to share the loss. These showmen/entrepreneurs attracted the best teams to the walkathon business. There were, in addition, other second level promoters who ran contests with teams who had less athletic skill and talent. At the lowest level, there were the "fly by night" operators who shamefully exploited both staff and contestants solely for their own profit. These short-sighted, "get-rich-quick" promoters were a menace to show promoters who attempted to run the dance endurance as a bona fide business.

The exciting action at walkathon contests invariably happened at the evening shows when crowds flocked thickest. This fact did not escape the attention of George Eells, who attended his first walkathon show in 1932, at The Palace of Wasted Foot Steps in Freeport, Illinois:

> I was eight years old and not overly precocious, but it took me only a couple of visits to realize that they [the walkathons] operate on the same principle as the weekly wrestling matches and were not too distantly removed from the melodramas that the Jack & Maude Brooks Stock Co. offered. (154)

Eells, as a young boy, saw contestants as living adventurous lives. Later, as entertainment editor, Eells commented:

> You didn't have to be very astute to figure out that something was wrong when shows that had big crowds always had strong contestants and shows that had small crowds had weak contestants...the bigger the show, the more potentially lucrative the spot, the higher the percentage of pros. (Interview)

Eells's early experiences with walkathon shows initiated a life-long interest. Following the walkathon "game" over the years, Eells made other observations. From his contacts with walkathon personnel and with professional contestants, Eells uncovered a number of practices which pointed to the likelihood that most, if not all, walkathon contests were rigged. He found, for example, that if a local amateur team were being groomed as "The Sweetheart Couple" for a forthcoming walkathon wedding, it was rare that this team would be disqualified before the wedding took place.

Eells learned of other practices. In the early morning hours, at 4 a.m., when few if any patrons were present, professional teams staged practice performances. Sprint races, for example, were carefully choreographed for optimum dramatic impact. In addition, these early morning sessions were used to gauge the relative strengths and weaknesses of each team since performances might vary from one night to the next. Legitimate sprints during these early morning trials proved which team was the strongest. At show time, the real winners might lose to a weaker team who were crowd favorites. Appropriate adjustments were made in the prize money. Eells also learned of "internal" arrangements made among professional contests. During the final days of the contest, with fewer than five teams remaining, an agreement would be reached to split the prize money.

The key to walkathon shows, true of today's professional wrestling events, was not the contest but the theatrical spectacle. What remained a well-guarded trade secret, kept from audiences and, strangely, from some professional contestants in the show, was the fact that every walkathon promoter carried a coterie of professional marathoners. He referred to them as "my teams," and paid them weekly sums ranging from $75 to $150 depending upon their ability to pull in customers.

The collusion between show promoter and professional contestant might take several forms. One practice occurred when the contest went into its final phase with only a few remaining teams. At this point, one of the paid professionals would be told to stage a fall with as much histrionics as possible. Jimmy Priori, who worked 10 years in dance endurance shows, remembers being told in several contests "to take a fall" so that a local team might win. Priori received a salary of $75 per week for five months in a South Kearney show (Interview). Another instance of this practice was reported by Frankie Laine who was offered $500 a week extra "to take a dive, put on a good show so that the hometown boy could win and please the paying customers" (Ripton 22).

Still other arrangements were made. If a portly contestant contributed entertainment to the show with his comic routines, he was kept in the contest even though his physical prowess might not have warranted his staying. At nightly sprint and derby events, he and his partner raced against other slow teams or against fast teams who modified their pace. Eells noted that the longer walkathon shows operated over the years, the more likely they were subject to collusive practices.

Ironically, the mid-1930s, when walkathon contests enjoyed their greatest popularity, was also a time of soul searching for concerned show promoters. Richard Kaplan, walkathon attorney, acting as the watchdog of the industry, continued to warn promoters that unless they banded together, the days of walkathon shows were numbered. Kaplan alerted promoters to the fact that while most of the court decisions in over 300 cases between 1928 and 1934 attested to the legitimacy and legality of walkathon shows, by 1955, half the states of the Union were enforcing statutes against endurance contests. In addition, many cities in other open states barred dance endurance shows by local nuisance ordinances (*The Billboard* 2 Feb. 1935, 27).

What remained a damning reality was the long history of abuse and chicanery which characterized dance endurance enterprises. From the earliest shows in the 1920s, both racketeer "slicker" promoters and inexperienced beginners, attracted by the promise of fabulous sums to be made in this form of show business, continued to exploit new territories, with dull shows, run with inefficient organizations in a haphazard manner. Racketeer promoters, using assumed names, advertised coming shows in desirable locations, then opened them in less promising areas or did not open them at all. Other opportunistic promoters held contests in facilities where sleeping quarters were filthy and poorly ventilated. Fly-by-night operators left contestants stranded in out-of-the-way places when they prematurely abandoned a contest. Such slicker promoters "burned up" territories by leaving a trail of unpaid bills owed to irate local merchants. When the show promoter ran out of the 1935 Denver show before it opened, it was "Pop" Dunlap and Ross who bailed out Dick Edwards by paying off the contestants and staff (*The Billboard* 28 Sept. 1935, 30).

Sabotage from within took other forms. The acrimonious rivalry between show promoters at times involved the law. Eells recounts how flirtatious Hilda, "a comedienne who looked like an animated Raggedy Ann," stabbed a rival promoter with a pair of scissors in the leg to protect her boyfriend/promoter (61). In another instance, a jealous contestant alerted plain clothesmen that Jimmy, her superstud partner, was having affairs with girls from the town. Eells writes: "...Jimmy's sexual athleticism was responsible for closing at least half a dozen Iowa towns to the endurance business" (Eells 154).

In one show held in 1931-1932, at the Mid-City Amusement Park Casino near Albany, New York, a dozen plain clothesmen in the audience stopped the show. They quickly acted after witnessing a female contestant being tripped by another couple, causing her to fall and cut herself. The show promoters were arrested. Charles Mooney, a police reporter on the scene, observed that army cots backstage had dirty blankets; male and female quarters were separated only by a tarpaulin hanging across the room. Talking with some of the contestants, Mooney noted several references made to "bedbugs." While in the audience he observed that the spectators were "hot-eyed" (highly excited). From what he could determine, many of the spectators were there "because they didn't know what to do with their time" (Interview).

Ross regarded walkathons as a business which should be run properly on a high grade business level, a "Family Man's Night Club." He featured Jane Shannon, a personable Irish girl who he called the "Blue Flame of Melody." Ross was known for running legitimate shows; his contests were never rigged; he did not program who would win, who would lose, and who would drop out. If a contestant fell down, he or she was disqualified, whether it happened at show time or at any other time. Despite the physically demanding regimen he enforced which required contestants to pick up their feet at all times rather than merely shift their weight back and forth, Ross attracted the best teams.

Ross identified the following key features of a successful show: never let interest in the show lag from the early entertainment stage to the time when audiences become identified with contestants; utilize special nights, costumed events and athletic features to turn on the heat, not too much, but enough to keep the crowd's interest; never try to milk your contest past its usefulness, causing a bad taste in the city you are playing; use a radio tieup but don't pay $350 a week for radio time and then hire a cheap emcee who will ruin your show; pay particular attention that food dishes be suitably prepared and dressed and that resting quarters be properly cleaned. Ross's parting advice: "Remember, an army fights on its stomach and so do walkathon contestants" (*The Billboard* 25 Aug. 1934, 43).

Ross saw the walkathon business menaced by two undesirable types. The first types were the "Racketeer" and "Slicker" Types who opened spots and killed them. These promoters started shows with backers who invested $500 to $1,000 when successful shows required opening sums which ranged from

$3,000 to $10,000. "Mr. Fly-By-Night" promoters had no location, no publicity, insufficient financing, and a harum-scarum organization hastily assembled. Bills were left unpaid and contestants stranded. A trail of dupes and victims with mediocre camp followers to seek more misguided sponsors and contestants resulted. Ross did not accept the excuse of show promoters who cried: "Hard luck" or "Not getting the breaks." Ross's advice to sponsors such as park and auditorium managers included the following cautions: make the man who approaches you show some real credentials; then check references from responsible business people, radio stations, banks, public officials and others he has done business with. Ross, himself, had a scrapbook of commendatory letters from these sources (*The Billboard* 25 Aug. 1934, 43).

One instance of the "slicker" promoter was reported in a 1933 newspaper under the headline: "DANCE CONTEST ENDS AS BISHOP CALLS IN POLICE. Failure to Provide Newly Married Couple with $100 Gift Causes Trouble." Rev. Charles Nelson, Bishop of the United Christian Church of America, had officiated at a walkathon wedding and later learned that the management had not kept its promise to pay the married couple. The bishop's outcry before the walkathon audience caused the disgruntled staff and contestants and the disenchanted fans to riot (Mathews Scrapbook).

"Slicker" promoters weren't the only undesirable characters in the walkathon business. Ross identified a second group, the "Beginners," novices who learned, too late, that it is a business learned by years of bitter experience (*The Billboard* 25 Aug. 1934, 43). Ross ended his article with these sobering words: "I shiver at some of the experiences of the past. I shudder when I think of the present and I am skeptical of the future unless we fight to keep the walkathon a clean, legitimate business and not let it degenerate into a racket." If proof were needed that walkathons could be a profitable business venture, legitimately run, *The Billboard* reported that Ross's show in Oklahoma City, in 1935, in which Hughie Hendrickson and Babs Evans won first prize, had a capacity crowd of 6,800 on the final night. Prices were raised to 25 cents and 55 cents for reserve seats; during the course of the show, 222,000 tickets had been sold (*The Billboard* 25 Aug. 1934, 43).

Added to the sabotage from within were equally strong pressures from without. Kaplan exhorted promoters to read the article entitled, "To End Marathon Menace," which appeared in *Box Office*, the publication regarded as the pulse of the motion picture industry (*The Billboard* 29 June 1935, 31). The statement in this trade publication was unambiguous, the intent clear: TO DRIVE THE ENDURANCE CONTEST OUT OF THIS COUNTRY BECAUSE OF THE ALLEGED DRAIN ON THE MOTION PICTURE INDUSTRY. One form of pressure was to encourage theatrical managers to stop advertising in media that carried news of walkathon shows.

More damaging to the future of dance endurance shows than this form of pressure were more indirect steps being taken. The theatre lobby instigated whispering campaigns aimed at parent-teacher organizations, and especially at ladies' protective associations such as "The Mother's League for Good Morals." Kaplan questioned the hypocrisy that allowed "the filth that some critics reported in so many current pictures to be permitted—no legislative body had dared to pass legislation prohibiting motion pictures—while walkathons were being outlawed for indecency" (*The Billboard* 29 June 1935, 31).

Ammunition for the campaign against walkathon shows was ready at hand; some promoters did operate illegitimate, disreputable shows. Kaplan felt organizations and clubs were being used as foils to influence city councils, commissioners, supervisors and legislators to pass prohibitory legislation. He denounced this legislation as unconstitutional and invalid, legislation which would not withstand a vigorous legal assault. Kaplan cited the case tried in San Jose, California, in which the court ruled that the evidence "demonstrated that the contest is not per se dangerous, but its evil rests in the way it is conducted...at most, the testimony showed need for regulation of the contest" (*The Billboard* 25 March 1935, 70).

Pressure to ban walkathon shows mounted during the early 1930s. On Feb. 2, 1933, the New York State Federation of Women's Clubs backed proposed legislation for a ban. On April 27, 1933, Governor Lehman signed a bill banning walkathon shows in New York State. Other cities followed suit: Boston, San Francisco, Los Angeles, Portland, Seattle and Tacoma. On the side of walkathon enterprises was the National Association of Amusement Parks which acknowledged that dance endurance shows were profitable and provided excellent entertainment during their average run of two to four months. This association informed its members that the marathon business was highly specialized, just as the park business, and that the best way to avoid grief was to work with the many reputable promoters who conducted clean, fair contests (*The Billboard* 17 March 1934, 25).

Walkathon shows, even without outside pressure from the theatre lobby, were periodically attacked in the pulpit. A newspaper article captioned "5 Couples Dance 106 Days, Labor Law May Stop 'em" reported that witnesses at the 1930 marathon were shocked at the spectacle which "rivals the most savage dances of primitive people." Reverend Roland Travers of the Mount Clemens Baptist Church, waging a campaign against a local walkathon show, sermonized: "It was the saddest most heart-breaking affair I have ever attended...it was not a funeral service over a dead body, but far worse...it was the slow death of the physical, mental and spiritual natures of nearly a dozen young people" (Mathews Scrapbook).

Unfavorable publicity exacerbated matters still further. There were claims that walkathon contests contributed to the delinquency of minors; that they destroyed peace and quiet and diminished the value of property adjacent to places where walkathon shows were in operation; and that walkathon shows were dangerous to the morals, health, and safety of participants. One incident cited was the fire which broke out in the Paradise Dance Pavilion in Hampden, Maine, in 1933, which claimed the lives of five contestants. Unfavorable publicity had similarly been directed at burlesque shows in New York City, spear-headed by local property owners, "legitimate" theatre managers, politicians and clergy who branded this form of show business insulting and outrageous, forcing them to close in 1937 (Toll).

There were incidents, however, in which walkathon promoters and show personnel were not the perpetrators of insulting and outrageous behavior. In Waterbury, Connecticut, a group of youths from the "south end" began heckling the walkathoners; one drunken youth started to sprinkle the contents of a whisky bottle upon the lumbering and trudging couples. Cautioned by both floor judge and security guard, the youth persisted in spraying liquor on the contestants giving his excuse: "It's only perfume." When the strapping trainer/masseur grabbed the ringleader and pulled him out of his seat, a riot broke out in which gang members fought against show personnel and contestants. With chairs and bottles flying, female contestants and fans sought safety. By the time the police arrived, the bellicose gang members had been ejected through the side entrance (Mathews Scrapbook). Such episodes made newspaper copy and soured the public on walkathon shows.

The abuses which critics of walkathon shows identified were usually exaggerated. In a rare report which appeared in a professional journal, Ruth Mix, a social worker in charge of the Girls' Protective Association, interviewed one female contestant in March 1934, to discover to what extent participating in a walkathon contest was injurious. In answer to her queries, her informant gave the following report:

"Yes," said Jessie, "I was in the marathon. Sure I liked it! We had a lot of fun. You see it wasn't really a marathon, it was a walkathon. I was in it for 112 days and I won the fifth prize which was $37.50. I thought it would be more when I went in but we make the most money on 'sprays.' (That's the money they throw you from the audience for your solo stunts.) I picked up $29 one night in a spray for me.

Did you hear me on the radio? Gee, I never knew I could sing before but one night, they gave me a singing lesson for my solo stunt. That was the night they sprayed me with $29.

No, we never had time out to sleep. We only had eleven minutes off out of every ninety. We used to sleep standing up. Honest! I've slept for three hours at a stretch moving all the time. At first, I couldn't, but after I got tired, believe me, I could. The idea is, your partner pushes you around while you sleep if he is a good partner, but some of them are mean. My partners were all good to me. I wore out five of them. But I was good to them too. They couldn't understand how I could push around Jimmy Donahue, when he weighed 150 pounds and I only weighed 116. But I did it.

Rough crowd? No, they're lovely people. And believe me, the management won't stand for any 'monkey business.' We were allowed 15 minutes a day for a hot shower. And every morning, the referee took us for a thirty minute walk out doors. You see we could do that because it was a walkathon instead of a marathon.

Folks were surprised that I stayed in so long 'cause it was my first time in a marathon. I would have been in it yet only I caught a cold and that made me collapse on the floor. But I gained four pounds! You don't think I look well? Oh nuts—I feel fine. Doctors can't understand how we do it. I'm going in another just as soon as I get a little rested. There's one going to start in Newark and I think I'll go down there. They say you can't stand being in more than three but I'll show them. If I go, I'll let you know so you can be sure to hear me over the radio this time." ("Forum" 169-170)

Mix's concern was voiced in *The Survey*, which reported that, in 1934, there were more marathons in operation than most people realized, and that the morbid interest they attracted was growing rather than diminishing. Characterizing walkathon shows as an "extraordinary form of amusement," she voiced considerable anxiety about a form of entertainment which recruited women locally, young girls who then followed shows from place to place and were exposed to all sorts of demoralizing conditions (53). Despite the general enthusiasm expressed by her informant, Mix concluded: "It is so emotionally stimulating that it takes away a desire for any honest work" ("Forum" 169-170).

Contestants were given a cursory physical examination before entering a walkathon show; no attempt was made to screen for psychological problems. Given the number of those who entered walkathon contests, it was not strange that the following story made newspaper copy. An 18-year-old girl was placed in a state institution after she had been in Steinel's show for eight days. Kaplan reported that the girl was disqualified after a few days, and that many days later, due to a disapproving love affair, she became mentally unbalanced. He added: "Let me point out once and for all that NEVER HAS A GIRL BEEN INJURED MENTALLY OR PHYSICALLY BECAUSE OF HER PARTICIPATION IN A CONTEST." Kaplan queried: "Was it the fault of the walkathon show she fell in love?" (*The Billboard* 22 Feb. 1936, 27).

As good spots continued to be used up and repeat shows became more and more difficult to book, increasing reliance was placed on "the patch." Acting as the walkathon public relations man, the patch functioned as a trouble shooter whenever there was opposition, both public and private, to the opening and continuation of a walkathon contest. Fixers ran through all itinerant show business enterprises. Walkathons were no exception; it was not far from the truth to say that there wasn't a promoter who didn't pay off someone in town. There was no one way to fix a contest; practices depended upon the promoter, the show, the year in which the show was held, etc. A good patch would bribe public officials from the mayor's office to health, fire and police departments, offering whatever minimum sums were acceptable.

Alleged attempts to shake down a promoter by public officials periodically made headlines. In October 31, 1931, *The Newark Star Eagle* reported: "Sheriff's Aide Charged With Dance Racket." The scandal began when Sheriff Huelsenbeck stopped the show operated by Zeke Youngblood and George Ruty in Atlantic City. In the ensuing investigation, Ruty charged that Charles Hummel, a Deputy Sheriff, had taken him to the store of George Washington Davis, a Republican politician, who demanded $5,000 from Ruty to permit him to start his contest. Huelsenbeck, in his investigation, found no validity to the charge of shake down. Twelve years later, in 1943, Ruty contended that he had to pay $100 a day to a Police Commissioner in order to keep his contest open (*The Billboard* 5 June 1943, 27).

George Pughe, another veteran promoter, felt similarly victimized. In answering a court order to close, Pughe reported that in his 1938 Derbyshow, sponsored by the local Lions Club, "Not a single penny of legal money was spent during the entire engagement." Further, Pughe claimed that his show, made up of professionals, "was not a contest because the show had a definite date to begin and end because trophies were awarded in his own discretion rather than as prizes" (*The Billboard* June 18, 38). Two years earlier, Pughe offered a $50 reward for information leading to the arrest of a party who represented Jimmy Parker as his advance representative, cashing checks and soliciting loans (*The Billboard* 28 March 1936, 30).

The big question throughout the Depression years when walkathon shows were in their heyday was posed by Kaplan: "Would the dance endurance contest be accepted as a legitimate form of show business or would it die?" Kaplan admitted that the industry should be regulated but cited the following court judgment in favor of walkathon shows: "Just because a few dishonorable and incapable men conduct a legitimate business in a rotten manner is no reason for passing legislation that will prohibit and prevent an honest and capable man from conducting that same business in an honest and capable manner" (*The Billboard* 25 Jan. 1936, 31).

In response to mounting criticism, Kaplan met with leading show promoters and presented a proposed program, "A Code of Fair Practice," as regulatory legislation for the industry. The National Endurance Amusement Association was formed with Hal Ross as president, George Pughe as Vice President, Don King as Treasurer, and Richard Kaplan as General Counsel-Secretary. The Board of Directors included Ray Alvis, Leo Seltzer, Guy Swartz, Hugh Talbott, and S.M. Fox. *The Billboard* reported the details of this landmark event which took place in Chicago on May 28, 1935 (*The Billboard* 8 June 1935, 28-29). The program had the following goals:

1) protect against operators who do not pay prize money or wages thus eliminating illegitimate competitors;

2) guarantee suitable working conditions for employees;

3) provide transportation for contestants who have walked more than 500 hours and who have been regularly disqualified;

4) protect both contestants and employees against abuse of power by operators;

5) protect the legitimate contestant against chiseling and conniving illegitimate operators and contestants;

6) arbitrate disputes which may arise between contestants, operators and employers.

The N.E.E.A. would serve to educate the public on the values of dance endurance shows. For example, Kaplan wanted the public to know that some 1,500 emcees, trainers, nurses and floor judges, along with 5,000 union and non-union workmen, were employed in this show business enterprise. Even more important in a time of closed factories and abandoned stores were the following significant figures: each walkathon show spent not less than $10,000 in the city or town where it opened and as high as $60,000 in a period of three months for groceries, workmen and supplies.

Additionally, the N.E.E.A. would act as a clearing house for latest information on pending unfavorable legislation. Promoters in legal trouble would have assistance. The N.E.E.A. could, in addition, arbitrate the claims of two promoters who wanted to open in the same location. Not the least value of the N.E.E.A. would be to keep a file, available to owners of arenas who rented space to walkathon promoters, of chiseler operators and hotel marathoners (*The Billboard* 19 Oct., 16 Nov. 1935, 28).

Kaplan estimated that some 20,000 people made their living in walkathon shows in 1935, as floor judges, nurses, trainers, emcees, publicity men, promoters, cashiers, dieticians and contestants. He noted that among those who competed, there were only "real contestants." He strongly urged that promoters use the real ones and bar the others who were "connivers," "food chasers" and "agitators" (*The Billboard* 16 Nov. 1935, 27). Kaplan exhorted all promoters to join the association and warned them: "We do not want court fights! We do not want FIXES!" He reminded show operators: "The public is amusement hungry...and you can give it to them without the bosh and the bunk which has been heretofore employed" (*The Billboard* 19 Oct. 1935, 28).

Joe Piccinelli, a respected "heat judge," sounded a similar warning. He said the future of the walkathons depended upon about 75 teams, "old-timers in the business, who were interested in shows as a livelihood, not in entering for the glory of it" (*The Billboard* 29 Jan. 1938, 30). Among Kaplan's "800 real contestants" and Piccinelli's "75 old-timer teams," included the following names (not already noted): Johnny Russo, Jayne Moon, Patsy Gallagher, Eddie Fox, Ray Leonard, Eileen Thayer, Helen Tyne, Phil Rainey, Johnny Hughes, Eddie Begley, Ruthie Booth, Fay DiMarco, Norman Lehman, Eddie Leonard, Ginger Rheudel, Buddy Jeffries, Jerry Guertin, Hazel Dietrich, Alice Simms, Don King, Margie King, Jackie Murphy, Peggy Collins, Dave White, Phil Arnold, Cecilia Keith McKinney, Joe and Margie Van Raam, Jack Stasik, Jimmy Firenzi, Jack Galuppo, Alice Donato and Benny Leonard.

In his weekly column in *The Billboard*, Kaplan identified many areas in which walkathon shows were open to criticism. He proposed that the name Walkathon or Walkashow be dropped at once and the entire form of the endurance contest be altered. He advised promoters to stop using the word "squirrely" in ads. He reminded the walkathon staff to keep resting quarters clean and sanitary. He further advised promoters not to permit a marathon wedding unless the parties to the contract were both single and had never been married to each other before. Kaplan cautioned show promoters that soliciting the sporting element to start a show would bring trouble. He reminded both beginning and veteran promoters that it was none other than Mrs. America, the housewife, who was the main support of the show; sell her, he maintained, and the contest was off to a good start. Kaplan outlined a series of athletic events which could be featured along with the entertainment that songs, dances, instrumental music, stooging and acrobatics provided. Not of least importance was his caution that it is of no help to use the radio as advertisement when emcees rattle words, singers can't sing and musicians can't play.

Concern about the future of walkathon shows came from contestants who wrote to Kaplan with these queries: "What shall I do? Continue as a marathoner or look for a job?" "Will the walkathon business last much longer or is the business dead?" "What are the operators doing to help restore the business?" Kaplan did attempt to give contestants sound advice as to how they could help the walkathon business (*The Billboard* 4 April 1936, 26).

Kaplan cautioned contestants not to go to locations where shows were to open until notified to do so. Once registered in the contest, he added these do's and don'ts: don't use profanity in quarters or on the floor; don't use vulgarity; do keep your hands to yourself; do be clean at all times, physically and morally; do help the nurse or trainer keep the quarters clean at all times; don't smoke while on the floor or in your quarters, and if you must smoke, do so while on your hygiene break where it is safe; don't speak out of turn; don't agitate on the floor; don't pay attention to other promoters' telegrams asking you to leave the show; do be courteous, friendly, gentlemanly and ladylike at all times.

Kaplan had advice for contestants in how to relate to audiences. He emphasized: "TALKING TO PATRONS ACROSS THE RAILS is bad...all notes or conversations shall be received through the floor judge for, to the public mind, there's always that false suspicion that someone is being framed" (*The Billboard* 21 Dec. 1935, 29). A deadly sin was to cross the boundary between the natural rivalry which exploded into a fist fight in front of the public.

Kaplan counseled floor judges as well. They were to dress appropriately and stand on an upraised platform off the floor away from the contestants. Familiarity between floor judges and contestants was absolutely forbidden. Since a floor judge was presumed to be impartial, he should keep his distance; all kidding or joking with contestants which could result in loss of power and control was ill-advised. Furthermore, all forms of heat, whistle blowing, handkerchief snapping and the use of chains or straps were to be eliminated forever. Kaplan went so far as to suggest that female judges should be used so that "the hard boiled attitude" which male judges adopted would disappear.

In cautioning floor judges, Kaplan attempted to eliminate such occurrences reported in a newspaper account with the following headline: "MAY FILE PROTEST AGAINST MARATHON: Citizens are Incensed Against Treatment of Participants by Floor Judge." In the Keansburg Marathon, Ernest Youngblood, the floor judge, had shown such brutality toward the participants that several fell unconscious to the floor. When Larry Troy, the show emcee, remonstrated with Youngblood, his actions precipitated a small riot in which several bottles flew and many ladies present fainted. The sheriff warned Jay Mans, the show promoter, to stop such occurrences or he would close the contest. Kaplan, of course, knew what audiences did not know; floor judges like Youngblood colluded with the show emcee in "working heat." Play-acting in this (and other) instances went beyond the bounds of propriety.

Kaplan cautioned emcees not to fall in love with contestants. The notice in *The Billboard* that an "Unloaded gun hurts Freddie Hall, emcee, shot in neck by girl amateur entertainer, who didn't know it was loaded," pointed to this practice. Kaplan adjured emcees to eliminate the affectionate terms "honey" and "dearie" in speaking to girl contestants, and to avoid getting "personal" with audiences. "With these changes," he added, "I defy the authorities or 'blue noses' to stop it [the show] by law" (*The Billboard* 29 Jan. 1938, 30).

Kaplan answered critics who claimed that participation in walkathon contests was injurious to health by retorting that "the kids must be in perfect physical condition to compete in daily elimination races; that through regularity of habit, they gain weight ranging from six to twenty-one pounds during a three month period...that they ACTUALLY SLEEP from eight to ten hours each day" (*The Billboard* 29 Jan. 1938, 30). He further claimed that in their recreation periods, in and out of the building, contestants could play games, read, run or do anything they wished. They also had seven minutes out of every hour for personal hygiene periods and seven minutes every hour for medical attention. In addition, contestants were given an entertainment period of 30 minutes each day, 16 minutes for cleanup every afternoon and not less than 20 minutes in which to bathe every morning. Beyond these intervals for health care and recreation, there were seven nutrition periods in which contestants were fed three heavy meals, each meal lasting 20 minutes and shorter periods for four light lunches (*The Billboard* 30 Nov. 1935, 37).

Richard Elliot, who ran several shows on his own (in addition to working with Ross), was more accurate than Kaplan in estimating how much sleep contestants did obtain. Theoretically, Elliot noted that contestants could get seven hours of sleep in each 24 period—15 minutes of every hour, plus an extra hour they might be given. In actuality, he estimated that after taking time going and returning to the dance floor, taking care of personal needs and preparing for the show, contestants probably slept no more than four hours in rest quarters which they supplemented with sleeping on their feet on the dance floor (Interview with R. Elliot 7).

In his defense of walkathon shows, Kaplan cited the fact that since 1879, when the first walking contest was held, the walkathon had not been responsible for the death or injury of a single participant. Compare this safety record, he reminded critics of walkathon shows, with the fatalities from high school and college football. In a four-year period, he noted that these sports were responsible for 150 deaths (*The Billboard* 18 Jan. 1936, 30). Kaplan added that baseball, boxing, wrestling, hockey, the rodeo and the circus all cause injuries. To drive home his point that walkathons were not injurious to health, Kaplan noted that "the kids MUST be in perfect physical condition to compete in the strenuous athletic races and could not do so if they indulged in alcoholic drinks, excess smoking, or dissipation of any kind." Kaplan declared, in fact, that "contestants, as a class, are just as moral as the citizens of the community and more so" (*The Billboard* 1 Feb. 1936, 28).

Kaplan, having adopted the role of watchdog which Will Hays played in the movie industry, for all his salutary recommendations to sanitize walkathon contests and keep them visible, avoided a core question: "Were walkathon shows legitimate?" Eells learned from floor judge Earl Clark that Hal J. Ross ran short, legit shows, that is, shows whose outcome was not prearranged. Clark added that he thought promoter George Pughe ran relatively legit shows. After inquiring from a number of sources, Eells generalized "that the earlier in the business that you talk about, the more likely it is that the contest was on the level" (Interview).

It is difficult to render any certain judgment as to the temporary or lasting medical and psychological effects that dance endurance shows had upon contestants. In 1929, Everett Perlman and G.W. Nelson wrote a small booklet entitled *The Marathon Guide.* In this booklet, the authors record their observations of the physical and psychological condition of contestants in three dance marathons in which Perlman was the house "doctor" (Martin 63). Though he acknowledged that the American public appeared to be equally divided for and against walkathon shows, Perlman viewed this form of show business as good clean entertainment, a splendid sport if properly conducted. He added, however, that walkathon shows did generate a spirit of "marathonitis" which gripped and fascinated audiences.

Perlman cautioned that contestants could suffer deleterious effects if they were not careful; young people, unprepared and untrained, would face hardships. He found that foot ailments and problems with posture could develop. He observed that as the contests wore on, female contestants developed marked stooped shoulders, sagging of the abdominal viscera and a slouching gait. He further noted that exposure, the loss of sleep and the continual exercise did lower resistance to colds, sore throats, eye inflammation and hand and finger infections. Even though attention was given to preparing healthy meals, contestants could develop gastric upsets if their voracious appetite drove them to eat food other than from the proposed menu. If contestants were careful, Perlman found that nearly all contestants put on weight and that blood pressure remained normal.

Perlman noted that mental disturbances among contestants were slight. Once again, however, despite this support for this form of entertainment, he did acknowledge that participating in the regimen of the walkathon show had psychological side effects. When contestants went "squirrely" for a certain period of time, they displayed behavior observed in patients who sleepwalk. In these states of semi-consciousness, contestants' speech rambled and was incoherent and when contestants were awakened, they were irritable. Perlman also noted that over time, contestants gradually lost interest in any form of amusement, in games, reading newspapers, or writing letters.

Perlman also did report the following episode and offered cautionary advice:

A girl was dancing with a young man. The doctors discovered that she was crying and investigation revealed that great areas on the upper part of the body were black and blue from his pinching, particularly around the chest. The couple was disqualified immediately and the girl placed under a physician's care. We mention this because the reader may have a daughter or sister under the same circumstances, and it may be said that dancers must be watched very closely. (Perlman and Nelson, 60)

Despite the need for reform, the N.E.E.A. never took hold. Kaplan attributed the demise of the N.E.E.A. to promoters who expected too much and contestants who wanted something for nothing. A modest membership fee of $100 for promoters, $10 for emcees, $5 for floor judges, trainers and nurses and $2 for contestants, could not explain the lack of response. Footloose professional marathoners, who often depended upon promoters to make their decisions for them, followed the lead of promoters and did not lend their support to the N.E.E.A. Part of the fault for the failure of the N.E.E.A. to take hold lay with promoters who considered themselves "loners," fiercely independent and unwilling to forget petty jealousies related to real and imagined grievances. One episode which illustrates that even reputable promoters were not above resorting to underhanded practices occurred when Zeke Youngblood discovered Fred Crockett slipping entry blanks to walkathon contestants in a show held in Trenton, New Jersey. Youngblood summoned the police to have Crockett ejected.

Earlier, it was noted that Seltzer, who had been a strong supporter of the N.E.E.A., sensing that the days of walkathons were numbered, left the field in 1935 to found roller derbies. By 1938, Seltzer was successfully operating roller derby shows on the west coast with attendances of 150,000. Despite his departure, Seltzer's impact on the walkathon field continued. Some walkathon promoters jumped on Seltzer's bandwagon. Milton J. Crandall, bumptious impressario of Madison Square Garden fame, before he was murdered, opened a Roller Skating Derby which folded after 15 days. Dunlap, though he cast his lot with the roller skaters, still had his hand in walkathons in 1940 (*The Billboard* 27 Jan. 1940, 26). A good number of walkathon contestants switched to roller derbies, among them celebrity contestant Helen Caldwell and well-known floor judge Lou Jarvis. Roller derbies, a clone of walkathons, replayed similar scripts including the animosity between show promoters. Seltzer sued Larry Sunbrock for infringing on his roller-derby copyright but lost the case. Walkathons were big business. Expenses for any one show ran as high as $60,000 for groceries, workmen and supplies. Hence the net profit which successful promoters accumulated was enviable. Mobs, small and large, some who backed shows, were envious and made certain that they received a share of the profits.

Over the years, some walkathon promoters were murdered. On Sunday, April 9, 1939, when long-time show promoter Charley Hayden walked out of the Park Casino in Chicago, where his walkathon was in progress, he was fatally shot. His assailant stepped out of a green car occupied by several other men. Questioned before he died, Hayden was unable to name the killer. Police suspected that Hayden might have been slain by racketeers he refused to pay or by amateur bandits or personal enemies. These speculations were based, in part, on the fact that mob money was involved in many walkathon shows, as it was in nightclubs during the Prohibition Era. Seltzer, who referred to Hayden as a "stand-up type of man," suspected that it was members of the West Side Chicago gang who earlier tried to rob Hayden's place. One tactic used by the mob was for a gangster to put his gun on the table and tell a promoter that "we're partners," or to suggest to a floor judge that they wanted a team they liked or sponsored "to be in there."

Show promoters, like other men who ran big businesses, saw to it that the mob got its share for protection against other mobsters and protection from the police. Part of the foul play uncovered in walkathon shows (as well as in other forms of show business) is attributed to the fact that show promoters were notoriously addicted to the rackets and to horse racing. Top promoters staked out territories for their shows and jealously guarded what they considered their turf. Ross returned to Washington, D.C. year after year; Brady went back to Kansas City. Neither Hayden's dying words nor others questioned at the show could shed light on his murder. Similar circumstances surrounded the mysterious shooting of Milton J. Crandall.

Kaplan, his counsel unheeded and his critics unappeased, acted the Cassandra of Doom and pronounced, in 1940, that the dance endurance field was finally dead, a prophecy he had hinted at five years earlier. If his obituary was premature by some 13 years, the heyday of dance endurance shows was clearly past. *The Billboard* discontinued reporting Derby Show News by December of 1943.

Though the heyday of walkathons from 1932 to 1936 had passed, King Brady continued to run a number of successful walkathon shows, both as promoter of his own shows, and as emcee in shows operated by other promoters. Brady, always the showman, (George Eells modelled the emcee/promoter in his play, *The Glory Walk*, on Brady whom he regarded as one of the best, if not the best, emcee/promoter in the business) remained optimistic over the future of walkathons and continued to draw crowds to his shows into the early 1950s. His Christmas cards to friends and enemies during the 1930s echoed his optimism: "My speaking may be wheezy/And my wise cracks rather stale/The Marathon dope all cheesy/And as a promoter I may fail/But things are looking better with liquor back and beer/So Now I Sure Can Wish You Merry Xmas and Happy New Year" (Mathews Scrapbook).

The new media of television, increasingly available to a mass audience in the 1950s, helped to bring the few remaining shows to a halt by 1953. Few mourned the passing of this form of entertainment which caught the attention and fancy of large numbers of Americans during the 1920s and 1930s. In its 30-year tenure, in the main, walkathon shows were stateside operations. However, a few promoters did take shows abroad. Ross traveled to Paris, Brussels, Frankfort and Nice and to Mexico City (Mathews Scrapbook, Program). Frederick Abarrategu, a Spanish promoter, staged several shows in Europe and Central and South America as late as 1941 (*The Billboard* 7 June 1941, 26). During that same year, a second Honolulu show opened and included among its 19 teams Chad Alviso partnered with Louie Meredith. *The Billboard* reported that the promoter of this show ran out and left the teams stranded in Hawaii. Contestants were forced to drive cabs and work at local clubs to earn return fare (*The Billboard* 10 May 1941, 27).

Why dance marathons did not catch on in foreign countries with the same fervor they were welcomed with in the United States raises questions for a future researcher. The answer may lie in the claim (which I shall make later in the book) that dance endurance contests were an aberration, and peculiarly American.

In the last decade of operation, there was a dearth of good contestants participating in walkathons. Top professional teams did continue to compete. Ruthie Carrol and Billy Harris won first prize and Chad Alviso and Louie Meredith second prize in the 1941-42 Coliseum Walkathon in Chicago, promoted by Sid Cohen. This show lasted six months and 14 days (*The Billboard* 2 May 1942, 27). By the early 1940s, some celebrity contestants left the dance endurance field for high paying jobs in war plants; others were drafted; others, disenchanted with being exploited by opportunistic promoters, dropped out altogether. Still others, determined to stay in show business, one way or another, went into carnivals, cabarets and nightclubs. Another sign of the changing times was the announcement that Jerry Green, in May 1942, took contestants to entertain soldiers at Fort Meade; they danced all the way to the fort and back in the bus. In keeping with the patriotic spirit of the times, Mary Rock married Pvt. William White on the contest floor (*The Billboard* 23 May 1942, 27).

In these latter days, it was a sellers' market for "flash teams" who, no longer naive or desperate and hungry, adopted a different psychology and were unwilling to obey a promoter's whim. Show operators were forced to deal differently with contestants not easily manipulated or intimidated. Celebrity contestants were allowed extra sleep in "kip" shows and were given the most desirable sponsors and hours to entertain, along with most of the prize money. One competitor, Jack White, complained in 1942 that professional contestants fraternized and snubbed the other contestants in the show. "The other kids are just fill-in-saps to entertain at the most undesirable hours and get sponsors if there are any left after the would-be-grandees get first choice" (*The Billboard* 10 Oct. 1942, 27).

There were complaints from other sources. Mrs. Olie Monroe, of Los Angeles, who described herself as a disgusted fan, was disappointed when she learned that a derbyshow contestant had quit because the winners were picked by the management. She remarked, "The public loses interest when the same kids win in every show" (*The Billboard* 26 Sept., 1942, 27). Dissatisfaction continued to be voiced in the pages of *The Billboard*. "My girl friend and I have been trying to enter a walkathon for some time. But as we have never been in one, we can't find a show willing to take a chance on two amateurs. Why don't promoters give amateurs a chance to break into the endurance field?" (*The Billboard* 15 Jan. 1938, 30).

The dog days of multiple dance endurance shows operated by temperamental promoters and emcees were over. In their place, the few remaining walkathon shows became more and more stylized; the same contestant sang old specialty numbers, performed in the same "schmaltz" skits, and told the same stale jokes. Hank Lewis, a former emcee, reported: "We went to a show in Sacramento last year and so help me, I sat there from 8 p.m. until midnight and called every bit of heat, every sleeping couple, and every gag and quip by the emcee 10 minutes before they were pulled" (*The Billboard* 16 March 1940, 27).

Crowds no longer attended matinee performances as they did before the war. Walkathons became more show business than contest. Eells notes that real fans didn't really believe in the endurance aspects though they screamed and hollered at the floor judge. Loyal fans came for the entertainment but complained that the walkathon show had become a farce; they no longer believed in the endurance part since the same contestants won in every show. Their prediction, more a hope than a reality, was that when promoters started running shows on the square again, "the kids would come back into the game." According to John Makar, walkathon shows came to a final halt in 1953 when the law closed down the contest in Monroe, Louisiana (Interview). A last ditch attempt, in 1958, to open a marathon show never materialized.

Dance endurance contests did change over 30 years, from fad to dance marathon to walkathon. What remained unchanged, after the fad craze and the short years of the dance marathons, were the basic ingredients of all walkathon shows, an impure mixture of vaudeville-cabaret acts and endurance sport events within a context of physical and psychological duress.

Leo Seltzer, before abandoning the dance endurance field in 1935, described the broad appeal of the walkathon show:

It cannot be denied that the urge that packs arenas for the knock-out punch, or the race track for the harrowing spill, resulting in death, is the motivating force behind this thing called walkathon.

The contestant is exalted to the position of combination gladiator and night-club entertainer.

Beyond races, the in-between entertainment from contests, or the hired or "drop-in" vaudevillians, the surge of the mob spirit in the crowd, the circus atmosphere of the blaring bands, the shouts and jeers of the spectators, the munching of hot dogs and peanuts, the moth to the flame, combined with the low admission charge and the no-limit stay, is the greatest universal appeal of the marathon. (*The Billboard* 29 Dec. 1934, 220)

Gingrich, less sanguine that Seltzer in acclaiming this form of entertainment as irresistible, nonetheless revealed his fascination for walkathon shows in the following stream of consciousness:

The whole thing juts with angles, but even though you know them all, and can tell in an instant just what's fake and what isn't, when you walk in the middle of one of those grinds and you don't really give a damn who wins and who loses, you can't remember that, somehow, when the fever surges up and yelling brotherly advice to some blank-featured youth with a sick sinking grin on his face and a glassy glaze over his eyes and how relieved you are when he finally snaps out of it and straightens up and goes over for the ice towel to revive himself and it isn't a fall and you knew of course that it wouldn't be because you've seen him go through all that before and anyway it's all phony but if you knew that all the time what did you go crazy for and stand up there yelling like a loon and you don't know and you feel foolish and anyway you never will again but you do the next night or at any rate within a week and if you do then you've got it and nothing can change you and that's the Walkathon. (*Esquire* Autumn 1933, 61, 104).

Part II

✧

How Long Can They Last?

Chapter Four
Poor Man's Night Club

The Poor Man's Night Club was an appropriate name for the walkathon contest since it placed this entertainment in the world of show business where it belonged. Simulating nightclubs, show emcees played straight men to comics and clowns; they introduced variety acts and song and dance routines. Like the nightclub, show patrons were invited to dance to the music of the house band or an orchestra brought in from nearby cities to keep the show fresh. Walkathon shows also aped vaudeville and burlesque by borrowing semi-risqué skits and speciality nights. In addition, walkathon shows featured sport events, a variety of athletic contests which involved running and fast-walking.

The ambience at walkathon shows, however, was not the same as at a nightclub. At the walkathons, the audience sat ringside or in bleacher seats, in an open auditorium, not at separate tables in a semi-darkened room. Nightclubs closed down for the night; walkathons remained opened 24 hours every day. Walkathons had matinee performances to which children as well as adults came. This genre of show business was unique in combining entertainment and sport.

Walkathon shows were built on the idea of endurance. Contestants were required to keep awake and upright, day and night, with short, fragmented periods of rest, for as long as it took to outlast all other teams in the contest. The show emcee exploited this idea of endurance by working heat, repeating ad nauseum: "How Long Can They Last?" The idea of endurance, the wear and tear of time, was carried over to the variety of timed, strenuous sprint and derby foot races.

The flavor of the walkathon contest as show business is captured in the following verse entitled *Marathon Memories* (Mathews Scrapbook). The enterprising contestant who composed these lines had them printed on the back of postcards which he sold to audiences during the 11-minute rest periods.

Marathon Memories

Life is just like a Marathon
You have to have nerve to stay,
It will help you to win
To continue to grin and help others along the way.

You will find if you follow the Marathon
That the finest of sport is there;
And all the pals and all of the gals

Show each other the finest of care.

There are laughs and thrills and heartaches and chills
That will pull you right out your seat
And you will discover there is more than one lover,
To watch them is really a treat

They will sleep on each other's shoulder
And keep right on walking the floor;
And after each rest they will do their best
To keep coming back for more.

You learn to mourn with the loser
And you will cry when one has to drop out;
Your heart will throb and you'll stifle a sob
When you learn what it's all about.

You will laugh when someone goes "squirrelly"
And starts picking flowers from the air;
He may roll up his pants and go into a dance,
There is nothing he wouldn't dare.

So pick out your favorite Couple,
And root for them loud and long;
If you bring cigarettes, you'll have no regrets
For each package you may ask for a song.

It's a tough old grind on this floor, Folks,
We all need your moral support—
When we're sleepy and sore, it will help all the more
To know that you are keeping our score.

We are all trying to earn a prize,
And we know it will be hard to do,
But a cheer and a grin will help us to win,
So you see it depends on you.

So, come on out and see us walk—
Bring your lunch and stay all night;
For we all know you will like our show,
And to please you is our delight.

Now we're counting on you to be here
And bring all your friends along, too:
If you like this rhyme, just hand me a dime
And I'll autograph a copy for you.

Successful promoters, unlike their nemeses, the "fly-by-night operators," had experience in show business enterprises before venturing into the walkathon field. Many had operated vaudeville, burlesque and nightclub shows. Though experienced, every show promoter knew that each contest was a gamble. Some walkathon shows "clicked" and made a lot of money; other contests broke even; still others lost money for a variety of reasons including luck.

Experienced promoters knew when to "turn on the heat," not too much, just enough to build up new enthusiasm for the show. They followed the principle: "Never leave anything to chance." It is not surprising that the outcome of mini sport contests, as well as for the grand prize, was not left to chance; most, if not all contests, were fixed. Contestants who were on salary were told when to take a fall and let another team win so as to generate greater interest in the show. Shows could be speeded up or slowed down according to audience response. Contestants were given extra sleep in "kip" shows in order to prolong the life of a show. At the same time, if a promoter wanted to close a show, he pushed contestants to their limit. Notwithstanding such chicanery, a shrewd promoter didn't try to milk a contest when interest in the show began to wane. He knew from painful experience that if he left a bad impression at the close of a contest, it would be more difficult to arrange for a return engagement.

Walkathon contests were promoted and operated by males. Those in charge of operating walkathon shows had autocratic titles expressive of patriarchal power: King Brady, General Hugh Talbott, Daddy Fox and Pop Dunlap. Paternal figures, they typically referred to female contestants as "girls" and male contestants as "boys"; the promoters and operators treated them as children and they responded with the appropriate behavior of dependent offspring.

Show promoters, benevolent and authoritarian by turn, were both respected and feared by staff and contestants. If a promoter wanted you out of his show, for whatever reason, he would find a way: contestants might not be wakened; sheets and pillow cases were taken away; requested medical treatment was delayed, etc. However, if he did want you in the show, he would make it worth your while by finding a sponsor and making you visible to the audience. Should you not respond to the call to return to the dance floor, there were smelling salts and an ice bath to revive you.

First and foremost, show promoters were businessmen. Their primary aim was to make money, as much as possible. The best ones used business acumen more than exploitation and chicanery, though the line between the two modes of operation was often thin. Some promoters like King Brady organized, financed and operated every aspect of the dance endurance contest, often doubling in his own show as emcee. Brady had "muscle." Other show operators, like Jack Steinel, rarely were seen after they raised the capital to start a show. Steinel left the running of the contest to the emcee who carried the responsibility for the show.

Walkathon promoters who had muscle set the rules for their shows and changed the regulations to suit their purposes. They worked in collusion with show emcees and the floor judge. For example, if during the early days of the contest a promoter felt that there were too many mouths to feed, or it was too crowded in rest quarters, he would alert the floor judge to eliminate contestants on any pretext. Later, if business continued at a brisk pace, the floor judge would become lax in ruling out contestants.

Paternal autocrats who regarded themselves a social class above their employees, walkathon promoters expected contestants to follow the rules laid down without agitating or complaining. Professional contestants were wary of the show promoter; they knew that they were at his mercy. Typically, promoters sought to instill "a fear complex" in contestants; they conned and manipulated staff and contestants to maintain control. Anyone who continued to stir up , trouble was given a verbal warning which was followed by a threat of physical punishment at the hands of the floor judge. If no form of persuasion was effective, Daddy would find a way to have the rebellious child disqualified.

A conscientious show promoter would see to it that a contestant who had been in the show for over 500 hours and was formally disqualified be put through a series of de-conditioning steps by the trainer to regulate a contestant's sleep before he or she left the contest. This measure was taken to lessen the chance that a contestant's muscles would stiffen or that paralysis would set in. The procedure went as follows: contestants were allowed to sleep for a half-hour, then awakened for two minutes; after another half hour, they were awakened again. At the end of two more hours, they were roused and made to walk for 30 minutes without stopping. This procedure was repeated three times at two-hour intervals after which contestants could sleep as long as they wished.

The key to a successful walkathon show lay in attracting strong teams. Promoters advertised in the pages of *The Billboard* for "their old teams to come on." Each promoter carried several teams he considered "his backbone," couples who were good athletes and entertainers. These "flash teams" had colorful wardrobes and knew how to get a contest started and "to stand the gaff" once the show was underway. These teams received special treatment from the staff—their requests for medical attention were quickly granted. Beyond subsidizing some teams with a weekly salary, promoters helped their favorite teams find a sponsor from a local seafood restaurant, brewery, army and navy store, bakery, laundry, coal company or bowling alley.

Show promoters had to decide what proportion of the teams in his show were to be made up of local contestants and what proportion professional contestants from out-of-town. If a promoter started out with a preponderance of local contestants, after the amateur locals dropped out for lack of training and stamina, they would take with them 100 to 200 fans who had made that local couple their favorite. Increasingly, over the years, experienced promoters came to rely on professional contestants to carry the show; they paid several celebrity teams weekly salaries to keep interest in the show high. A successful walkathon promoter who expected a smooth running contest hired a number of specialists. His staff would include show emcees, a day and night floor judge, publicity man, day and night trainer, secretary, physician, day and night nurse, a masseur, day and night cashier, and a reserve seats' cashier. In addition, attached to walkathon organizations were carpenters, plumbers, electricians, door and counter men and police officers.

The publicity man acting as an advance representative solicited loans and secured the services of cleaners, podiatrists, barbers and beauticians, if possible bartering services for advertisements in the show. He contacted newspapers, set up display advertisements in local stores and posted banners in the show auditorium along with blown-up pictures of favorite contestants. To promote the show, he arranged for radio broadcasts, an important medium to draw customers to the show. He supervised the printing of the *Marathon News* a house publication, which reported the ratings of each team, their strengths and weaknesses, evaluations based on the judgment of the floor judge and training staff. The publicity man was a promoter's antenna whose job it was to sense how people felt about the show—whether it was "peppy" or "lazy." Importantly, he also sounded out the community's general attitude toward the show and its contestants.

The head male trainer with his assistant kept rest quarters clean and sanitary. More importantly, trainers were responsible for keeping contestants in good physical condition particularly during the first 500-hour "breaking-in" period. It was the job of the trainer to awaken contestants; if a contestant did not respond to the warning bell, it was a trainer's job to carry the contestant, sound asleep, to the dance floor to hand over to a partner. Trainers and nurses humored their charges when the strain of the contest began to affect their attitudes and behavior. They put up with contestants' mental quirks, listened to their complaints and protected them from the annoyances and pranks perpetrated by fellow marathoners. A local physician was hired to take care of minor injuries and respiratory ailments which might develop during the contest. If there was any question as to the fitness of a contestant to continue in the show, or any possibility that a contestant was injuring himself or herself, the physician's ruling was final.

One member of the staff not acknowledged in the official program was "the patch." His job was to smell out trouble, and, if necessary, to grease someone in power without spending too much "legal money." Promoters who gained the cooperation of city and parish officials before opening a contest were fortunate. Most often, promoters had to resort to fixes and bribes to open a show and stay open. Police departments shook down promoters in exchange for protection; health and fire officials withheld licenses and permits when not suitably compensated. A good patch could get away with all kinds of things; a bad one could cost a promoter his show.

An efficient patch would counter the pressure applied by ministerial and civic-minded organizations (who had been influenced by competitive theatre interests) by reaching public officials with enough influence in the Mayor's Office to restrain the issuance of a nuisance warrant. Promoters enlisted local organizations, the American Legion or the Veterans of Foreign Wars, for example, to sponsor a show in return for 10 to 25 percent of net profits from admissions and from refreshment and parking concessions. This exchange, which might involve considerable sums of money, was one means of gaining acceptance from the community.

Walkathons were big business. Shows which succeeded were backed with capital investments that might range from $3,000 to $10,000. Expenses for any one show ran as high as $60,000 for groceries and labor. Promoters who opened shows with as many as 75 couples found themselves incurring expenses which included (in the first week) the following purchases: 75 dozen eggs, 500 pounds of meat, 12 bushels of potatoes, 400 loaves of bread, and 75 gallons of milk. A sample menu compiled by physician Dr. Everett Perlman and G.W. Nelson, in their small booklet written in 1929, listed the following diet which, even by today's standards, appears healthy (Martin 58):

7:00 a.m. - Breakfast
One-half grapefruit
Boiled oatmeal (sweetened with syrup)
One soft-boiled egg
2 slices of whole wheat toast (buttered)

10:00 a.m.
Cookies
Glass of Milk

12:00 Noon - Lunch
One cup of soup (puree or thickened soups)
Vegetable salad (oil dressing)
Cottage cheese
Two slices whole wheat bread (buttered)

3:00 p.m.
Apples
Oranges
Celery

6:00 p.m. - Dinner
Soup
One slice of meatloaf
Small baked potato
Cabbage salad (oil dressing)
Two slices whole wheat bread (buttered)
Milk

9:00 p.m.
Apples
Oranges
Celery
Cookies

12:00 Midnight
Whole wheat sandwich of jelly or relish
Black coffee

3:00 a.m.
Celery
Apples
Cookies
Black coffee

A contest which opened in a good location, in a building that was well lighted and had advertisements posted on the outside walls, was off to a good start. To reduce the risk of financial failure, two or more promoters joined forces making it possible to run several contests simultaneously in different locations. Other promoters were highly competitive and operated on a "dog-eat-dog" basis, double-crossing each other, harboring petty jealousies and nursing personal injuries, real and imagined. Among the underhanded methods used by such promoters was to attempt to lure popular professional teams by mail while a show was still in progress; the wary promoter of the contest countered by withholding mail from contestants. Another method that seemed unfair to contestants was for a promoter to take a share of the kitty, the sums earned by contestants in performing for the public.

Promoters with muscle established claim to certain territories, cities and towns to which they regularly returned, year after year. In order to ensure their territorial rights, show operators came to rely upon protection from official and unofficial sources. Public officials were paid off to open a show and keep it open despite public criticism; crime syndicates were paid off to protect against petty racketeers. The bitter reality for dance endurance promoters, true also in other itinerant forms of show business, was that both public servants and criminals wanted to get a share of the profits. Amidst territorial claims and mob pressures, some promoters were murdered. Endurance contests, like other forms of show business, were plagued by other forms of pressure. Promoters who solicited "the sporting element" to support a show could expect pressure to influence the outcome of a contest. Mobsters did sponsor teams in the show. They let promoters and floor judges know that they had a stake in who won and who lost in the contest.

Show promoters were plagued by "inside" practices as well. Contestants referred to as "hotel marathoners" and "chiselers" would receive advance money for food and gas and either never show up at the contest, or, having been housed at a local hotel, leave before the show began. Other contestants, "glorified hoboes" and "itchy-foot marathoners," left one show to join another without being properly disqualified. In addition, show promoters had to contend with male contestants who caused trouble by fighting in public or even more seriously, seducing minors in the audience. Though setting strict rules against using drugs, "Daddy" would come to the rescue of a male contestant who was apprehended by the police for smoking marijuana. "Pop" did fulfill a supportive role by giving protection to female contestants assailed by an ardent hoodlum who "wanted to buy her off the floor."

Critical to the success of any walkathon contest was the talent of three emcees, showmen who mixed corn and con. A seasoned emcee was a seat-of-the-pants psychologist who knew enough to afford audiences, the majority women, the opportunity to mix laughter with tears. Timing was all. To keep things going, popular songs and dances were mixed with comedy skits and fast paced foot races. Novelty if not originality was prized. To open a show, the emcees would sing the Marathon theme song, played to the tune of "Baby Face" (Mathews Scrapbook).

Marathon, we've got a great big jolly Marathon
And all we do is just keep Dancing on
Marathon, our poor feet are aching
We sure are hesitating
Carry on, no one will know how long
Until, we'll all be gone
For we won't shed a tear
If we stay here a year
In this great big Marathon.

The emcee played "straight man" to his staff of comics and clowns who assailed audiences with a barrage of gags and slapstick. His stooge emcees, "Popeye," "Pee Wee," "Wiggley," "Puddin' Puss," and "Big Bang," modeled their antics after the "hells-a-poppin" format of vaudeville and burlesque. In a typical restaurant skit, the waiter would correct his first order for soup by shouting to the kitchen: "Hold the chicken, make it pee." In another skit, the stooge who proclaimed that he liked flowers would receive a faceful of flour. Show promoters who relied on comic talent alone to carry the show soon found that the novelty of pie throwing, shirt tearing and water spilling wore off. It was the ability of the master of ceremonies to sell contestants, to get each team a good following within three weeks after the contest opened that ensured a show's success.

One way of increasing contestants' popularity was to call them to the stage to perform their speciality act, to sing "California, Here I Come," "Give Me Five Minutes More," and "Ain't She Sweet," or to do a fast-paced dance like "The Lindy Hop," whistle or do an impersonation. When a contestant had no demonstrable talent, the emcee prefaced his introduction with: "If there is anything you like about him.lthe way he wears his hair, his tie, etc." However amateurish these performances or modest the talent, the master of ceremonies urged patrons to acknowledge each effort: "Open up your hearts and your purse...give a silver shower of pennies, nickels, dimes and quarters...at the count of 1, reach into your pocket and grab a coin...at the count of 2, raise your hand...at the count of three, throw the money on the floor."

An effective way to advertise walkathons was through radio broadcasts at 3 p.m. and 8:30 p.m.; show emcees used this medium to paint word pictures, what was happening on the walkathon floor. To entice listeners to the show, an ebullient emcee described the entertainment at last evenings' show time, the songs, dances, comic routines, which, in addition to the featured sprint and derby races, brought a spirited response from audiences who "hollered, screamed and whistled."

Before performing their act, both professional and amateur teams were introduced by the emcee, who made an unabashed appeal to elicit support for "all these marvelous kids...who are depending upon you to see them through the long weary hours in the days and weeks ahead...lets get behind them and let them know you care."

When a contestant was forced to solo after her partner had been disqualified, the emcee appealed for audience support by describing the plight of " their own hometown girl who is sticking it out to the very end because her mother needs an operation and does not have the money." Or the emcee would make an appeal for Charlie, a dead ringer for "Al" the unbelievably dumb ballplayer in a Ring Lardner cartoon. Charlie, prompted by the emcee, would then mumble "Thanky" to a stout middle-aged woman with frizzled hair who had sent him a carton of cigarettes. Such "formulas" to elicit sympathy were interchangeable with approaches used in radio soap operas. Emcees sought to ingratiate themselves with show patrons by posing as the protector of the "courageous kids," protesting that the floor judge was being too harsh or unfair. Both emcee and floor judge, unbeknownst to walkathon audiences, colluded with each other since both were in the hire of the show promoter. Floor judges reminded the show emcee "to sell what you see!"

It was the job of the show emcee to alert patrons to signs of weakness in the couples milling around the dance floor. Fans were encouraged to warn their favorite team if they saw them faltering. In the athletic acts, an underdog couple was lauded as having "lots of guts." Endlessly, an emcee's appeal was that the audience get behind all contestants, to "let them know you care."

Celebrity contestants who had "flash" needed little prompting by show emcees. Norma Jaspers, a seasoned contestant adept at working heat, responded in an interview: "We were professionals, we knew exactly what we were doing" (Martin). There were some contestants, neither daring nor imaginative, whom the show emcee prodded. Eells remembers Hazel Dietrich, "a fat girl with a pretty face who couldn't run or entertain" (154). In intentionally coercing her to sing, the emcee had aroused sympathy for the shy contestant who was rewarded by a "silver shower" of coins after her inept performance.

A promoter hired his entertainment staff "to show his way," his personal style. (Female promoters were a rarity.) Those promoters who catered to the sporting element chose an emcee who would exhume burlesque skits and suggestive vaudeville acts. Emcees used the familiar, "honey" and "dearie" to introduce a female contestant to the audiences. Entrepreneurs who pitched their appeal to "Mr. and Mrs. America" advised show comedians and emcees to do "clean blackouts and bits." Some vaudeville skits, like "The Farmer's Daughter," and "A Night in a Turkish Harem," though risqué, were performed in shows billed as "family entertainment."

The protracted, enforced contact between staff and contestants created a hothouse climate such that some emcees were easily disposed to return favor for favor. Some female contestants were called to the bandstand more frequently than others to do their speciality act; others were chosen to be the "Sweetheart Couple" of the month. Periodically, a male contestant emotionally involved with his partner called a lecherous emcee to account.

A boon for walkathon contests were stage, screen, radio and sport celebrities who came to see the show. The presence of such popular figures was acknowledged by the emcee who invited the celebrity to the band stand. When such offers were accepted, an emcee's efforts to sell the show were greatly enhanced. Occasionally, an alert emcee would be quick to exploit the windfall of a local evangelist in the audience who approved and had expressed interest in the show...in saving the soul of the female contestants.

Dance endurance contests were adjudicated by two floor judges, a day judge and a night judge. Their role was crucial. It was the judge, more than the emcee, who improvised the actions which the emcees reported over the microphone. During the walking act, with a "one fall and out rule" in effect, the floor judge was quick to disqualify a contestant when both knees touched the ground. Anyone who fell during a sprint or derby race and was unable to recover to an upright position by the count of ten was ruled out of the contest by the floor judge. Any contestant who accumulated a designated number of penalty points heard from the floor judge. Promoters left the final decision to disqualify contestants to the floor judge. He was the boss; his word was law!

The floor judge maintained a constant surveillance over the milling couples during the walking act to make sure they kept in motion. When a contest began, with the floor dense with couples, he had to be particularly alert. His constant reminder to contestants was "to pick 'em up and put 'em down." A contestant whose knees began to sag during the walking period felt the sharp sting of a ruler snapped against the calf of the leg by the floor judge. As overseer, the floor judge was vigilant; any contestants who broke a rule or regulation were penalized.

If contestants complained or agitated the dance floor by starting a fight, their behavior brought swift physical retaliation from the floor judge. Punishment could also take the form of delaying permission for medical assistance. Though he favored the professional contestants who participated in one contest after another, he had to be wary of how these same professionals harassed the amateurs in the contest. The floor judge acted as a watch dog; he kept track of what contestants were doing. A request for a "hygiene break" required the consent of the floor judge. Emcees who called a contestant to the bandstand to do their speciality number reminded them to first obtain the permission of the floor judge.

Floor judges earned their fearsome nicknames: King Kong, Dracula, Simon Legree and Frankenstein. Characteristically adopting a hard-boiled attitude, they never smiled, had a "sour puss" and were "poker faced"; they talked through clenched teeth and exaggerated their gestures for full effect. Floor judges were the villains of the show, a role the most successful judges performed with flair. In addition, during the early morning hours, floor judges coached professional teams to dramatize the nightly sprints and lap races. It was the judge's decision to choose a team, an experienced professional couple, to set the pace for a particular race at the evening performances.

Floor judges who were most strict were most hated. Acting as both villain and adjudicator, floor judges walked a fine line between chicanery and fairness. Collusion between the floor judge and professional teams hired by the show promoter was kept a secret from audiences and amateur contestants. Amateur contestants who expected impartial treatment from the floor judge found this not to be the case. Still, when a contest began nearing the end, the few professional teams expected the floor judge to go by the rules.

The role of the floor judge was vital in walkathon shows. Acting the role of the heavy, he knew how to rile the emotions of the audience by picking on the crowd favorites and by favoring their underhanded rivals. He treated the contestants he favored the worst to gain them the most sympathy. Another important contribution of the floor judge was to gauge the strengths and weaknesses of each team in the contest. He would then alert the promoter how long a contestant might last, how much time they might get from each of the remaining contestants. His daily stint over, the floor judge was well advised to leave the arena and not attempt to make any contact with the audience. During working hours, he was similarly cautioned not to joke or gossip with contestants for such familiarity might cost him control and respect. The best floor judges, those who heeded this advice, earned the reputation as "The Meanest Men in Town."

The interaction within "The Family Man's Night Club," between the show promoter, his staff, the contestants and the audience provided a fluid set of interrelationships. While it is true that promoter, staff, and contestants set the stage for what was to happen, audiences also controlled, to some extent, what did happen. Martin observed that "the power of purchase" gave audiences a feeling of superiority (*Drama Review*). Fans supported their favorite team by requesting a speciality number which they generously rewarded with money and gifts. Contestants, on the other side, attempted to control audience responses by "working heat." As Havoc noted: "Our degradation was entertainment; sadism was sexy; masochism was talent" (42). If walkathon personnel and contestants colluded in projecting a climate of sado-masochism, they did so with the expressed knowledge that it was the audience who wanted and desired this brand of entertainment.

Chapter Five
What's Your Story?

Walkathon shows called for a new breed of professional contestant, women and men with physical stamina and prowess, who had extrovertive personalities and were adaptable to whatever schemes the show promoter or emcee invented. Professionals who made walkathons their work, if not their life, were the celebrities of the show admired by devoted fans. Despite limited education and work skills, the top professional contestants were effective actors and actresses in the world of walkathon show business.

Going from one show to another, professional contestants met competitors from other shows but also other professionals and amateurs who were new to them. Professional or amateur, they asked the same question: "What's your story?" Of course, every contestant had a story and without much prompting told it. Each storyteller revealed motives, real or made up, to explain why he or she was in the show.

Stories reflected family and neighborhood backgrounds; most professional contestants were from a lower-socio economic class than that of the show promoter. Many contestants were in their late teens or early twenties; not all had finished high school. Without benefit of status and valued work skills, contestants saw the walkathon contest as "a glory road," an accessible means of moving to the right side of the tracks.

Stories of professional and amateur contestants reflected the times and the place. During the 1920s, when dance endurance contests were considered a fad, men and women, young and old, attempted to better the record of other Americans and so earn a special place in history. With the change from fad to dance marathon, contestants entered dance endurance contests "for a lark," or because they were "just crazy about dancing!" Winning the grand prize money meant buying a car, making a down payment on a home, saving for a vacation or a marriage and honeymoon, paying for an operation, opening a business and, for newly arrived immigrants, an opportunity to send money to aging parents in the old country.

In the years of the Great Depression, when dance marathons evolved into walkathons, contestants were driven by needs more urgent than any of the reasons already mentioned. Young men and women, without family support, with little more than a grade school education and minimal job skills, hitched or rode the rails hundreds of miles to join a show for free room and board. Destitute couples entered walkathon contests to survive, feed a family, save their home from foreclosure, all the while hoping for a new start in life.

The increasing popularity of dance endurance shows during the 1930s did provide an opportunity to satisfy needs other than those of survival. Unmarried and married women, middle-aged divorcées and widows, lonely and bored with the daily routine of housework, satiated on afternoon radio soap operas and movies, sought to dispel psychological depression by entering a walkathon show. Younger women from crowded cities, nurtured on a daily diet of stories in the *Silver Screen* and *True Romance* magazines, were seduced into believing that they could follow the path taken by Hollywood star Joan Crawford, who, they read, had once entered a dance marathon contest. Girls in their mid-teens from small towns, rebelling against puritanical upbringing, ran away from home and signed up for a contest. Some runaways succeeded in their search for independence; others were brought back home by a worried mother or apprehended by a truant officer. Waitresses and salesgirls were recruited by professional male contestants with glib promises of easy money and fame.

Among the varied backgrounds of show participants were women who alternated between this new profession requiring them to stay on their feet with an older profession which kept them on their backs. O'Day recalls meeting a "pretty prostitute who made jokes about dancing shows until her feet got tired, then going into a house until, to quote her 'my ass gets tired' " (O'Day 38). The hard times of the depression years particularly affected performers from vaudeville and the cabaret. Some vaudevillians swallowed their pride and entered walkathon shows even though they did not regard this form of entertainment legitimate show business.

Males entered walkathon shows for a variety of reasons. Not content with working in a brewery or driving a cab, they wanted to work in a job with more excitement. Dance hall habitués hoped to use their skill in ballroom dancing to become celebrities. Other men, self-styled Don Juans, entered walkathon shows with the intent of gaining easy access to women as dance partners or as admiring fans. Greek and Polish immigrants and their first generation cousins who lived in big city ghettoes hoped that by becoming a winner in a walkathon contest, they might gain recognition in a country where the doors to success were no longer easily opened.

Other reasons to join a show bordered on the absurd. Fugitives from alimony payments and a patient from a mental institution joined the walkathon show as an escape. When Eells first met Al, "a schitzy personality," he was astounded when the contestant openly announced that he had been in mental institutions a number of times. In a fit of temper, Al produced his commitment papers and shouted, "Don't bug me! I'm crazy and I've got papers to prove it!" (154).

Show emcees in the opening days of a walkathon show sought to "sell" each team by telling their story, stories which turned out to be part fact, part fiction. Seasoned masters of ceremony knew that walkathon fans, a large portion women, were ready and eager to identify and emphathize with the plight of those contestants who, it appeared, were less fortunate than themselves. Drab life dramas were transformed into heroic struggles in the telling. Typical were the tales of ex-boxers and former track stars trying to make "courageous" comebacks, or the sad tale of a show comedian whose face had been disfigured in an accident, who wanted to return to the "big-time."

Show emcees embroidered contestants stories by drawing upon scripts with which all could identify and feel strongly about. Male contestants were described as former veterans, soldiers, sailors and marines who had fought in World War I, "the great war to end all wars," "men who were once again fighting a battle for life, this time, not with their buddies in the trenches, but in the walkathon arena with the help of a faithful wife or girl friend." Every contest had its Sweetheart Couple, the Janet Gaynor and Charley Farrell of the show, who aspired to be discovered and catapulted to stardom as happened in the movies.

Dance endurance shows opened with a mass of contestants, usually 25 to 50 couples. Some promoters aimed for a 50-50 balance between amateur and professional teams; others favored a preponderance of professional teams. Each had a rationale for their preference. Local amateur teams were readily available, eager young adults, many in their late teens, ready to try for the big cash prize of $1,000. Promoters knew that local teams attracted a following of family and friends that helped to get a show started and served as a form of insurance to gain community support. Amateur couples, however, were often unable to meet the rigorous physical demands during the first 500 hours after the contest opened. They soon dropped out or were disqualified from the contest. With more professionals than amateurs in the show to begin with, such an eventuality did not endanger the success of the contest for there were always the professional contestants to keep the show going.

Promoters carried a number of flash teams who were the celebrities of the show, extroverts given to exhibitionism. On opening night, after the Grand March, these energetic couples would make early contact with the audience; male contestants went through the stands kissing the middle-aged housewives on the cheek; female contestants greeted the bald-headed men with a kiss on the head. During show time, flash teams appeared in colorful costumes entertaining audiences with their speciality acts, a popular song or a dance like "The Lindy Hop." They acted in vaudeville skits, "The Paper Hanger Act," or in playlets such as "School Days." Between staged performances, male contestants with a flair for comedy heckled the emcee, mimicked the floor judge and took pratfalls.

In addition to entertaining crowds with these acts, flash teams captured the attention of fans by "working heat." In gruelling races like the Dynamite Sprints and the Bombshell Races, these athletic performers dramatized their actions for full effect. Appearing to be "good sports" by being magnanimous in victory and by accepting defeat gracefully, flash teams were well aware that these actions increased their popularity with the crowds.

Dance endurance shows were billed as contests in which each contestant had an equal opportunity to win. Amateurs soon found out otherwise. Flash teams were favored; they received quick medical attention while other teams were forced to wait. At show time, flash teams were similarly favored by having first crack at performing. Though both amateur and some professional contestants (not so favored) might grumble, there was little they could do about this preferential treatment since the promoter and staff were behind these teams.

A show promoter considered these flash teams his mainstay. He sent letters inviting them to join his show and wired travel fare if they lived a distance away. Most, if not all, promoters secretly paid their teams a weekly salary ranging from $50 to $125 depending upon how each contestant was valued. A show promoter saw to it that "his teams" received sponsors early in the show. In return for advertising their product, sponsors supplied their team with a weekly stipend and matching show outfits. Professional contestants supplemented their earnings from the sales of photographs showing their participation in "The Ice Act," or posed in dance position.

The largest single source of income at a walkathon show came from winning one of the grand prizes: $1,000 for first prize; $600 for a second prize, and $250 for a third prize. If only one grand prize was offered, the few teams battling it out might decide to split the prize money evenly though, for the benefit of the public, one team would be declared the winner. Since winning the big prize money was always problematic, (contestants varied in their performance from contest to contest depending upon how well matched they were with their partner, and also depending upon their current state of physical and mental health), professional teams competed in mini-athletic contests. At show time, first place winners received $3, second place winners $2, and third place winners $1. Celebrities visiting the show might offer larger sums to the winners of these mini-contests.

Celebrity professional teams were hustlers. When contestants with "flash" performed their speciality number, a song or dance or comedy routine, they were rewarded with "sprays," a shower of coins thrown from the audience onto the dance floor. When show patrons requested a specific number, they were generous in contributing everything from a pack of cigarettes to sums of money ranging from $1 to $20.

There were still other sources of income for professional contestants to tap. A popular couple in the show who agreed to be the bride and groom at at Marathon Wedding was given $100 or more to get married. In addition, the newlyweds received numerous gifts from merchants who contributed goods or services to this gala event. Promoters agreed to pay for an annulment should the couple desire it. Not the least bounty came from fans who sent gifts to the wedded couple, presents which were later redeemed for cash.

Additional small sums could be garnered by "working the stands" during intermission by selling boxes of candy. Like the "candy butchers" at burlesque shows, canny professionals saw to it that their loyal fans received the boxes which contained prize money. Appreciative fans returned the favor at show time by rewarding these contestants with a shower of coins after they performed their speciality act. These sources did add up over many weeks and months. During the dark days of the depression, after a six to eight week stint, it was not unusual for some teams to come away from the contest with sums ranging from one to three thousand dollars.

Flash teams comprised only a few of the professional marathoners who entered dance endurance contests. They were the stars of the show. Other professional teams were regarded as "The Iron Men and Women" of the walkathons, tough competitors with strong bodies and dogged persistence. While their exhibitionistic peers were knocking themselves out entertaining, the "horses," as June Havoc referred to them, conserved their energy. Unwilling or unable to play to the crowds, they eschewed popularity for winning cash prizes in the athletic acts. In nightly sprints and derbies, they seemed all but indestructible. Amateur couples were the fodder of dance endurance contests. Young men and women, stage-struck, viewed the walkathon show as a short-cut to becoming a celebrity and an easy way to make money. Whatever illusions of easy fame and quick fortune amateur contestants entertained before entering the contest, these expectations soon faded as the contest ground on and on.

All walkathon contestants had to follow the rules and regulations set down by the show promoter upon pain of disqualification. Though each promoter had his own requirements, the following list is representative:

1. Contestants will spend 45 minutes on the dance floor; 11 minutes in rest quarters, 2 minutes to get there; 2 minutes to return to the floor;

2. When dance music starts, floor-judge blows his whistle and everyone must be in dance position and remain so until dance music ends;

3. Any contestant who shall leave the floor without permission from the judges is automatically disqualified;

4. All male contestants must be clean shaven at all times. Regulation clothes for female contestants were as follows: no shorts, no halters or abbreviated covering; no trousers for girls except at late, hours;

5. No smoking on dance floor. No gum chewing except at events or late hours. No spitting;

6. Contestants must get an excuse from the floor judge for hygienic purposes. 2 minutes is the time limit;

7. Showers are compulsory. The floor judge permits 20 minutes in respective shower rooms every 12 hours under supervision of matrons and trainers;

8. All contestants are forbidden to receive candy, gum, cigarettes, food or anything to be placed in contestant's mouth from any other than regular authorized sources and at designated time. Any contestant violating the rule may be disqualified and ruled from the floor;

9. Contestants must behave as ladies and gents at all times;

10. The management reserves the right to disqualify any contestant who is not in good physical condition at any time on the advice of a competent physician;

11. Fighting means immediate disqualification;

12. Floor rules will be interpreted by the floor judge on duty and no appeal may be had from his ruling;

13. During any 45-minute walking period, if a contestant should touch both knees to the floor, he or she is immediately disqualified;.

14. During a dynamite sprint, should a contestant fall, he or she is allowed five counts to be back on their feet and in action. Should they touch both knees in the danger zone, they are automatically disqualified;

15. Should either team member be disqualified, the remaining partner may solo until a new partner becomes available.

There was little difficulty getting into a walkathon contest. A cursory physical examination included screening for venereal disease and body lice. A contestant who used drugs for whatever reason, medical or otherwise, was not accepted into the contest. Proof of age was often overlooked. Some promoters claimed that they screened contestants from "a character viewpoint"; how this screening was done was never made clear. The proof of a team's fitness soon became evident. Contestants who had problems with their feet or who entered the contest with ill-fitting shoes were in immediate trouble. Professionals sought to build up a thick callus on their feet as cushion and protection against rawness and bleeding.

Amateurs and professionals alike were subject to a number of physical ailments due to the stress upon the body from the walking athletic acts. Leg muscles cramped and ankles swelled; shoulders stooped and abdomens and buttocks sagged; faces became pallid and eyes bloodshot. In the opening days of the show, contestants' resistance to foot and hand infection was lowered; colds and sore throats were easy to catch. With the introduction of sprint and heel and toe races, in addition to sustaining shin splints and hip locks, contestants ran the risk of ankle and knee injuries especially when there was a pile-up on the dance floor. The management continued to warn teams that unless they followed the balanced diet provided by the management, gastric upsets might follow from ingesting food from other than official sources.

A medical staff consisting of a doctor, dentist and podiatrist was on call; there were also several nurses and trainers always in attendance. Contestants were treated at the marathon hospital equipped to handle minor physical problems which arose in the course of every walkathon show. Anyone with more serious ailments or injuries was disqualified.

Contestants were housed in separate quarters, one for women, the other for men. Living was a make-do operation with minimal comforts. There was no privacy. Quarters were cramped, especially during the early days of the contest when there was a mass of contestants. Everyone slept on cots and lived out of his or her luggage. The smell of stale tobacco, sweating bodies, liniment and disinfectant hung in the air. During the brief 11-minute rest periods, contestants took aspirins to dull aches and pains and smoked cigarettes for relaxation. A female contestant in a deep sleep who did not respond to the warning call was brought to consciousness with smelling salts; a male contestant who did not respond to any other means of awakening might be dumped into a tub of water with floating blocks of ice.

Communal living, both on the dance floor and off, fostered a sense of camaraderie. Professional teams helped other couples particularly if they proved to be assets in the show. An amateur team who had audience appeal would be literally carried by a professional team during the walking act to keep them from being disqualified. Should a valued professional lose a partner, he or she would be given support from intact teams until a new partner was available. Beyond friendship, the reason for helping a competitor was to prolong the life of the show and, hence, to make more money.

Friendly banter was mixed with horseplay and practical jokes, rowdiness with smut, to lessen the tedium of the daily repetitive regimen.

Teams, as did individual contestants, exchanged photographs suitably autographed. Group and individual pictures taken by a professional photographer were mounted in a scrapbook. In one suggestive photo, Chad Alviso posed with a female contestant (dressed in a suit) who had her arm around Chad's shoulder; both were seated behind the base drum upon which were hung a pair of women's underpants; tacked to the face of the drum was a large sign with the number 69. In another photo, Chad, with her partner, posed with four other teams, in clowning poses; one team pointed toy pistols at their head or toward another contestant; another team wore a scarf as headpiece and balanced a serving tray with one hand.

The key to survival and to winning prize money was team effort. Men ran against men or women against women only in grudge fights. Partners who gave each other both physical and emotional support stood a better chance of lasting in the contest. It was probably true that female contestants maintained a better emotional balance than their partners, though there were many exceptions. Noble "Kid" Chiseel commented: "The best place to judge a woman is in a marathon...her disposition...her attitude...her consideration...a lot of happy marriages were made at marathons" (Interview).

Though a sense of camaraderie was part of the ambiance at walkathon shows, there was also a keen sense of competition and jealousy. Both men and women gossiped, not merely to pass the time, but to fan rivalries and create dissension between and among couples. A cunning professional team practiced the art of deceit on the popular Sweetheart Couple. She would be told: "I see your boyfriend was hanging around with...." He would be told: "Did you know that your ole lady was flirting with ...." The result of these not so veiled innuendos was predictable; the Sweetheart Couple would fight and be disqualified.

Professionals resorted to the practice of "sharp shooting," aiming barbed criticisms to devalue a competitor who threatened their popularity as show celebrities. Flash teams bragged about their talents and exploits as a means of bolstering their egos against the criticism of their peers. As Johnny Makar put it: "They all wanted to be the Big I!" (Interview).

Professional contestants who made their living working in marathon shows were wary of a talented amateur who might detract from their own popularity. They contrived any number of ways to eliminate possible competitors. For example, helpful advice took the form of recommending that the newcomers wash their socks in hot soapy water before putting them on, as preparation for the walking act. When June Havoc, as a novice contestant, took such advice, she suffered from painfully swollen feet, a condition which almost caused her disqualification.

Psychological warfare between contestants took more subtle forms. A chorus of voices singing a round, "Row Your Boat" while a contestant tried to sleep, was sufficiently disruptive among female contestants to result in a fist fight and hair-pulling, grounds for disqualification. Males resorted to putting red pepper in an opponent's shoes or slipping a potent laxative or sleeping pill into a rival's drink at mealtime. Such practices, once discovered, brought swift retribution from the victim who was expected to settle "the matter of honor" with a fist fight. In such events, the floor judge was judicious enough to look the other way.

Survival in a contest, beyond dealing with rivals, depended upon cooperating with one's partner. Teammates helped conserve each other's energy by holding up their partner when they were asleep or resting. Couples matched in height carried each other by lacing their arms around the back; if there was a marked discrepancy in size, a towel wrapped around a partner's buttocks was used to gain leverage. One male supported his partner by having her stand on the top of his shoes as he moved around the floor. It was important not to awaken a partner when shifting a supporting position. A team member saddled with a partner who was a "lug," who went limp as he or she fell asleep, was sorely taxed. Extreme measures were sometimes needed to awaken a partner who had become dead weight; partners resorted to slapping the face, kicking shins, even sticking a finger up the nose.

Cooperation between teammates was crucial in the athletic acts. In Heel and Toe Dynamite Sprint races, a male whose stride was noticeably longer than his partner's had to shorten the length of his steps. Though it was not unheard of for a male contestant to drop his partner if a more attractive or talented female became available, ordinarily contestants did rely on and trust their partners.

Competing in a walkathon show was always a gamble. Running daily foot races especially on an unraised floor, night after night, was hard on the feet. During sprint and heel-and-toe races, there was always the possibility of leg cramps, shin splints, or more seriously, turning an ankle. Using the Danger Zone for a brief respite to recover during a lap race was fraught with peril; falling on both knees in this area brought instant disqualification. Seasoned contestants knew that every show depended upon a number of variables, your partner, the feeling of the floor judge, the breaks, etc.

Contestants came to rely on the support and recognition of fans who had contacted "marathonitis," the disease of the addicted fan. Teddy Schwartz, an addicted fan, after hearing a walkathon radio broadcast, wrote the following verse (Interview)

I'm sitting near the radio
My throat is parched—my head aches so
My nose is clogged—I have a cold—
I'm weak—I must be getting old.
And since there's nothing better on,
I tune in on the Marathon.
I turn to W-A-A-T—
I hear a groan—What can it be?
Some fellow's gasping out "My Mom"—
I'm wond'ring where his strength comes from.
And then, the voice of Larry Troy,
Encouraging each girl and boy,

Assuring them that it's worthwhile,
When courage slips, to wear a smile.
One lad, though his spirit's waning,
Bravely sings "I'M NOT COMPLAINING."
I compare myself with him
And find my cold a childish whim.
Then Arthur Harman, tired and worn,
Sings "THE NIGHT WHEN LOVE WAS BORN"
And following this dark-eyed boy,
And more, the voice of Larry Troy
Says "So long, folks, now we're through";
And if we have appealed to you,
I'd appreciate it so
If you'd write and let me know.
And as Larry sang his theme,
My poker face began to beam,
And with a pen, in a few minutes time,
I scribbled down this little rhyme.

Contestants dreaded Sundays since, generally, there were no crowds to buoy the spirit. On all other days of the week, devoted fans brought food and fruit to their favorite teams even though contestants were discouraged from accepting this fare. On Christmas Eve, the yule tree was piled with gifts. Louie Meredith observed "They can't do enough for us!" Some professional contestants kept up their correspondence with fans over the years.

Though there were many advantages which professional teams enjoyed for working in walkathon shows, there was a price to pay. Gingrich referred to walkathon as "The Innocent Jail." This metaphor was not altogether off the mark: contestants were confined to the building for the duration of the contest; they obeyed a list of rules and regulations; women and men were segregated in living quarters, etc. There was no privacy. When Hal Ross introduced the fledgling Richard Elliot to the world of the walkathons, he took his assistant to the the girl's dressing room where some of the women were partially dressed, others totally naked (Martin).

It was true that an undercurrent of eroticism did pervade dance endurance shows. This ambiance of sexuality was partly built into the format of the show and partly resulted from the way contestants were housed. Contestants, both men and women, were discouraged, if not prohibited, from fraternizing with the other sex, whether contestants or fans. The strenuous physical demands of the walking and athletic acts did diminish the ardor of contestants who might otherwise have been disposed to follow their sexual urges. Some contestants followed a strict moral code and accepted the restrictions imposed by the show promoter. Other contestants, however, both female and male, satisfied their sexual appetite whenever there was an opportunity.

Female contestants responded to the seductive advances of show promoters and emcees who returned favor for favor. Joy Rogers remembers accepting a gift of an automobile from the Mayor's son, one of her admirers. Johnny Makar, known for his erotic athleticism, who identified with the image of the "macho" male, made the most of every opportunity to sustain this image. With well-meaning conceit, he once attempted to convince a contestant, a declared lesbian, that if she would go to bed with him just once, she would be cured of her "disease."

A show promoter sometimes allowed his favorite married teams to spend time alone in his office. Fans who inquired after a couple who did not appear on the dance floor were told that the team was receiving medical attention. Couples not so favored with the use of "The Snake Room" resorted to fornicating during the walking act, in the early morning hours, in a darkened corner of the dance floor. This act was consummated behind a large army blanket wrapped around a couple—the blanket was a standard gift from fellow contestants to the bride and groom after a marathon wedding. During these sexual encounters, the floor judge looked the other way. Given the repressive milieu of the walkathon show, contestants resorted to stealth in arranging clandestine meetings with other contestants under the band stand, in the storage room, in the toilet or the shower room.

Sexual encounters with members of the audience took place under the bleachers. A female fan who signalled her interest by sitting in the stands with legs apart, without underpants, elicited the response of "beaver" from male contestants ever ready to respond to such an offering. An illicit liaison between a female fan who was underage with a Don Juan in the contest, when discovered by an irate parent, could cause a promoter grief by forcing him to close the show.

"There were many homosexuals in the business..." notes George Eells. He continues, "Among the girls, the ones who were actually known as lesbians were given a pretty hard time...some of the heterosexual women would go to bed with the lesbians because of the fact that they were cut off from their husbands; it was the same thing with their husbands" (Martin, Interview 17). Richard Elliot found that a lot of the females he came in contact with in walkathon shows were women off the street; one boasted to him that she was a "five-way girl; she could have sexual relations five different ways" (Martin, Interview 9). Despite restrictive living conditions, it was probably true that the sexual behavior practiced within a walkathon show was not dissimilar to that practiced outside. Many professionals who married in walkathon contests did remain faithful to their mates; others who did not marry kept to a strict moral code.

Contestants were subject to an extensive list of rules and regulations dictated by the management. Among this list was the caution not to use alcohol or drugs like marijuana, referred to as "tea." Some celebrity contestants believed that using "tea" was addictive and feared being busted. Walkathon contestants, as was true of other show business personnel, were prone to drinking, gambling, using drugs and engaging in a range of deviant sexual practices. In general, the longer professionals stayed in walkathon shows, the more likely their behavior deviated from norms dictated by the larger society.

Professional marathoners traveled a fairly well defined circuit. They formed their own "in-group"—a society within a society. Becoming a professional contestant meant identifying with others of their kind who were looked down upon by middle-class citizens. Contestants also recognized that show promoters regarded themselves in a class above those he employed. When not participating in a show, professional contestants felt themselves to be social misfits. It was not strange this group of show people were clannish.

With bitter experience, professional contestants carefully chose which promoter to work for. Even with the more reputable promoters, contestants knew they were at the mercy of the show promoter who could be vengeful if one was not loyal to him. Flash teams gravitated toward shows which had strong contestants, the hallmark of any successful walkathon. Before finishing one show, professional contestants planned ahead, when to leave one show to start in another, whom to choose for their next partner, etc. After a particularly strenuous contest, some contestants "walked" the next show by working in some capacity other than as a contestant, for instance as a trainer or floor judge.

The regimen of walkathon shows was demanding but there were compensations for professional contestants. They did earn substantial sums of money. They were celebrities, the object of admiration of devoted fans. If scrambling for coins was viewed as demeaning to an outside observer, from the inside perspective of the professional marathoner, being a contestant was easily preferable to waiting on tables, driving a cab or being on the dole.

Professional contestants, some who competed in dance endurance shows over a 20-year period, shared many characteristics with their peers inside the walkathon business and with those in other show business ventures. They were men and women who were tough, determined, with inflated egos. Though uninvolved in social and political issues of the times, they had a confirmed faith in the gullibility of people, a sustaining hope in the crowd's appetite for painless and exciting entertainment, and a large charity for their own kind.

Chapter Six
"Natural Heat," "Working Heat"

Bunions, Corns, Blisters, Fallen Arches
and They Still GO On
Trills, Spills, and Chills!
Dancers, Singers, Comedians
100 Athletic Entertainers
How Long Can They Last?

Walkathon promoters relied on the "natural" heat generated by such ads placed in local newspapers and trade journals to attract customers to their shows. Show emcees used melodramatic appeals to get the contest off to a fast start. With the show underway, he exploited the natural heat endemic to walkathon shows by making the following pitch:

Face to face, toe to toe, around and around they go. That's the routine of the contest, day in and day out. Already the weary tramp has begun to wear them down. Remember they are out there twenty-four hours a day and no end in sight. This is where they eat, sleep, love, hate, and carry out all functions of a normal life. This is their world in toto, their lives in a microcosm. Some will become acclimated to the routine, thrive and grow fat; the others will drop by the wayside. What will happen? What will develop? Only time can give a final answer. (Eells, Act 3, Scene 2, 1)

Large signs, boldly painted and prominently displayed, added to the natural heat generated by the show emcee:

THIS IS A PLACE OF REFINED AMUSEMENT
Whistling, Stomping of Feet
Catcalls or Drunkenness or Any Obnoxious Noises
Will Not Be Tolerated at Any Time.

WARNING: CONTESTANTS ARE NOT PERMITTED TO ACCEPT
CANDY, FOOD OR LIQUOR FROM SPECTATORS.

DO NOT TOUCH CONTESTANTS!

The idea was to keep fans emotionally involved in the show by appealing to a variety of conscious and unconscious needs and fantasies. Audiences, conditioned by radio soap operas and movie serials, were easily receptive to barrages of announcements aimed at the heart. Natural heat was additionally

76

generated through the lighter fare of standard burlesque and vaudeville show features.

A shrewd walkathon promoter reminded his staff as well as his hired professional contestants that up to 75 percent of the audience were women. Hence, he advised: make them laugh and make them cry. A typical comedy routine was performed by Squirmy, the show comic, who did a brief hopping dance in which he sagged and bent his knees creating the effect of being crippled. Such light fare exhumed from burlesque and vaudeville acts was an effective means of generating natural heat to put audiences in a receptive mood.

The most powerful form of natural heat came from the contestants themselves. Their progressively worsened condition during the opening ten days of the contest was unmistakable: countenances became drawn and haggard; eyes were sunken and bleary; faces had a fixed vacant grin. Beyond fatigue were tell-tale signs of exhaustion as couples hunched over each other in what seemed a death embrace. Spectators watched with morbid fascination the mass of male and female contestants milling around the floor, bodies draped over each other, torsos contorted in every imaginable way.

One form of natural heat was, indeed, tied to nature. During the early morning hours, from 3 a.m. to 6 a.m., contestants went "squirrely." Fatigue brought them to a state resembling a coma, a state which seemed to offer relief from the soreness of the day's travail. During these episodes, contestants hallucinated, became hysterical, and had delusions of persecution. Anita O'Day vividly remembers seeing Jesus when she went squirrely. During these temporary states of altered consciousness, contestants acted out daily rituals: they talked to an imaginary companion, grinned vacantly and snatched objects out of the air (39). Chissell remembers a female contestant who disrobed in preparation for a shower during one of these episodes (Interview).

Staff members referred to these episodes which resulted from sleep deprivation as "goofiness"; nurses and trainers were not seriously concerned about these temporary bouts of dementia since these states disappeared after a short time, though they could continue on for several hours. These episodes did bring distress to the victimized partner who was struck and whose face was clawed by a teammate. In these twilight states, contestants were highly suggestible and, like the hypnotized subject of a stage demonstration, responded readily to even the most ludicrous cues. The suggestion from a fellow contestant that "The Indians are coming!" propelled one sleepwalker into rapid motion around the dance floor in a state of panic.

If, as some dream researchers have suggested, it is the function of the nocturnal dream to allow us "to go privately crazy every night," going squirrely appears to have had a similar function to dreaming. To maximize their sleep time and hence minimize going squirrely, some contestants practiced a form of self-hypnosis; as soon as they lay down for the 11-minute break, they trained themselves to fall into a deep sleep. Similarly, during the walking period, they quickly succumbed to sleep despite the music generated from amplified, scratchy old phonograph records.

As one might expect, audiences present at these happenings reacted differently. With the onset of the squirrely state, some fans grew anxious and tense; they leaned forward, bit their lips, clutched and twisted their handkerchiefs. These often ludicrous displays fascinated audiences, like seeing a freak at a carnival side-show. Walkathon promoters set the stage for exploiting the theme of endurance shows, "How Long Can They Last?," by creating an atmosphere of stress and emergency. Grim reminders of the tenuous nature of being a contestant in a walkathon appeared on either side of the band shell, in rectangular frames which kept audiences informed of the progress of the contest:

Couples Started	Days Danced
(51)	(7)
Couples Remaining	Hours Danced
(30)	(168)

Last Dancer Out
(Boy: No. 4)

The feeling of impermanence coupled with a sense of foreboding was present in still another sign which was prominently displayed:

BUY A SOUVENIR PICTURE OF YOUR FAVORITE
HE MAY NOT BE HERE TOMORROW.
MM. PRICE 10 cents.

Further reminders of impending danger to contestants came with the presence of nurses and trainers in white uniforms. Off to the right of the bandstand, up a ramp, stood a room with an overhead sign: "Marathon Hospital." This room usually had an open side or glass wall which gave the curious spectator a partial view of the contestants receiving attention for an injury. When the curtains were pulled, in instances where the case was extreme or required discretion, fans projected their fantasies as to what was going on behind the drawn curtains.

The flavor of emergency is highlighted in several literary depictions of walkathon shows. In *Marathon 33*, Dankle, the show promoter, relies on natural heat by capitalizing on Jean Reeds' appearance. She is small, skinny and looks anemic. He bills the 14-year-old vaudevillian as "The Little Mamie" of the show. "There's a depression on outside of right here. My spectators got a real need to feel sorry for somebody that's more depressed than themselves...it's human" (15).

Ruddy, the show emcee, follows Dankle's lead by referring to Jean as "The Baby of the Show." His pitch to the morning customers includes calling their attention to how tired Jean looks and how much she needs encouragement from the audience. Later in the day, the floor judge, Mr. James, described as a combination bouncer and Simon Legree, snaps a long ruler to sting her calves as a reminder to keep moving. His action generates additional sympathy for the struggling young girl.

On Cot Night, advertised as "A Fascinating Glimpse Behind the Scenes," audiences were able to view contestants sleeping on cots in the middle of the dance floor during their 11-minute rest period. Using the occasion to generate heat, show emcee Ruddy, his voice mellow and "personal," reminds the audience that the "brave kids will have to give up the few minutes each hour they have known of privacy." He reminds the crowds of the coming event, the "grinds," a protracted period of time when contestants cannot receive help from nurses or trainers unless they fall. Under these circumstances, he repeats, ad nauseam, "How Long Can They Last?"

Jean soon learns how natural heat is generated by the walkathon staff and also learns how to work heat to elicit sympathy from the audience. Not without some initial pangs of conscience, Jean fakes exhaustion by affecting a slow motion gait and causing her voice to falter. Her acting has the desired effect. Two teen-age girls seated at ringside reassure her of their support and encourage her not to give up. At one point in the contest, Jean attempts to use this mode of eliciting sympathy by affecting hysterics when another contestant is doing her speciality act. Once again, her acting is effective though the floor nurse tells her that to act squirrely when another performer is working heat is considered unethical by the other contestants. Dankle encapsulates the powerful effect of working heat in his cynical observation that all audiences love watching the "death agony." Audiences did become mesmerized by watching the slow moving couples mill around and around during the repetitive walking act to the continuous music played on the Victrola. To liven up the show before the rest break, the show emcee would have the band play a brief animated selection which brought contestants back to life as they attempted to match their movements to the up-tempo music.

If a contest was generating sufficient natural heat from the spectacle of watching contestants struggle through the opening days of the contest, and from the vaudeville-cabaret entertainment, the introduction of athletic acts was delayed. However, once there was a slackening of interest after the initial novelty of the show had worn off within a ten-day period, further heat was introduced. The sequence of events followed a predictable course. The floor judge, appropriately called the "heat judge," publicly remonstrated with the show emcee that contestants were "too strong" and were not dropping out fast enough. His demand that more stringent elimination tests be introduced to narrow the field of competition was met with initial resistance by the show emcee who posed as a protector of the "kids" in the show. Despite the emcee's spirited defense that further elimination features be delayed, the floor judge remained adamant in his demands. Within the prescribed ten-day period, sport features, strenuous sprint and derby races were introduced at the evening show. Behind the facade of the emcee as protector and the judge as villain was the actuality: both floor judge and emcee were in the hire of the show promoter. As far as the public knew, however, the floor judge was an outside referee.

Audiences responded with mixed feelings to the announcement that elimination features were to be introduced into the show format. Fans both feared for the fate of their favorite team and looked forward to the coming attractions, the sprint and derby races, which would bring "thrills, chills, and spills." The appeal of novelty and the promise of excitement soon superseded any sense of concern fans might have felt for contestants put under additional stress with the introduction of these foot races. Predictably, the new show features increased box office receipts.

The introduction of sprint, heel and toe, and lap races signaled the true beginning of the walkathon contest for professional teams. These sport features served a dual purpose: they virtually eliminated all but a few amateur couples and also gave flash teams the opportunity to earn extra money. Each race carried prize money which might be increased by the show promoter, the team sponsors and occasionally by fans. These sums seemed hardly commensurate with the sustained effort it took to earn this revenue.

The introduction of athletic events to generate heat in the show called for close cooperation between partners and between teams. In sprint races, male and female faced each other and maintained four hand contact as they alternated between going forward and backward around the dance floor in dance position. This race, modelled on a fast-paced dance called the Peabody, took skill and practice to execute effectively especially navigating the corners of the rectangular dance floor. Sprint races gave a clear edge to professionals over amateur teams.

Another athletic feature to generate heat was the heel-and-toe foot race. Teams lined up at one end of the dance floor ready to begin; the floor judge had selected a lead team to set the pace. At the sound of a pistol shot, the house band began with "The Washington and Lee Swing," played in moderate tempo to allow contestants to warm up. Males executed a fast-walk; females had the option to run or walk. The race underway, the judge sounded his police whistle, the signal for the band to pick up the tempo. At this point, any couple might challenge the lead team and set a faster pace. When this happened, all the teams began hurtling around the outer edge of the dance floor converted into a miniature track. Teams pushed, shoved and elbowed their way trying to remain out in front so as not to finish last (Eells, Act 1, Scene 2). Sprint races which lasted a half hour or more took a toll, particularly on amateur teams who succumbed to exhaustion. The climax of these races roused audiences to a fever pitch.

In the late 1930s, walkathon show promoters introduced some of the practices used in roller derbies to generate heat. During the early morning hours, professional teams practiced "jamming," choreographing a heel-and-toe derby. They practiced which team would surge ahead or drop behind, which contestant would trip, bump, or push another contestant. The floor judge would monitor these practice sessions to optimize their dramatic impact.

Amateur contestants were careful if not ingenuous in not incurring any penalty points which might jeopardize their standing in the contest. Not so for professional walkathoners whose intent was to keep fans in a state of apprehension by working heat. With a "three-fall-and-out rule" in effect, professional teams took two falls early within the designated period. Subsequently, they brought themselves to the brink of disqualification by having one member of the team gradually sink to the ground. At a prearranged signal, both teammates suddenly straightened their knees amidst cries of relief from fans who feared the worst. Forced to go apart during the walking act, the solo professional worked heat by yawning, pretending to be in a trance on the verge of falling asleep, bending over as if ready to pitch forward to the floor.

The point system afforded contestants still another opportunity to work heat. Flash teams would break one or more of the following rules and thereby incur penalty points which placed their position in the contest in apparent jeopardy:

Standing still 15 seconds.

Leaving the floor without permission.

Not wearing chains or breaking contact with partner by dropping chains.

Striking partner.

Using profane or vulgar language.

Being late for bell on floor.

Failing to face partner and refusing to dance on judge's whistle.

Engaging in an extended conversation with spectators without the floor judge's consent.

Working heat, contestants faked pain. It was true that walkathoncontests had pain built into them. Skeptical newcomers to walkathon shows heckled contestants with the accusation that the walkathon show was a "put-up-job" and "a racket." Seasoned contestants, in defense, would remind their critics that they had thick callouses on the balls of their feet, that their ankles swelled and that, at the end of each walking period, they were exhausted. There was, of course, truth on both sides. "Putting fans on" by confirming their worst imaginings was some compensation for the real travail of walkathon contests.

Throughout the walking periods, show emcees described the protracted struggle of teams who were in various stages of exhaustion. Repeatedly, audiences heard the refrain: "Let's get behind them folks. Let them know you care. Every team is on the brink of disqualification...who will be the next to go?" Additionally, the walking act gave "heat judges" the opportunity to generate excitement. A contestant who had fallen in a sprint was ordered by the floor judge to the Danger Zone in the center of the floor. The emcee signaled the band to stop the music. In the ensuing quiet, as the beleaguered contestant's knees inched to the floor, the floor judge was down on his hands and knees, his right hand raised, whistle in mouth, ready to signal a disqualification. Floor judges who "knew how to run a floor," sought to keep audiences in a state of uproar. Working heat, they abused popular contestants while abetting the knavery of The Trouble Makers by feigning ignorance of their unfair tactics. Conversely, they were quick to punish retaliatory measures taken by The Sweetheart Couple.

Audiences took delight when the "heat judge" became the victim in place of victimizer. Crowds roared their disapproval each time the floor judge chalked up a penalty point against a favored contestant and derived huge delight at the antics of a show comedian who imitated the mannerism of the villain behind his back. Fans were amused when a playful contestant "accidentally" bumped a faltering couple into wakefulness. Predictably, patrons cheered when the floor judge was struck from behind without being able to identify his assailant.

The introduction of the athletic acts afforded further opportunities to the professional staff and professional contestants to work heat. In *The Glory Walk*, floor judge Dracula Brown is described as a huge, demonical-looking creature who paces the floor like a caged lion (Eells, Act 1, Scene 1). He is a man of action who uses verbal threats and physical force to enforce the rules and regulations. Dracula Brown grimaces and scowls; at the first signs that a team is faltering, he snaps a ruler against the calves of the exhausted couple. In the fiercely contested athletic acts, the "heat judge" races around the floor, urging teams along by snapping his handkerchief in their face and blowing his whistle in their ear.

When speed derbies are introduced into the contest in the film, *They Shoot Horses Don't They?*, Rocky works heat as he addresses the audience: "There is a lesson for all of us in this race, ladies and gentlemen,...You don't need to be Number One as you amble down Life's Highway...but don't be last!" (McCoy 215). Midway through the race, with teams frantically shoving and elbowing their way so as not to finish last, Rocky exhorts the audience, already at a fever pitch of excitement, to cheer their favorite teams "...because each one of them is fighting down pain, exhaustion, weariness...struggling to keep going...battling to win...and isn't that the American way folks!" (McCoy 221).

Walkathon shows, particularly in later years, relied on familiar melodramatic formulas to "work heat." Teams labelled "The Trouble Makers" looked the part: the women were dark and buxom, the men, strong and mean looking. Their adversaries, "The Sweetheart Couple," were attractive and usually light complexioned. The struggle between good and evil was particularly dramatic when acted out between female adversaries.

In sprint and derby races, "Gypsy," the distaff side of the Trouble Making couple, openly telegraphed her malevolent intentions to the crowd. She appeared remorseless in the grudge match with her fair-haired adversary, pushing, shoving, elbowing, tripping, jabbing in the ribs, and striking from behind. Her behavior elicited boos and cries from the audience who felt compelled to shout their warnings to the crowd favorite, all to no avail. Notwithstanding the difference in sport, the attraction of the walkathon show was little different from that enjoyed by fans in a wrestling arena. Showmanship was first and foremost.

During this perpetrated mayhem, the floor judge's attention was, of course, directed elsewhere. Insult was added to injury when the victimized contestant attempted to retaliate and discovered that the floor judge was quick to penalize the abused victim-turned- aggressor. These episodes always left audiences cliff hanging at the end of one race before the beginning of the next. Would the Sweetheart of the walkathon show get revenge on the Trouble Maker? When and how would she do it? Or would the victimization continue despite all the effort made by the audience to give the abused heroine help?

Lap races gave professional contestants a good chance to prove their mettle as athletes and provided a prime opportunity to excite audiences. Rivals in a hotly contested lap race alternated in gaining sympathy from the audience by clutching at their side (as if they had a stitch) and by falling to the ground writhing from a charley horse. A contestant who fell in a lap race was forced to the safety zone (the "Danger Zone") in the center of the floor; they remained there until the other member of the team had run two extra laps. Now handicapped, the Sweetheart Couple seemed destined to lose to the Trouble Makers. Crowds went wild when The Sweetheart Couple propelled themselves over the finish line just seconds before their adversaries.

Each night some new feature would be introduced, or an existing feature made harder. If speed derbies were run for ten minutes one night, the next night an additional minute would be added; in lap races, contestants were required to do additional laps. To reduce the number of contestants, walkathon promoters initiated a grind period, a determinate or indeterminate period of time when rest and hygiene breaks were curtailed and food and drink was withheld. At show time, during the grind period set from 7 p.m. to 2 a.m., with a "three-fall-and-out" rule in effect, there was to be no help from trainers or nurses in any way except after a fall.

Vaudeville and cabaret acts provided numerous opportunities to work heat. In the novel *The Dancing Madness*, a professional contestant coached his partner to sing "Why Was I Born?" a question some spectators might have asked themselves during the height of the Depression (Ames). In the film version of McCoy's novel, Rocky calls a pregnant, female contestant to the stage platform to sing "The Best Things In Life Are Free" (221). Whether heat was natural or worked, the important point was this: no matter how amateurish the performance, fans were generous in demonstrating their appreciation by throwing coins on the dance floor for the performer.

Professional contestants, in addition to working heat in the speed and lap races, also used the vaudeville-cabaret acts to generate interest in the show. The emcee rehearsed teams to act in a variety of vaudeville skits like "School Days" and "The Shotgun Wedding." In addition, he called contestants to the bandstand during the repetitious walking act to do their speciality act. A request to sing "Ace In The Hole" from the boisterous crowd of hoodlums in ringside seats brought a generous tip of $20. The emcee worked his own brand of heat by cajoling a female contestant, whom he addressed as "Cutie Pie," to come to the bandstand to do her speciality number. Her rendition of "Roses of Picardy," though sung in a whiny voice and with a monotonous cadence, brought a shower of coins from the audience.

A typical bit of stage business borrowed from burlesque and play-acted by a walkathon couple with a flair for comedy would go as follows: "I thank you from the bottom of my heart," (stuffing a dollar bill down her bosom, a "spray" from an admiring fan). He: "I thank you from by bottom," (this line delivered in a way-over bent position facing away from the audience).

Though cautioned not to fraternize with the audience, contestants "worked the rails," a calculated ploy to generate heat. Teen-age girls were prone to develop a crush on some attractive male contestant. Betty Herndon Meyer remembers that, as a 14-year-old girl, she wrote brief notes to her favorite contestant in which she expressed her tender admiration and sympathy. "We thought these people brought this kind of world with them from Hollywood and New York into our small town," she reminisces.

Jimmy Parker, the object of her crush, replied to her notes with the following message:

> Dearest Red: [Betty has red hair]
> I think you are a mighty sweet girl—I hope I can see you when the walkathon's over—I would like to dance with you at the Playmore. Thanks for rooting for me.
> 'Dancingly yours'
> Jimmie Parker
> (Martin, Interview with B.H Meyer)

Though Meyer never met Jimmy, this exchange kept the impressionable teenager coming back every afternoon. Not all exchanges between contestants and fans were innocent. It did happen that a promoter was forced to close his show when an ardent male contestant seduced an underage female admirer.

Promoters enticed potential customers to the walkathon by generating heat over the radio. Several times daily, live from the walkathon arena, listeners were kept abreast of the latest happenings at the contest. The emcee, much like a sports announcer, reported which contestants had survived the previous night's ordeal and what the outcome was of the sprint races. In addition, the emcee described the mayhem created the night before by the comedians and clowns for the evening's entertainment.

The radio emcee described the fun and games at the walkathon show but also the sadness. "Believe me, ladies and gentlemen," the softened voice of the broadcaster continued,

...a more sorrowful sight you wouldn't want to see...the elimination that occurred last night...her partner tried desperately...really, it was a dramatic picture to watch the boy straining, striving feverishly to keep that girl up on both feet...gradually, yet surely, she kept slipping away...finally, her arm grip, which he had been attempting to maintain about his partner's waist, broke loose...he lunged forward to grab the belt, but missed and his hand fell short of the belt...soon you could see his hands separating from his partner's back and as his hands separated from each other, he couldn't possibly bring them back together again...his partner kept slipping closer and closer to the track...the boy tried to get her up...he tried for minutes to stand that girl on both feet...soon the boy with tired muscles, couldn't hold the girl up any longer, and she slipped to the track for a heavy fall...he, too, almost fell to the track, but the girl went down...the trainers picked her up and carried her from the floor....A greater dramatic picture could not be unfolded in any walkathon contest. (Mathews Scrapbook)

Advertisements placed in trade journals and newspapers were another form of generating heat:

COUPLES CHAINED AFTER 572 HOURS
TRAINING QUARTERS ABANDONED
NO MEDICAL ASSISTANCE
NO ASSISTANCE
GOODBYE FOREVER

Periodic exposés of shady practices did damage the image of walkathon shows. On the other hand, newspaper stories with headlines like the following: "Sex Morals Shot By Dizzy-Grinds" and "Good Girls Turn Bad in Sleep Sex Orgies," added a measure of natural heat and lured customers to the show to see if the stories behind the headlines were true.

Walkathon show promoters and emcees added the natural heat generated by the human body in abbreviated costume to heighten interest in the contest. Voyeurs in the audience were attracted to the eroticism of special features such as Bathing Beauty Contests, Cellophane Walkathon Weddings, and the Ice Act, in which a female contestant, clad in a bathing suit, entered an ice tomb. At show time, in the heel and toe derbies, female contestants wore shorts and tee shirts. During these fast paced races, the motion of breasts and hips was not unnoticed. On rare occasions, in the heat of summer, when males removed their tee shirts, females stripped to their brassieres. An added aphrodisiac was the proximity of female and male bodies, almost within reaching distance, sweating and straining through the nightly ordeals. Not to be overlooked in these displays of the senses was the music of the house band playing hot jazz and Dixieland.

Among the variety of acts featured at walkathon shows, none was more strange than the Ice Act. Several large blocks of ice, hollowed to receive a human body, were placed on a table supported by saw horses. The table was placed before the bandstand for easy viewing. A professional contestant of either sex, always a crowd favorite, chose to be "frozen alive in 1200 lbs. of cold, frigid ice" (Eells 154). Clad only in a bathing suit and wooden clogs, the daring contestant climbed into the ice coffin, with head and shoulders only protected against ice burns by a towel.

The entombed body exchanged signals with a fellow marathoner using a flash light. To further heighten the suspense, the emcee would report that the encased marathoner had temporarily lost the flashlight. When 50 seconds elapsed without an answering signal from within, the house physician ordered the contestant chopped out by the crew of men standing by. After a short period of recovery in the marathon hospital, following a rub down, the thawed-out contestant was greeted with applause. That evening, at show time, the contender "who had set a new record in the ice," or who had beaten the record of an arch rival, was generously rewarded after performing his or her speciality act. Additional revenue came from postcard pictures of the act which were sold for ten cents a piece.

To heighten the effect of this act, show promoters had a resuscitator standing nearby the ice block while the act was in progress; as an added fillip, an ambulance was parked out front. Contestants who participated in the Ice Act knew what audiences did not know. If the seams of the ice blocks were properly sealed and there were no drafts, the interior of the ice block, reputed to be thirty degrees below zero, would not cause a contestant undue discomfort for an interval upwards of thirty minutes, the time the act usually lasted. This feature was staged when the show was two weeks underway.

From a grab bag of events which were featured night after night, ever popular was Amateur Night which gave local talent, old and young, an opportunity to demonstrate their talent. Some programs were earmarked for women, wedding showers, engagement parties and anniversary celebrations. There was still more—groceries given away and prizes raffled.

The *pièce de résistance* of walkathon shows was a walkathon wedding. The emcee introduced this coming attraction by announcing that this gala was "in line with the management's policy to give you nothing but high-class entertainment." This popular event combined both natural heat and working heat and was particularly effective in attracting female fans. Walkathon weddings were both real and mock. Most often, professional contestants were invited to be the bride and groom since they were the celebrities of the show. Occasionally, if an amateur team caught the public's fancy, the show promoter would approach the couple with an offer to be the "Sweetheart Team of the Month." He explained the benefits in accepting this prize: the team would be built up to be the most popular team on the floor and reap the full benefits from this box office attraction.

Walkathon weddings were changed from real to mock if there were some legal restrictions which prevented one or both parties from being married. One good reason to switch from a real to a mock wedding was discovering that the bride-to-be was underage. O'Day remembers the events which led up to her mock wedding as a walkathon bride. Brady, the show promoter, had persuaded the ingenue's mother to put in an appearance at her daughter's shower. When her mother appeared, she demanded that the wedding be stopped because her daughter was underage. Making the most of blackmailing Brady, O'Day's mother stormed around the emcee's stand and threatened to have him jailed. Brady, having incurred expenses involved in making the bride's cellophane wedding dress and the bridesmaids' gowns, gradually persuaded the apparently aroused parent to go along with the wedding plans. She agreed when he promised to perform a mock wedding by substituting for the actual minister. For playing her part so well, Brady reimbursed O'Day's mother by paying her return bus fare along with a bonus of ten dollars for her cooperation (35).

Mock wedding or real, a walkathon wedding called for careful preparation. In the weeks prior to this celebration, one night was set aside for an Engagement Party, another for a Bridal Shower, etc. The special day arrived with much excitement. The drab enclosure which housed the band was decorated with festive colored streamers and a large, white wedding bell was suspended above the band box.

Preceding the ceremony, merchants who contributed goods or services for this event were publicly acknowledged: bakeries and florists, a loan company, a doctor who donated Wasserman tests and, oddly, a funeral home. Congratulatory letters and telegrams from fans and fellow marathoners were read from the bandstand. The bridal party, having carefully rehearsed earlier in the afternoon, made its entrance in full traditional attire. Invariably, when this act was staged (and restaged, later that evening), there was *standing room only*!

Walkathon weddings gave show emcees a prime opportunity to work heat. Rex (a fictional character in *The Glory Walk*, who was modeled after the real show promoter King Brady) instructs the audience at the outset of a walkathon wedding. He reminds the expectant crowd that the contest is first, last and always; that audiences should honor with silence the ceremony. However, if a team is in trouble, fans should do everything in their power to alert their endangered favorites (Act 1, Scene 1). Rex's instructions are acted upon when Grandma Malone, lulled by the monotonous tone of the minister's voice, sinks to her knees. Fans yell and shout their warnings to the aging contestant as her partner slaps her with his fist and then uses a wet towel to revive her.

Walkathon shows exploited Americans' perennial preoccupation with love and romance. Emcees used the occasion when a contestant lost his or her partner to capitalize on this preoccupation. *In The Glory Walk*, when Marcella, scheduled to be the bride at a forthcoming walkathon wedding, is disqualified, Rex, always an opportunist, announces that the Sweetheart Couple will be married even with her disqualification, since the couple is in love (Eells, Act 2, Scene 1).

A couple groomed for a walkathon wedding was rarely disqualified before the event took place—show personnel saw to it. Solos were given 72 hours to find another teammate or face disqualification. Just prior to the deadline after a new partner became available, the jubilant emcee would announce: "Boy meets girl...boy loses girl...boy gets girl. Well, folks...isn't that the American Way!"

The fact that professional contestants traveling the same circuit over two decades married, divorced and remarried the same partner, or different partners in successive shows, did little to shake the belief of walkathon fans, reinforced by the rhetoric of the show emcee that "The Dance Marathon is the Original Home of Romance!" Louie Meredith added this observation about walkathon weddings. The fact that the story-book romance and marriage of The Sweetheart Couple could not be formally consummated during the run of the contest (at least, so it seemed) elicited sympathy from fans who empathized with the newlyweds who were forced to put off their honeymoon for many weeks, sometimes months.

The winners in walkathon shows were crowned "The King and Queen" at a Celebration Ball. The losers, those who had survived the first 500 hours, were given a Disqualification Ceremony. This partying ritual was carefully staged to evoke a strong emotional response; parting brought sweet sorrow. Emcees played a crucial role in this performance. Here is how a Disqualification Ceremony was staged: The disqualified contestant appeared in a bathrobe, a towel swathed around the head and parts of the face. At a signal from the emcee, the contestant's partner approached from behind, circled in front of the chair and kissed the ill-fortunate teammate. Fellow competitors followed suit in bidding the departing competitor farewell.

Many spectators cried openly, especially when "The Marathon Songbird" sang the official song for the disqualification ceremony (O'Day 35):

> Oh, how we'll miss you tonight,
> Miss you when lights are low.
> Oh, how we need you tonight
> More than you'll ever know
> You did your best on the floor
> Now you're not here any more.
> Though your poor heart is aching,
> Now our hearts are breaking
> Old pal, how we miss you tonight.

Following the song, the emcee would make his final appeal, reminding audiences what lay in store for the disqualified contestant in a world caught in the throes of the Great Depression. Fans were genuinely if momentarily unhappy to see someone they had come to care for drop out of the contest. They were unusually generous in providing the departing contestant with a small cushion to fall back on as they made the transition back to the outside world. Fellow contestants who felt some kinship with the disqualified contestant—after being in hourly contact over a period of weeks and months—also felt sorry to see their friends drop out of the show. The disqualification ceremony was a perfect vehicle to afford an emotional catharsis for all present.

If audiences continued to respond at the box office, promoters sought to keep the contest going by introducing easier rules and less strenuous athletic features. In the later 1930s, some walkathons were "kip" shows, contests in which teams were permitted to have extra sleep. If inquiries were made about an absent contestant, fans would be told that he was getting a pedicure or a haircut, or that she was scheduled for a physical exam or was having her hair set.

Periodically, to reduce the number of contestants (and to reduce suspicion that the show was not on the "up-and-up"), a positive elimination feature was scheduled. The message was that of the Circus Maximus: "Tonight, someone must go!" A professional contestant in the hire of the show promoter would be told "to hit the deck anyway you know." Another means of quieting criticism was to have someone disqualified, not at show time as was the usual practice, but at some other time. To close a show, a series of exhausting athletic events was introduced.

Walkathon contests operated on P.T. Barnum's premise that the American people want to believe and they want to be fooled. The American passion for humbug was well understood by walkathon promoters who banked on this American trait. Americans, they believed, were willing not only to suspend belief but sound judgement as well. By combining natural heat and working heat in their shows, show promoters and their staff of emcees, floor judges and professional contestants proved anew that Barnum was right.

Hal J. Ross European Walkathon, 1935. Ross ran big shows and promoted them as 'The Family Man's Night Club."

Small walkathon show with matinee performance for mothers and children.

Three remaining couples in Kearny Dance Marathon after 3356 hours (nearing five months).

Jim Priori and Jeanne King with matching costumes donated by sponsor Dantis Cafe and Bar.

Partners doing the Lindy Hop with names on matching sweaters.

Professional contestants, an unglamorous look.

Professionals clowning. Rare instance of Trouble Maker, Chad Alviso smiling (front, two from the right).

Erotic overtones back stage. Chad Alviso and friend in spoof.

Milling around during the walking act. Frankie Lane, 19 years old (upper right hand corner), and Frank Miller, 56 years old (in front line, between two couples).

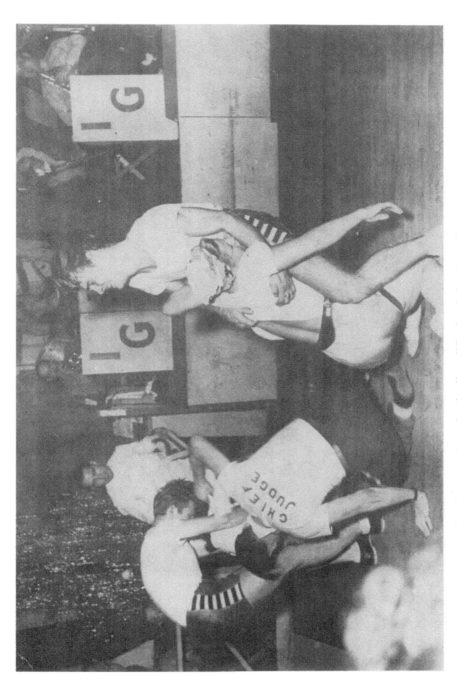

Struggling to keep upright. Chief Judge ready to signal a disqualification during the walking act.

Audience raptured waiting for the end. Nurse and Frankenstein, the floor judge, vigilant. Notice couple connected with dog chains to prevent separation.

Jim Priori takes a fall during a Zombie Treadmill. Contestants had eyes bandaged for this act performed in darkened arena.

Contestants in tortured postures during the walking act. Floor judge (bad guy) eager to signal a fall, with emcee (the good guy) offering support. Both colluded to heighten the melodrama.

Dynamite Sprint with menacing floor judge. Partners changed from promenade to closed dance position rounding corners; this maneuver gave professionals edge over amateur contestants who lasted 500 hours.

Exhaustion at end of Heel-and-Toe foot race. Part real ("natural heat"), part fake ("working heat").

One, two three, four, five...and out. Floor judge waves towel used to slap couples from behind to keep them moving in Bombshell races.

Women had the greater stamina.

The Vaudeville Cabaret Act...Emcee, Ted Brown, between Clown, "Wiggles Royce," and Comic, Jimmie Fierenzi.

Comedy on Country Store Night. Ted Brown offering turbaned spectator pigs head.

Country Store Night. Food baskets were a welcomed prize during the Great Depression.

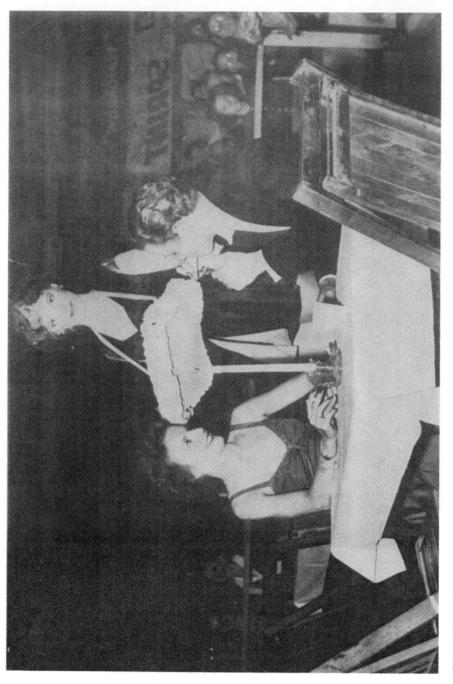

Night Life in Chicago. Cabaret act with a touch of class.

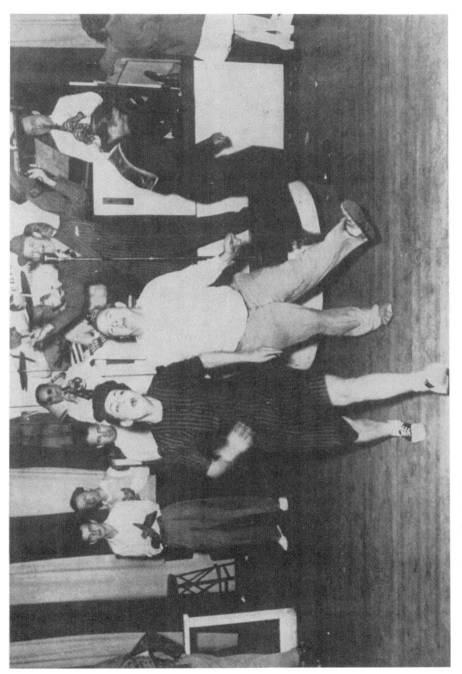

Down home entertainment for the folks.

School Daze Review with Prof. Ted Brown. Contestants in short dresses and rolled up pants.

Johnny Makar before setting world record in Ice Act. Postcards commemorating event sold for 10 cents a card.

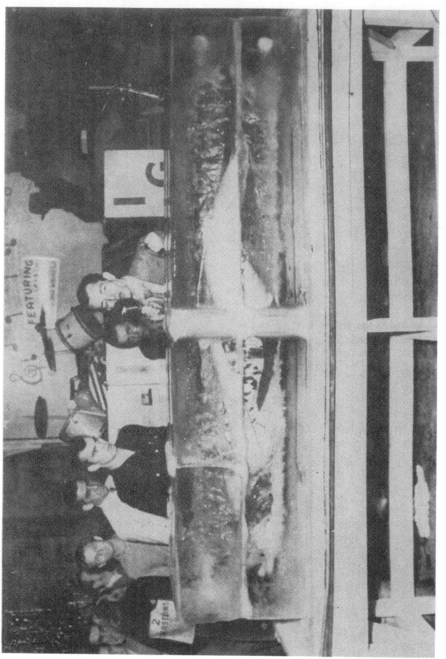

The Ice Act: "frozen alive in 1200 lbs. of cold, frigid ice." Birdie Cortez in total immersion.

Cot Night: An intimate peek behind the scenes.

Audiences absorbed watching trainer work on feet of contestants on Cot Night.

Walkathon Wedding. "Standing Room Only Sign" posted at each performance of legitimate and mock weddings.

Double Walkathon Wedding. The old gang (see photo p. 95) dressed up. The Sweetheart Couple and Trouble Makers married in a double wedding. Villain, Chad Alviso, strikes her characteristic "sour puss" pose.

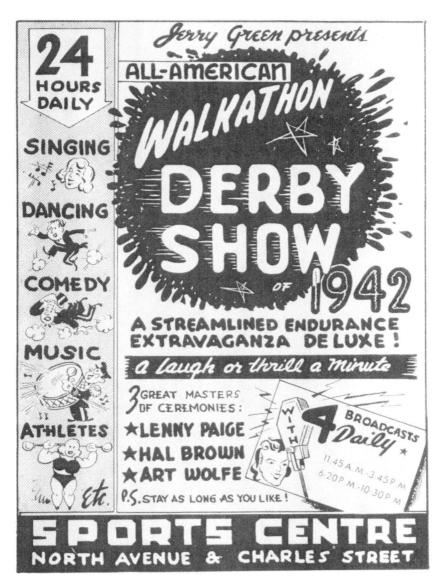

Official Program Guide. Listing teams, sponsors and coming events. Ten couples and two male solos after 888 hours.

The
COLISEUM WALKATHON
proudly presents the
ALL-AMERICAN CHAMPIONS
1500 SOUTH WABASH AVENUE, CHICAGO

CASH PRIZES UP TO $1500.00

Masters of Ceremony
Austy Dowdell — Jimmy Bittner — Duke Hall

Music by
ARTIE STARK and HIS ORCHESTRA

BROADCASTING 9:15 and 10:45 MONDAY TO
NIGHTLY   FRIDAY
WIND   9:15 and 10:00 Saturday
             8:00 and 10:45 Sunday
TUNE IN WHEN YOU CANNOT ATTEND

PHONE CALUMET 6798

Chicago's Own Walkathon
Presents
ENTERTAINMENT plus SPEED
Thrilling . . . Exciting . . . Amusing

Advertising Walkathon Shows. Radio broadcasts and Specialty Nights drew audiences to the arena.

Part III

The Palace of
Wasted Footsteps

Chapter Seven
Dance of the Godfathers

Walkathon promoters fancied their shows a family man's night club. However exaggerated this conceit, the idea of the walkathon show as an extended family did have some truth. The parent-child relationship found in father-dominated families was characteristic of the interaction between walkathon promoters and contestants. "Pop" used the familiar address "kid" with contestants; he expected and received their respect and often their loyalty. The "kids" recognized the authority of "daddy" (or that of his staff) who gave his children free room and board and the opportunity to earn some money. Eells notes: "The contestants were like kids; the promoter took care of them and helped them make decisions. He got them out of jail; he helped them if they got into a financial bind" (Martin, Interview with G. Eells).

A benevolent paternalistic promoter provided his dependent children with clean living facilities, a nutritious diet, adequate medical help and most importantly, a guarantee that siblings would receive the promised prize money. In addition, the "good father" promoter honored his obligations in the community with a shrewd eye to doing repeat business. Hal Ross personified the benevolent paternalistic show promoter, and there were few others like him in the walkathon business.

The paternalistic promoter also protected his female charges from the lewd advances of drunken gangsters and hoodlums who attempted to "buy a woman off the floor." It was not unusual for a promoter to post bail for a male contestant arrested for smoking marijuana. As head of the family, he was not always successful in handling the misbehavior of all the other members of the walkathon family, especially when an errant son seduced an underage girl from the audience and incurred the wrath of her parents. Such an incident was enough to close a show. In general, show promoters, as business entrepreneurs, regarded themselves in a socio-economic class above that of contestants and staff.

Sometimes it was the show emcee who assumed the role of strong father figure. When a show promoter was away, he left the responsibility for the contest in the hands of the emcee. As surrogate father, the emcee demonstrated his support for family members by helping to find sponsors for each team in the show. Another father surrogate was the floor judge who, in addition to adjudicating the contest, had the responsibility of monitoring the unruly behavior of family members when they stepped out of line.Contestants fortunate enough to join a show with a promoter and staff that was supportive could look to nurses and trainers to give them the attention of sympathetic aunts and uncles. In this model image of the walkathon family, the large contingent of women fans, old and young, like well-meaning relatives, were generous in giving contestants praise and encouragement.

Under such favorable conditions, a sense of camaraderie was likely to develop among contestants. A positive family ambiance softened the impact of the hardships contestants had to endure. In each new show, it was quite common to meet rivals who traveled the walkathon circuit, competitors from previous shows with whom days, weeks, even months had been spent together. Joining a new show, especially a contest billed as "The Battle of Champions," was like old home week. This sense of belonging to a family in-group was important: professional contestants felt themselves outsiders from society as a whole, itinerant gypsies looked upon with suspicion by the middle-class who disapproved of dance endurance shows.

This positive image of the dance endurance contest as "happy family" is, however, not the description portrayed in literary accounts and film documents (nor in newspaper and magazine accounts). The walkathon promoter in these sources is depicted as a paternalistic authoritarian in charge of running a "family protection racket." His self-aggrandizing stance is not unlike the posture of the stereotypical movie mogul afflicted with a godfather complex who maintains a co-dependent relationship with actors and actresses. Eells notes that, more often than not, show promoters took advantage of his teams and made a lot of money off them (Martin, Interview with G. Eells). This co-dependency also defined the walkathon promoter's interaction with rival promoters and with members of the community where he opened his shows. The pattern of interacting in the walkathon family between show promoter in a co-dependency relationship with other family members is the mode of relating characteristically found in neurotic families.

Eric Berne's theory of family dynamics helps us understand the dark underside of the walkathon contest as a family protection racket. In Berne's view, dysfunctional families engage in a series of transactions which are, in the main, destructive games. Families which exhibit marked neurotic symptoms play "two-handed games" for ulterior motives with a "payoff" that is lethal to both victim and victimizer. When the entire family is in collusion, as is often the case in the neurotic family, the two-handed game takes the form of a family protection racket.

The walkathon show as a family protection racket is the image projected in most, if not all, literary and cinematic portrayals. In *Marathon 33*, June Havoc describes her disillusioning initiation into the world of the walkathon contest. In this play, as in her autobiographical novel *Early Havoc*, Havoc portrays the fierce sibling rivalry which she encounters in the world of the walkathon show. The ingénue performer—she is a 14-year-old vaudevillian when she joins her first show—follows the advice of a professional contestant who tells her to tape a 50 cent coin under the metatarsal of each foot before putting on her shoes. Instead of toughening her feet, this action results in bleeding, inordinate swelling and excruciating pain. Challenged to name her victimizer by Dankle, the show promoter who decries the act before the audience as an old crooked trick to force amateurs out of the contest, the street-wise vaudevillian remembers the promoter's earlier admonition to keep her mouth shut. She does.

Jean Reid, the stage name Dankle gives her, is identified by the emcee as "the baby of our show." Soon Jean adopts the code of the insider and begins to collude in the game of family protection racket. Though disenchanted by the underhanded treatment she has received from a fellow contestant, Dean rationalizes that "her lie" not to name her victimizer, was "good marathon manners" (57). In playing the two-handed game of family protection racket, Jean remembers having comparable experiences as a vaudevillian. Her career in vaudeville taught her an important lesson: show business performers were at the mercy of the mogul promoter; if you wanted to stay in his show, you needed to cooperate or get out.

In the game of family protection racket, show personnel and contestants, though identified predominantly with one role, that of being victimizer or victim, Top Dog or Under Dog, alternated in acting out both roles. The interaction between the show promoter, members of the community and fellow promoters showed the same kind of extreme polar fluctuation. This stance of being victimizer and victim, Top Dog and Under Dog, exploiter and exploited, sadist and masochist, is typically found in the authoritarian personality and in members of a dysfunctional family. The format of the walkathon show reinforced a contestant's sense of being an Under Dog. As Jean debates whether to sign up for the walkathon show, the staff nurse is curt in reminding her: "Nobody wants your act...vaudeville bums come a dime a dozen and they're all like you" (19). Jean is further disenchanted when Ms. Jones, described as "a nice-looking, motherly woman," throws a handful of coins on the dance floor, encouraging the contestants to "scramble, children, scramble." Similar episodes follow which do little to bolster Jean's sense of self worth. Nightclub celebrity Texas Guinam offers Jean the opportunity "to join her entourage of girls who are known all over...to meet rich guys old enough to appreciate you—might even find yourself a sugar Daddy...." Jean refuses but ponders whether she has sacrificed her chance for success, happiness and fame by not accepting this offer during the dark days of the Great Depression (60).

Walkathon shows were based on team effort, on the cooperation of both female and male partner. Despite what appeared to be gender equality, female contestants in this male-operated form of show business were most often exploited. A blatant form of exploitation was the practice of having female contestants take the brunt of the burden in the day-to-day routine of the contest. Jean is the victim of this mode of exploitation when she is first introduced to the world of the walkathon show.

Out of work and desperate, Jean is enticed into her first walkathon contest by Dankle, the show promoter, who teams her with Patsy, a professional contestant whom the show promoter regards as "his personal property." Jean's role is to support her partner so that he will be fresh during show time to perform his comedy routines. The teen-age vaudevillian soon learns that Patsy is a lug "who sleeps all apart, whose knees constantly cave in without warning...who shifts and changes his positions wildly, fights in his sleep and is constantly falling with great tearing motions" (49).

Jean is disillusioned by her experiences in this first walkathon show. After four grueling months in the contest, she is shocked to discover that her second prize earnings amount to $50. The devious show promoter reminds her that he has had to deduct the expenses Jean incurred for extra food and dry cleaning. In the film version of McCoy's novel *They Shoot Horses, Don't They?*, Rocky, the show emcee, informs Gloria that should she win, she will be docked for the extra expenses she has incurred. "Naturally," Rocky adds, matter-of-factly, "you don't win, you don't pay....I'm not out to cheat anybody" (308).

Female contestants in walkathon shows were exploited in still other ways. In *The Glory Walk*, in order to increase his profits, Rex, the show promoter, attempts to influence Marcella, his loyal and long-time girlfriend who is a contestant in the show, to become the bride in a pre-advertised walkathon wedding (Eells, Act 2, Scene 2). Though strongly resistant, Marcella agrees to this arrangement if Rex will stop harassing her friend on the staff. Later, Rex tries to convince Marcella (whose idol is Joan Crawford who, reportedly, was once in a dance marathon) to entice the Mayor's Aide to accept a bribe of two thousand dollars so that the show will not be closed after a fire in the walkathon arena causes the death of two contestants.

Exploitation, as a mode of operation in running a "family protection racket," was built into the format of walkathon shows. "Working heat," contestants played at being Top Dog and Under Dog so as to manipulate an audience's emotions. They faked pain in the walking act and acted out their aggressive drives in the athletic acts, giving credence to Havoc's observation that in walkathon shows, "sadism is sexy...masochism is talent" (37). The game of sadism and masochism, Top Dog and Under Dog, was played in more subtle ways by walkathon contestants. In brief ringside exchanges with show patrons, professional contestants took some comfort in knowing that they "put people on" by exaggerating the ordeals they faced in the contest. In this way, the Under Dog might momentarily feel the Top Dog.

In most written accounts, walkathon show promoters are depicted as authoritarian personalities, as highly competitive men who practiced a dog-eat-dog ethic. Power and control define their attitude in dealing with others. They double-cross other promoters, harbor petty jealousies and nurse personal injuries, real and imagined. In the two-handed walkathon game, show promoters are motivated by two ulterior motives: exploitation and opportunism. Their payoff in the walkathon game is to be Top Dog.

Rex Keller in *The Glory Walk* personifies the show promoter with a godfather complex. He is described "as a kind of foster father, a beefy athlete gone soft, who is cruel, kind, vigorous, dictatorial, hard-boiled, sentimental and animally attractive" (Eells, Act 1, Scene 1). A shrewd man, Rex has learned to ferret out the weaknesses of those with whom he comes in contact; when necessary, he uses this information to force his will upon staff and contestants. When a team leaves the show after being shamefully exploited, Rex comments cynically, "They don't know what they are looking for...they'll be back...whoever heard of anything getting better?" (Eells, Act 3, Scene 1).

Contestants in shows run by autocratic patriarchs reacted with symptoms

Freud identified in patients with an Oedipus complex: they feel castrated. In *The Glory Walk*, Tommy "Muscle" Menken is embittered at the treatment he has received from Rex, the show promoter-emcee. Tommy remembers that when he first entered the walkathons, he aspired to become a show business celebrity. He blames Rex for undermining his dream of becoming a comic like Red Skelton who, he remembers, once worked in walkathon shows. Rex, like King Laius in Sophocles's drama *Oedipus Rex*, is depicted as a tyrant, a destructive father figure.

The theme of castration surfaces as an intrinsic part of dance endurance shows. The name Oedipus in ancient Greek, means "swollen foot." Freud noted with brilliant insight how, in dreams and symptom formation, through the dynamics of displacement and substitution, parts of the body, like the feet, legs, arms, neck and head, associated with the properties of extension and erection, may come to symbolize the male sexual organ. These body parts were subject to particular stress in the walkathon contest.

Walkathon shows were public exercises in collective castration. The goal of the endurance contest was to induce stress, to progressively weaken contestants through sleep deprivation. In addition, teams were required to be on their feet 45 minutes out of every hour, night and day. Pain from footsores and bowed postures were particularly acute for newcomers during the first 500-hour breaking-in period. Within 10 days of the show opening, sprint and derby foot races were introduced which put further stress on the body.

Still later in the contest, additional stress resulted from the grind periods, intervals during which contestants were given no support from medical personnel for hours, sometimes days on end. When grinds were in effect and contestants were forced to solo, partners were cautioned against making any attempt to help their teammates keep awake. In the final stage of a walkathon show, the contest was thrown into Nonstop. Show promoter and emcee were imaginative in increasing the amount of stress to bring the few remaining teams to the breaking point.

Perhaps the most dramatic illustration of symbolic castration occurs at the climax of McCoy's novel. Robert, at his partners's entreaty, shoots Gloria in the head. This act of homicide triggers the memory of a traumatic event of his early childhood. Robert remembers when a beloved horse accidentally broke its leg running in an open field; the young boy is traumatized by his grandfather's decision to shoot the crippled animal so that it would not suffer.

Freud, in an oft-quoted metaphor, compared the id and ego, the relationship between the power of instincts and the mechanism of control in the personality, with a horse and rider. The death of the horse in McCoy's novel signals the devitalization of the power of the instincts in an animal, the result of an accident of nature. McCoy may have equated the death of Gloria with that of the horse; both are parallel psychological events. In each instance, there is the loss of vital power; a horse's broken leg is difficult to heal, and so the horse is no longer useful in the marketplace. Similarly, a human being who has been broken in spirit, who has been castrated, will not heal and is no longer useful in the marketplace.

Viewed from the perspective of psychoanalysis, Robert's behavior could be interpreted as an example of infantile "acting out" of repressed anger triggered by his participation in the walkathon contest. Robert identifies with his grandfather's role when he shoots his partner, but there is this difference. Though Robert's intent in shooting Gloria may be motivated, in part, by compassion for her suffering, his decision to perform this deed is, at the same time, an ultimate act of reductionism in which human is equated with animal. Freud describes the pull between the expressive forces of the id, in this instance Robert's aggressive drive, and the repressive forces of the super ego, represented alternately by the judge in the courthouse and the floor judge in the dance arena. Unable to master the original trauma associated with the death of his beloved horse, Robert's repeat performance with his walkathon partner indicates that he is the victim of a repetition compulsion, a symptom which announces the surfacing of dark unconscious forces in his psyche.

The walkathon family protection racket operated, as well, outside the walkathon arena in the communities where show promoters opened their shows. It was the job of the patch, an unofficial member of the walkathon organization, to "smell out trouble." If the patch sensed opposition by community agencies or public officials to the opening of a new show, it was his job to "grease" someone in power without spending too much "legal money." Walkathon show promoters, secretive about the operation of running a family protection racket, were well aware that this *modus operandi* was practiced in most other show business enterprises. In big cities and in small towns, show operators had to contend with the greed of officials in the police, fire and health departments who wanted a share of the "family" profits.

Promoters, afflicted with a godfather complex, were both victimizers and victims in the game of family protection racket. In McCoy's novel, Socks (named for the blackjack he carries in his pocket) introduces the first of a series of exhausting foot races as "a little novelty guaranteed to pack 'em in." He cautions contestants: "You play ball with us and we'll play ball with you!" His idea of playing ball is to offer the Sweetheart Couple the opportunity to be the bride and groom at a walkathon wedding, "just a showmanship angle" (35).

Socks feels himself a victim when he is forced to stop the contest after a hoodlum fires five shots into the crowd; one shot claims a walkathon fan. Even before this fatal event, "The Mother's League for Good Morals" threatens to close the show. Adopting the position of public watchdog, these self-appointed guardians brand the walkathon show "immoral and degrading" for permitting a pregnant contestant to compete in the show. They also demand that Socks abandon an advertised walkathon wedding which they feel is "a sacrilege" (McCoy, 93).

Walkathon contests, like other itinerant show business enterprises, came under a fair share of criticism and opposition from community organizations. Such attacks were fueled, in part, by newspaper accounts headlined: "Sex Morals Shot by Dizzy Grinds—Good Girls Turn Bad in Sleep Sex Orgies." Such reports did not always have the intended effect. In some instances, such accounts were enough to close a show; in other instances, these lurid stories stimulated new business. Not to be overlooked in the game of dog-eat-dog was the role of competing theatre interests, particularly movie owners, who aroused local opposition to take action against the "immoral" influence of dance endurance shows.

Show promoters felt themselves victims from pressures inside as well as outside the business. Hotel marathoners and "chiseler" contestants received advance money for food and gas from a show promoter and then would never show up, or, having been housed at a local hotel, would leave before the contest began. Other contestants, "glorified hoboes" and "itchy-foot marathoners," left one show to join another without being duly disqualified. The bane of walkathon contestants, both male and female, were fly-by-night operators who abandoned their show and left contestants stranded in remote locations.

By supporting walkathon shows, audiences were implicated in the walkathon game. The contest offered fans a means of satisfying masochistic needs by allowing them to identify with the ordeal and plight of their favorite teams. At the same time, as contestants pushed, shoved and elbowed each other in grueling sprint and derby races, the cheering fans gave vent to unconscious sadistic cravings not satisfied in normal, everyday living. Viewed from the perspective of psychoanalysis, walkathon contests, predicated on the idea of deprivation and delayed gratification, exemplified the denial of the pleasure principle which Freud saw contributing to the discontent of civilization. At the same time, this entertainment allowed contestants and spectators the opportunity to release sexual and aggressive drives normally suppressed by society. Like the nocturnal dream, the dance marathon as a form of waking dream was both the disease and the medicine.

In the main, writers, critics and social commentators highlight the destructive aspects of the walkathons. In their descriptions and commentaries of this form of show business, aggression is directed both toward the self and toward others. In McCoy's novel, a spectator dies from a gunshot wound; protagonist Gloria Beatty is shot to death by her partner. Robert, her executioner, is condemned to death for murder. Before these fatal events occur, a contestant is apprehended on the dance floor for murder. *The Glory Walk* ends with two contestants dead by fire. In *The Benefits of American Life*, Takiss Filliss, a contestant, becomes tubercular after ending his career as a professional marathoner; he returns to his homeland, Greece, to die. The heroine in Wilson's short story *The Lonesome Pioneer* also dies an early death.

The most garish death occurs in the play *Marathon*. In this drama, a promoter murders his partner by using a hypodermic needle. In the film version of *They Shoot Horses, Don't They?*, Sailor, a middle-aged contestant, meets his death from heart failure while a female contestant, Alice LeBlanc, suffers from a psychotic episode. If no death occurs in *Marathon 33* or in *Hard Times, Hard Times*, both contestants in their teens reflect upon the human waste which this form of entertainment engendered.

The walkathon show depicted in literary and film sources is portrayed, in the main, as a show business enterprise run by a paternalistic authoritarian show promoter in charge of running a family protection racket in collusion with show personnel and professional contestants. In contrast to the image of the walkathon show as hoopla, entertainment which blended the time-honored fare of vaudeville, burlesque and nightclub with sport, literary and film accounts reveal that dark unconscious forces were at work below the surface of this popular amusement. Interpreting this form of play from the vantage point of psychoanalysis, the walkathon show is a study of repression rather than expression, of the victory of Thanatos over Eros. The dance endurance contest was a true child of the Great Depression which pointed to a disease of the spirit as much as a crisis in the economy.

Chapter Eight
The Glory Walk

The Glory Walk, the title George Eells gave his insightful play about the world of the walkathon show, identifies a basic motif in the literature of the dance endurance contest: the theme of being a winner. Professional contestants who made a living working in walkathon shows regarded competing in these contests as perhaps one of the few accessible roads open to them to becoming somebody, to becoming a hero. Becoming a contestant did provide professional contestants an opportunity to embark on the journey of the hero, however pedestrian the road. Without intending, these athletic entertainers were out to prove that the myth of Horatio Alger was still alive in America during the dark days of the Great Depression.

Joseph Campbell explores the theme of the journey of the hero in his classic study *The Hero With A Thousand Faces*. The archetypal hero, Campbell observes, ventures beyond the normal range of achievement to give his life to something bigger than himself. In this spiritual quest, the hero attempts to experience life more fully, to find the meaning and significance of his life. On the mundane, less exalted level, the goal of the hero is to be a winner. What is uncovered in literary and film depictions of the walkathon contest is how the hero is ultimately defeated in his quest for finding his true self. In McCoy's novel, Robert Syverten begins the journey of the hero as a walkathon contestant in a show held in an amusement park, by the sea, on the outskirts of Hollywood. The call to adventure comes from Gloria Beatty who wants him to enter the contest as her partner. The immediate boon he will gain in this hero's journey, if he is successful, is a grand prize of $1,000 and perhaps an entree to the world of the movies.

Robert's experience in the walkathon show follows the traditional script of the hero's journey. First, he undergoes a series of severe tests in the walkathon contest. On an external, conscious level, he must face the challenges of the walkathon contest: confinement in the building for the duration of the contest; sleep deprivation and strenuous physical tests in the walking and athletic events. On an internal, unconscious level, Robert must encounter his dark unconscious self, his shadow. This inner journey is sometimes portrayed as undergoing the night-sea journey in the belly of the whale. At the termination of the contest, McCoy invokes this symbolic image by having Robert remark as he looks back at the building where he has been confined for weeks, "Now I know how Jonah felt when he looked at the whale" (35). Through his participation in the walkathon show, Robert undergoes a transformation of the self, but into a failed hero.

The building in which Robert is cloistered during the contest and later, the jail cell in which he is incarcerated, represent on a symbolic, archetypal level, the suffocating presence of the Great Mother. Robert's descent into his collective unconscious necessitates that he face not only his dark shadow side but also his anima, the female aspect of his personality which is projected through the various women with whom he comes in contact. More about this shortly.

Campbell describes how the hero undergoes his supreme ordeal with the aid of helpers who aid him in his quest. If the hero is successful in his quest, he (or she) will gain one or more rewards: elixir theft, a sacred marriage and/or father atonement. If he is unsuccessful, if he is defeated by unfriendly powers within himself and/or from without, the hero gains no reward. Pursued by the Furies, dreaded messengers of the Great Mother, the hero may be dismembered and die (Neumann). If he escapes this fate, he may still face castration by a tyrannical father figure, the male archetypal counterpart of the Great Mother.

Robert's journey formally begins when he leaves his home town in the open plains of the Midwest to reach the Pacific Ocean. Robert dreams of becoming a famous movie director. Once he arrives in Hollywood, Robert traverses a labyrinth of movie studios making the daily rounds traveled by hordes of movie extras. His quest to achieve fame and success is that of the American Adam.

In McCoy's novel, the two phases of the journey which Robert embarks upon are in tandem: the earlier phase, as a Hollywood extra, and the later phase, as a walkathon contestant. Both phases are part of a similar quest: becoming a hero. Robert's fantasy as a walkathon contestant is that he will be singled out by a Hollywood talent scout and offered the opportunity to become a movie director. Robert's defeat as ego hero is prefigured first by his failure to become anything other than a Hollywood movie extra, and later, by his failure to become a walkathon winner. That his defeat is more the fault of external circumstance than internal motivation makes his story all the more tragic.

Robert's story is inextricably entwined with the story of his walkathon partner Gloria Beatty. As a fellow traveler in Robert's journey, she is no helper but lures him to destruction. The story of her journey as heroine is filled with misfortune. Gloria leaves her home embittered from the treatment she receives at the hands of a promiscuous aunt and lecherous uncle. She dreams of becoming an overnight movie star like Katherine Hepburn and Margaret Sullivan. This fantasy is nurtured by reading an article in a screen magazine which encourages her to come to Hollywood and become a star overnight. Her illusion is soon shattered after her arrival in Los Angeles where she joins the ranks of an army of unemployed movie extras. In Robert's mythic journey as hero, Gloria personifies the archetypal Great Mother in her aspect as young woman, the virgin. She is a projection of Robert's anima, the unconscious feminine side of his psyche. Importantly, she is a manifestation of the destructive virgin, a priestess of the Great Mother, who, along with other female characters in McCoy's novel, ultimately contributes to Robert's defeat and extinction as an ego hero.

Gloria's hope, like that of her partner, is to be singled out and recognized by a Hollywood scout. Both want to gain admission to Central Casting, the agency which hires movie extras. Gloria, ill-tempered, foul-mouthed and cynical to the point of nihilistic despair, becomes further embittered by her experiences in the walkathon show. She infects Robert with her pessimism and with her dismal outlook on life. Gloria is a loner who gives her partner little encouragement and support. When Robert is given a jock supporter in preparation for the evening derby races, Gloria quips that her partner needs only a small size. During the contest, she has clandestine sex with the show emcee. Most devastating is the effect of her bouts of depression on Robert. She repeats over and over again to her partner: "I wish I were dead....I wish God would strike me dead" (McCoy 76).

Socks, the show promoter, approaches Robert and Gloria with a proposition—that they become husband and wife in a walkathon wedding. Gloria adamantly refuses the offer complaining that she has enough trouble looking after herself. Robert equivocates in his response to the promoter's offer fearing retribution should he fail to cooperate.

Gloria's morbidity increases with each successive day in the contest. She tells Robert: "This whole business is a merry-go-round. When we get out of here, we're right back where we started" (McCoy 76). She feels a sense of futility chained to Ixion's wheel as she circles round and round the dance floor. After the show is in progress for several weeks, a deranged hoodlum fires five shots into the audience. One bullet kills a walkathon fan. Socks is forced to close the show. This event precipitates Gloria's total breakdown. She voices her despondency: "I'm going to get off this merry-go-round....I'm through with the whole stinking thing...life" (McCoy 125).

Forced to leave the show prematurely, Gloria sinks further into depression. She attempts to shoot herself. Unable to complete the act, she pleads with Robert: "Shoot me...it's the only way to get me out of my misery" (McCoy 127). Robert tries to dispel her despondency; failing in this effort, he initially refuses to be her accomplice in her suicide. Dispirited from his experience in the walkathon show, however, he acknowledges that there is truth in what Gloria says and finally agrees to be her accomplice.

As Gloria hands him her pistol, Robert remembers an incident when he was a child on his grandfather's farm. On that fateful day, a work horse dear to the young boy breaks her leg. His grandfather is forced to kill the animal. He tells his grandson: "It was the kindest thing to do...she was no more good...it was the only way out of her misery" (McCoy 127). At the conclusion of McCoy's novel, when the arresting officer questions Robert about his motive for killing his partner, Robert's reply is: "She asked me to." Pressed further by the officer: "Is that the only reason you got?" Robert's answer resonates with this early episode with his grandfather. Robert's response to the officer is: "They shoot horses, don't they?" (McCoy 128).

In this ultimate act of reductionism, in which Robert equates animal and human, an act motivated in part by pity, Robert signals his defeat as a hero. His dark destructive shadow side has gained control; his ego is further undermined by the emergence of his anima which has him in its power. These inner aspects of his personality, his shadow and anima, potentially regenerative sources for the fortunate hero, are emptied of vitality and contribute to his defeat as a hero. Robert's homicidal act emphasizes what happens when the hero fails in his quest to actualize his authentic self. McCoy's story is that of the failed hero who loses his innocence and becomes corrupted.

Robert encounters other destructive females in the walkathon contest besides Gloria—all priestesses of the Great Mother in her negative aspects. Rosemary Loftus, an attractive contestant in the show, represents a second destructive anima figure. Desperate for affection in the barren atmosphere of the walkathon arena, Rosemary beckons Robert to follow her under the stage platform. Rosemary tells Robert: "I've seen you with a thousand different expressions on your face...sometimes I got the idea you were badly frightened" (McCoy 56). When Gloria sees Robert emerge from the trysting place under the stage—though she has been in this space and for a similar reason—Gloria feels abandoned and even more alone.

Robert is affected not only by these two younger furies but by an older anima figure. Ms. Leyden, a faithful attender at the walkathon show, chooses Robert and Gloria as her favorite couple and succeeds in getting them a sponsor. Appearing as a supportive mother figure, Leyden has, however, an ulterior motive. In the course of the contest, she attempts to undermine Robert's trust in his partner. Before her accidental death from a stray bullet, Leyden reveals that her interest in Robert is more than platonic; she informs him that she is rich and that she can arrange employment for him after he leaves the show.

Other women play the role of destructive mother figures in McCoy's novel. Ms. Witcher and Ms. Higby, representatives of The Mother's League for Good Morals, attempt to close the walkathon show for its allegedly immoral and indecent practices. Gloria accuses these self-appointed censors of being sexually perverse; she tells them that they remind her of the matron of a home for delinquent girls where she was sent. "There was a dame just like you in charge...she was a lesbian" (McCoy 95).

The destructive effects of archetypal, mother-virgin, anima figures is compounded by Robert's encounter with male figures, men who personify the archetypal castrative Great Father. Socks, whose nickname derives from the blackjack he carries with him as a weapon, is manipulative and an opportunist. Rocky, the show emcee, is a woman-chaser. At the close of the contest, when Robert is put on trial, the court judge gives Robert the severest penalty, the death sentence. The judge is not moved by Robert's disclaimer that he was doing his partner a favor, that he killed her out of pity and friendship.

Early in the contest, Robert is surprised to learn that a fellow contestant, Mario, has been apprehended for murder by two detectives in the audience. Unconsciously, Robert identifies with Mario, his archetypal shadow self, when he reflects: "He was one of the nicest boys I'd ever met....Now I know you can be nice and be a murderer too" (McCoy 45).

It is Robert's misfortune to suffer defeat in his hero's journey at the hands of both the Archetypal Great Mother and Great Father. His partner Gloria, in her journey, suffers a similar fate. At the end of the novel, Robert, as tragic hero, has gained no sacred marriage; his partner refuses to marry him even in a sham marathon wedding. Robert's initial optimism has turned to cynicism and resignation. There is no elixir in his life; he receives little nurturing from women nor support from men. In addition, he has lost contact with nature, a source which once nourished him. The Pacific Ocean which regenerated him when he first arrived in California becomes associated with sickness after he enters the walkathon contest. He feels the ocean pounding through the balls of his feet, night and day, as if they were stethoscopes.

When Robert first arrived in Hollywood, he aspired to become a famous Hollywood film director. His dream was to make epic movies, to join the Olympians who control the Hollywood pantheon of movie gods and goddesses. His allegiance is to Apollo, the sun god, the god of illusion and the dream. Each day, as the rays of the afternoon sun fade through the skylight over the dance floor, Robert rises on his toes and performs a ritual sun dance to Apollo. He tries to maintain contact with the diminishing light and warmth of the sun for as long as possible. Soon, however, the coming darkness of the night makes him feel trapped in the dance arena.

Robert's identification with Apollo is not fulfilled in his role of movie extra, a cog in the Hollywood Dream Machine. One of the few parts Robert has acted is, prophetically, a dead villager in a film entitled "Fallen Angel." Despite the discrepancy between dream and reality, Robert remains an apostle of Apollo. Unlike his partner, who is belligerent towards authority, Robert cautions restraint. Instead of Gloria's pessimism, Robert has blind hope in the American dream. Restraint and blind hope define the Apollonian posture.

Robert, however, is fixated with Apollo the adolescent narcissist. It is Apollo (and his sister Artemis) who must suffer for his willful adolescent acts by cleaning the excrement of other gods. Robert, young, inexperienced, an unknown movie extra, pays for his grandiose dream of becoming a movie director by having to perform a dehumanizing act by killing his partner.

Gloria's dream of becoming an overnight movie star, like Robert's fantasy, is equally unrealistic in light of her lack of dramatic training and her ordinary appearance. Unlike her partner, however, Gloria's unconscious identification is with a wrathful Dionysus. Gloria, like other female characters in McCoy's novel, represent the Maenads, representative of the archetypal Great Mother in her dark aspect. The Maenads are akin to the Furies who accompany Dionysus on his rampages. Gloria's character, like that of Dionysus, is driven by excess. Her goal is self destruction; ultimately, she destroys both herself and her partner.

McCoy's novel is situated between two locations: the walkathon arena and the court room where Robert is being tried for murder. Both settings are identified with the shadowy underworld. Gloria's effect on her partner suggests contagion; the action at the walkathon show is a form of epidemic dance. Further, the theme of McCoy's novel deals with the tragic drama of a couple who aspire to join the deities of the Hollywood pantheon. In the pursuit of her elusive goal, Gloria is driven to the brink of hysteria. Shadowy underworld, epidemic dance, tragic drama and hysteria signal the ominous presence of Dionysus.

Dionysus further reveals himself in the walkathon contest. Robert and Gloria are reduced to the level of the elemental, to a preoccupation with bodily existence. They are required to keep moving, night and day, to eat and sleep in an upright position. The ultimate sign of Dionysian pathology appears in the momentary state of madness which contestants periodically experience. Allowed only intermittent periods of sleep, deprived of normal dream time, dance marathoners periodically act out the irrational behavior found in the nocturnal nightmare. They go "squirrely" and hallucinate.

It is not only Dionysus whose image haunts the dance endurance contest. In his entourage, in addition to the Maenads, Dionysus is associated with a rag-tag band of followers who contribute to mayhem in the walkathon show. Priapus is the patron of the freak event, the judgment of many critics of walkathon shows. Pan, the irrational and violent purveyor of panic, is especially evident in McCoy's novel in the episode in which the gunman at the walkathon goes on a shooting spree. Silenus made himself known in the lewd behavior of the show emcee, Rocky.

Perhaps the most powerful member in the Dionysian company is Eros, god of love. In contrast to the great romance between Eros and Psyche celebrated in Greek mythology, Robert and Gloria are propositioned by Socks to be the bride and groom at a walkathon wedding. For Socks, the mock wedding is "just a showmanship angle," a stunt designed to draw in the crowds by creating the illusion of romance. Gloria refuses to participate in this charade of love for fear that her tenuous hold on sanity will be further threatened. For Gloria, there is little to choose between a debased Eros and his counterpart, Thanatos.

Gloria had encountered Eros long before her meeting with this mythic deity in the walkathon show. Eros, in early Greek mythology, the child of Chaos, appears to Gloria in his cruel and imperious aspect as the god of sensual desire. Gloria's life is chaotic, in part, because of her experiences as a young woman. Her lecherous uncle tries to seduce her; after leaving home, she meets a restaurant owner who wants to have sex on the kitchen table during the lull between customers.

Gloria's lethal identification with Dionysus is unmistakable. Where there is sickness, pathology, darkness, perversion and death, the tragic characteristics of the walkathon contest in which Robert and Gloria participate, there is Apollo's nemesis, Dionysus seeking retribution. Dionysus is personified on an individual level in the character of Robert. Dionysus reveals his presence as Robert's shadow when Robert kills his partner. Dionysus also makes his presence felt through Gloria who, turned a fury, represents Robert's female side, his anima.

The dramatic encounter between these brother gods in the walkathon show reflected in the conflict between Robert and Gloria point to this psychological truth; when we live our life in imbalance by overvaluing one set of values and undervaluing their polar opposites, we become victims of that which we repress. In the context of Greek mythology, it is often the role of Dionysus, "Born Rat

Catcher of Conscience," to challenge his brother who has a propensity to devalue his brother's worth. Dionysus performed this necessary service through the dance endurance contest.

At the termination of the contest, unlike Jonah who is liberated from the belly of the whale, Robert leaves the innocent jail of the walkathon show for a prison cell. His descent into the dark unconscious of his soul has no return passage. Both Robert's and Gloria's journeys end in Hades.

McCoy's novel offers the richest source for mythic analysis. However, similar archetypal motifs and figures of myth found in McCoy are present in other literary works which portray the walkathon show. In the interest of brevity (and because the yield is less rich) reference will be made to a few typical examples from the walkathon literature.

Farrell depicts the myth of the journey of the hero in his short story, *The Benefits of American Life*. Takiss Filliss, a shepherd, leaves his homeland in Greece to come to Chicago, "a paradise where men had their pockets lined with money." Like his ancient predecessor Odysseus, Takiss faces a series of severe trials in his hero's journey. He receives no help from his own countrymen who have immigrated earlier; instead, they exploit Takiss by having him labor in harsh working conditions for little pay. His ordeal continues when Takiss becomes a professional marathoner; again, he labors in an inhospitable environment for minimal compensation. In one of his first contests, Takiss is assigned "a girl of his dreams," blonde and beautiful Marie Glenn. As the contest grinds on, his goddess turns into a fury who is "blowsy...and looked like a worn-out prostitute" (Farrell 308). Takiss is sexually aroused by being shoved and pushed against his partner, a siren who looks feverishly in his eyes, telling him smutty jokes (Farrell 308).

Five years later, after competing in a succession of walkathon contests, Takiss receives momentary recognition by his fellow countrymen as a walkathon celebrity. Unlike the successful hero, there is no sacred marriage with any of his Anglo-Saxon partners who appear to promise ecstacy, but, instead, reveal themselves as Furies. The elixir he obtains, his earnings of five thousand dollars as a professional contestant, pays for his return journey to his homeland. But it is not a triumphant return like Odysseus. In his hero's journey, Takiss is mortally afflicted with tuberculosis. Shortly after arriving in Greece, Takiss is stricken.

The hero and heroine have a somewhat different fate in Wilson's short story *The Lonesome Pioneer*. Jim and June, who are in love and catch the marathon fever, leave their small town in Kentucky to enter a walkathon contest near Louisville. An itinerant salesman narrates the story of this couple who want to become the champion marathon dancers of America. In relating their story to his cronies, the narrator describes how Jim and June talked a lot about dancing through life together and how he found this idea beautiful, the idea of dancing through life together.

The narration continues. The aspiring couple is approached by the show promoter and asked to be The Sweetheart Couple of the walkathon show. They are delighted to accept his offer. As part of the preparation, the Sweetheart

Couple is displayed in a little space that is covered over by artificial orange blossoms that has an arch light over it that advertises BRIDE and GROOM. In Wilson's story, the already confining space of the dance arena is further constricted by placing the betrothed on the tiny stage.

Misfortune strikes when the bride-to-be is disqualified before the gala event. After the departure of his partner, the enterprising contestant, now a solo, adopts the name The Lonesome Pioneer. He invests in a set of fancy pioneer suits made out of silk with an imitation coonskin cap. Misfortune befalls him a second time when his beloved ex-partner is taken ill and dies. The Lonesome Pioneer assembles a scrapbook which depicts, in picture and text, the events leading to the death of his fiancée both before and after she is disqualified. He distributes the scrapbook to walkathon fans to collect money to build a mausoleum as a fitting memorial for his intended mate. Never a real groom in life, the Lonesome Pioneer is betrothed to his partner in death.

The Lonesome Pioneer is disqualified from the contest when his then current partner, Mary Frances, complains to the promoter that her partner had made improper advances. Jim's defense is that he had kissed Mary Frances while she was asleep; she reminded him of June. Jim is reinstated in the contest when the narrator intercedes for him. The episode of Jim's lapse of conduct and his behavior leading to an "honor wedding" are also included in his scrapbook. The grand theme of the hero's journey is reduced to a radio soap opera melodrama.

There are very few references in the literature of the dance marathon contest which reveal the positive transformative power of either father or mother figures. In *The Glory Walk*, female contestants are characterized as "bums," "queers" or as a "little chick with a loving heart" (Eells, Act I, Scene 1). This latter reference is to Marcela, the only positive anima figure in the play. It is her fate to have to contend with Rex, her lover, the show promoter-emcee, described as "cruel, dictatorial and hard-boiled" (Eells, Act I, Scene 1).

Marathon 33, and *High Times, Hard Times* are written by female contestants who portray themselves in a positive light surrounded by non-supportive father and mother figures. In *Marathon 33*, Havoc describes Texas Guinam and Helen Morgan, two well-known celebrities who visit the walkathon show, as exploitative and dissolute. For adolescents Havoc and O'Day, there is little to choose from between the corrupt worlds inside and outside the walkathon arena. In Ames's *Dancing Madness*, the narrator's sister commits suicide after being abandoned by her partner in a dance endurance contest. *Marathon*, one of the earliest plays to use the dance endurance contest as thematic material, tells of a married female contestant who is sexually harassed by her marathon partner and by the show promoter (Dawn and DeGaw).

In the film version of McCoy's novel, released in 1969, Gloria Beatty, portrayed by Jane Fonda, is a strong personality, an outsider, someone who is hard and hostile. Her partner Robert is decent, if naive. Rocky's role as promoter-emcee is given prominence in the film version of McCoy's novel. A man in his early 40s, Rocky is portrayed as a complex, powerful person. When a female contestant has an anxiety attack, he effectively dispels her paranoia.

Later Rocky unscrupulously confiscates another contestant's makeup kit and clothes so that she will drop her glamorous facade. This action precipitates her psychotic breakdown. When Robert asks the promoter-emcee why he has committed this unethical act, Rocky's reply is direct: "For the good of the show!" (McCoy 247).

The mythic figures and themes identified in the literature of the dance endurance contest are associated with sickness, castration, dismemberment and death, characteristic signs of the archetypal Terrible Mother and Tyrannical Father. Both female and male characters who appear in these literary accounts, both as parent and offspring, old or young, are largely negative and destructive. As projections from the collective unconscious, these literary characters and events, often based upon actual people and happenings, reveal the world of the walkathon show as corrupt and debased.

Chapter Nine
Danse Macabre

The walkathon show with its mechanical regimen was an expression of the absurd, a seminal theme in the literature of twentieth-century existentialism. How absurd the underlying idea and mode of operation of the dance endurance contest. How absurd that women and men, coupled as teams, were to keep in motion 45 minutes out of every hour, day and night, and participate in exhausting foot races at show time until all but one couple collapsed on the floor. How absurd that contestants were housed, fed, and given medical attention to keep them fit for this ordeal. The Creator rested on the seventh day, not the marathoner.

McCoy's novel *They Shoot Horses, Don't They?*, like the works of his existential mentor Kafka, depicts the world as absurd. Gloria and Robert are portrayed as strangers alienated from themselves, from others, from nature and from God. They live a life without real purpose or meaning. Their existence as contestants in the walkathon show is an extension of their sterile, mechanical lives as Hollywood extras.

McCoy describes their day-to-day attempts to find employment by making the rounds of film studios and Central Casting, the organization which hires actors and actresses for small movie roles. After becoming contestants, Robert and Gloria continue their daily rounds in the walkathon arena where they are required to circle round and round the dance floor during the walking act and race round and round the dance arena during the athletic acts. Both environments, the Hollywood environs and the walkathon arena, reinforce a routinized existence.

Contestants labor like Sisyphus who is condemned to roll a huge stone up the hill only to have it roll down again and again. Camus sees Sisyphus going through his motions eternally and ineffectively rolling the stone back up, yet Camus imagines Sisyphus happy, the existential hero who can affirm his fate. Not so Gloria who feels that her fate has been sealed; her life is like being on "a merry-go-round." Gloria daydreams that a Hollywood talent scout in the walkathon audience will discover her and make her into a star. This daydream soon begins to fade; her despair deepens. With each new day, she feels empty and alone with no involvement or commitment to life.

Existence for Gloria prior to entering the walkathon contest is a Kafkaesque nightmare. Her world is filled with nausea even before moving to the west coast. As a young girl, she has had to contend with her two guardians, an alcoholic aunt and a rapacious uncle. Her condition worsens when she leaves home and encounters a lecherous restaurant owner. Growing desperate, she makes an amateurish attempt at stealing so that she can be caught by the police.

139

Her motive is not that of a criminal but of a person who wants some attention paid, who wants to be cared for.

Feeling useless and without love, Gloria tries to commit suicide. She is unsuccessful even in this attempt at self-destruction. While convalescing in the hospital, Gloria reads an ad in a movie fan magazine that promises quick fame and fortune for the Hollywood extra. Filled with hope, and as a last resort, Gloria travels to Los Angeles but is soon disenchanted. What she finds in Hollywood are legions of other women and men who have been similarly lured by the propaganda of the movie magazine.

As a movie extra, Gloria lives a meager, uneventful, boring existence. But becoming a contestant in the walkathon show only increases her sense of futility. She anguishes over her future and is pessimistic about what she can do to change her luck. Gloria expresses her sense of helplessness in the face of the absurd: "Maybe it's just the whole damn world's like one big Central Casting—and they've got it all rigged before you even show up" (McCoy, Film Adaptation 313).

When the walkathon contest is closed down prematurely by the local authorities, Gloria, disillusioned to the point of despair, chooses suicide to a life devoid of meaning and hope. Her decision to die rather than live a meaningless existence might have been commendable had it not been for the way she implicates her partner. Unable to shoot herself, she entreats Robert to kill her and " pinch-hit-for-God" (McCoy 127). She does not accept the responsibility for her own death nor for the destructive effect her act will have on her partner. Unlike the existential hero, she cannot or will not transcend her fate.

Camus reflects that there are two truly philosophical problems facing all persons: the problem of suicide and the problem of killing others. McCoy confronts these two issues in his novel. He suggests a parallel between the events at the walkathon show and the ongoing trial in which Robert is being tried for the murder of his partner. In both settings, Robert stands accused: in the contest, he is an accomplice to his own death as a person; in jail, he is being tried for the death of another person.

Robert, initially depicted as innocent, basically decent and good natured, is corrupted by his experience in the walkathon contest. Like Camus's existential anti-hero, Messuralt, Robert undergoes a metamorphosis and becomes a stranger. When the arresting officer asks Robert why he killed his partner, his response is " She asked me to" (McCoy 127). His act is performed without malice, without much feeling of any kind. Pressed further by the policeman, Robert's reply seems to have cold reason and logic: "They shoot horses, don't they?" (McCoy 128). His reaction is prompted by the realization that in an amoral world, nothing is immoral, nothing is meaningful. At his trial, Robert insists to the prosecuting attorney that Gloria did not die friendless and in agony. He remembers that just before shooting her, she was smiling for the first time. Robert reiterates to the lawyer that "I was her very best friend. I was her only friend" (McCoy 11).

In Sartre's existential philosophy, Robert's existence in the walkathon contest is a life lived *en-soi*, an existence permeated by habit, in contrast to *pour-soi,* in which one comes to grips with a challenge and acts with awareness and responsibility (Sartre 47). Robert's automaton-like response in killing his partner is indistinguishable from that of a lower animal acting instinctively out of its essence. Robert fails the unique moral challenge presented by human freedom and intelligence, to question one's basic values, to respond out of his essence as a human being. Failing to meet this challenge, Robert acts in bad faith.

Camus, in his novel *The Plague,* describes the large, French port of Oran off the Algerian coast as "thoroughly modern." Oran is an ugly city, with a smug, placid air, a place where citizens stifle in their banal existence; their main goal is pleasure and making money. The plague in Camus's novel is nothing less than "the absurd," an event having no real meaning or value. By forcing upon its victims an increasing solitariness, the plague reveals the essential loneliness and emptiness of modern existence.

Hollywood for McCoy, like Oran for Camus, is a state of mind and a location, a place where the distinctions between reality and illusion are blurred. Both are thoroughly modern cities. McCoy associates Hollywood with capitalism, hypocrisy, perversion and deceit. In setting his dance endurance contest in the environs of Hollywood, McCoy makes a harsh commentary on the walkathon show and on Hollywood, a symbol of glamour, money, success and retribution, "a graveyard of broken dreams" (Johnson 1). One example showing how Hollywood and the walkathon show were alike was the advent of a public wedding, a spectacle in which artifice masked shoddy reality. A Hollywood nuptial was a press-agent's dream; a walkathon wedding always played to "standing-room only." The sacred ritual of marriage as promoted in Hollywood and the walkathon contest were show business spectacles.

Hollywood movies and walkathon shows had their vocal critics who branded these amusements a visitation of the plague. In a climactic episode in McCoy's novel, Gloria has a confrontation with Mrs. Hibgy and Mrs. Witcher who condemn the walkathon contest as a plague (McCoy 100). Though she bitterly denounces these women as hypocrites, their reference to the walkathon as a plague does describe the devastating effect the walkathon show (and being a Hollywood extra) has on Gloria's tenuous hold on existence. Becoming a contestant exacerbates Gloria's sense of loneliness and emptiness and increases her feelings of isolation and powerlessness. Instead of asserting her will to attain her goals, she sees herself the pawn of fate and destiny, of forces beyond her control. She is a victim of the modern plague, a social disease which afflicts the spirit and body alike. McCoy indicts the dance endurance contest, its violence, exploitation and chicanery, its decadence, as a modern plague. This amusement mirrored for McCoy the epidemic which had spread in America during the early years of the twentieth century.

In Ames's novel *The Dancing Madness,* two spectators similarly refer to the walkathon show as reminiscent of the dancing madness at the time of the Black Plague. Participation in a walkathon show in this novel brings a plague upon the family: the eldest daughter commits suicide after she is disqualified and betrayed by her walkathon partner. The sense of the dance endurance craze as plague, a collective contagion, is reinforced by the shady and unethical methods some walkathon promoters practiced. Staunchly individualistic, walkathon promoters established their own code of business ethics. At the extreme were the "fly-by-night" operators who acted in bad faith. This breed of exploiters abandoned contestants in out-of-the-way places, leaving them stranded without fare to return home. The more successful promoters, while they did not resort to such trickery, may have been motivated less out of moral scruples than from the knowledge that such behavior would make it difficult to recruit top professional teams for their next show.

Leslie Miller's observation that "a pretense of caring is essentially to regulate, to control, ultimately to coerce," does accurately describe the motives and behavior of show promoters in dealing with their staff and with contestants (Miller 83-91). If a spirit of bad faith was present in the behavior of some, perhaps many, of those who promoted and participated in walkathon shows, audiences were willing to collude. In Farrell's novel *Studs Lonigan*, the hero is callous toward the plight of contestants whom he views as making "damn fools of themselves, and then, too, there's the dough" (Farrell 284). In Marathon 33, Patsy, a professional marathoner, veteran of 55 dance endurance contest, instructs his inexperienced partner Jean Reid when she questions the legitimacy of the walkathons as show business. "I guarantee you...there'll always be more bums in the bleachers howling for blood, than satin asses whistling Gotterdamerung...there'll always be the marathon...the world couldn't do without it" (Havoc 75).

The literary and film depictions of the dance endurance contest are a literature of alienation. Those who participated as both amateur and professional contestants were depicted as estranged from the world. According to most written accounts, the sense of time and space, the experience of one's body and the mode of relating to people were adversely affected by being a contestant in a walkathon show.

Time in walkathon shows was serialized and fragmented. Contestants experienced the passage of time at the extremes, like working in an automated factory which enforced periodic speed-ups after a slow-down. At show time, fast-paced derby races in which couples hurtled around the dance arena alternated with the hourly walking acts when couples barely moved around the dance floor. Walkathon contestants were in bondage "to the time table and the schedule which subordinates the emotional necessities of lived time to the mechanical necessities of clock time" (Levi 265).

Walkathon shows also adversely affected a contestant's consciousness of space. Contestants were confined to the walkathon arena for protracted periods of time, extended intervals which could last weeks, even months. Leaving the building was immediate grounds for disqualification. Inside the building, women and men were segregated into two large dormitory rooms where they slept on army cots and lived out of a suitcase; even legitimately married couples were required to live apart. There was no privacy.

McCoy describes the change in consciousness of space which Robert experiences after entering the contest. From the open plains of the Midwest, he is confined to the narrow confines of the building where the show is in progress. Robert's attempts to maintain some contact with nature and the world outside are restricted to catching a glimpse of the Pacific Ocean when the janitor momentarily opens a back door of the walkathon building to take out garbage. At dusk, when couples are permitted to solo during the walking act, Robert rises on his toes to catch the fading rays of the sun streaming through the overhead skylight on the dance floor. This sense of confinement and loss of contact with nature is further intensified when he is imprisoned in a jail cell.

Keen observes, "A man's body is his bridge and model of the world; therefore, as a man is in his body so will he be in the world" (148). In the walkathon show, contestants contorted their bodies into tortured postures as they supported and dragged each other around the dance arena during the 45-minute walking acts. In the derby and sprint races, teams pushed, shoved and elbowed other couples as they sped around the perimeter of the dance floor at accelerated speeds. When one couple fell, those in close pursuit piled up on one another.

Interpersonal contact between show personnel, contestants and audience was characterized by an "I-It" mode of relating, the mode of manipulation and exploitation (Buber). In place of an "I-Thou" relationship, walkathon shows undermined the practice of authentic dialogue by treating persons as objects and commodities. There was little sense of authentic community between show personnel, professional contestants, and amateur members of the walkathon family. Narcissistic monologues of contestants were disguised as dialogues. Show emcees used program dope sheets to describe the strength and weaknesses of each team as if they were describing horses at a race track. Technical dialogue substituted for genuine dialogue.

From the perspective of existentialism, the walkathon contest was a study in absurdity. Pretending to be a legitimate form of show business, walkathon contests featured pseudo-events masked as authentic experiences. Eminent American historian Daniel Boorst in *The Image, Or What Happened to the American Dream* introduces the concept of the pseudo-event to analyze American culture (9). Before illustrating how walkathon shows substituted pseudo-events, simulated, spurious, artificial experience for the real and genuine, a brief digression to the world of myth to deepen our perspective.

It is Apollo, the god of dreams, who creates fair illusion through the inner world of fantasy. Apollo can make our illusions so vivid and persuasive, so realistic, that we can live in them. When blinded by his own light, tempting us to replace our ideals with images, with pseudo dreams, this sun god menaces us with unreality. Behind our grandiose illusions is the false persona of Apollo; we live these illusions through pseudo-events. It was Apollo, as artificer, who hovered over walkathon shows.

Pseudo-events are "dramatic," according to Boorstin. In the walking act, couples "worked heat" to create the illusion that they had reached the limits of their endurance; appearing to be on the point of collapse, they miraculously recovered, each time cheered by the crowd. Similarly, in the athletic acts, The Dynamite Sprints and Bombshell Derbies, flash teams "worked heat" by stunting falls and perpetrating mayhem.

Pseudo-events are showcases for the celebrity. Walkathon fans imbued with a sense of Apollonian illusion clamored for their favorite contestants to be made into the apotheosis of show celebrity with whom they might identify. Show promoters carefully groomed their flash teams for the role of Sweetheart Couple or for the role of The Trouble Makers. Celebrity teams rehearsed comedic and melodramatic skits designed to encourage fans to form empathic bonds with them. Transformed into show celebrities, contestants became mere caricatures of persons. Fans could project their illusions, irrational fantasies and extravagant wishes upon the persona of the celebrity contestant. Dionysus, god of theatre and the mask, was on hand to create havoc at the walkathon house of illusion.

Pseudo-events require careful preparation. Preceding the walkathon wedding, whether real or mock, there were rehearsals and attention given to proper wedding attire, the presence of a minister, etc. The bride and groom, usually chosen from among the flash teams in the contest and billed as The Sweetheart Couple, were made the center of attention; their prosaic life story was embroidered to give it romantic appeal. What was reinforced through this pseudo-event was the illusion that the walkathon show was "The Original Home of Romance." In reality, contestants married the same or different partners in a succession of shows. Each time a real or mock walkathon wedding was performed, audiences were led to believe that the bride and groom were being united for the first time.

Pseudo-events were repeatable. The walkathon wedding, because of its popular appeal, was often re-enacted the succeeding evening. Within a six-week period, a second Sweetheart Couple might be married. At each performance, the Standing Room Only sign was prominently displayed.

Pseudo-events expended money to make money. Walkathon weddings were especially targeted for women in the audience; as true believers, they sent the bride and groom carloads of presents (which were quickly redeemed for cash).

Pseudo-events were well advertised. Announcements of a walkathon wedding were repeated over the radio and show patrons were frequently reminded of the gala event from the bandstand.

Pseudo-events spawned other pseudo-events. A walkathon wedding was preceded by engagement parties, bridal showers, etc. These events were made convenient to attend and became the occasion for fans to converse and feel momentarily bonded. A walkathon promoter, inspired by Apollonian conceit, was wont to refer to his show as "A Place of Refined Amusement." Reality belied these words. Places where walkathon shows were held were, more often than not, sleazy auditoriums rather than grand ballrooms.

The walkathon wedding, as a pseudo-event, symbolized the metamorphosis of people into machine; the "Sweetheart Couple" was transformed into a mechanical bride and groom. Secular spectacle substituted for sacred ritual. In this transformation, Apollonian artifice was countered by Dionysian pathology; lust replaced love. Hours after the public ceremony, in the early morning, the couple, wrapped in an army blanket, a wedding gift from fellow competitors, consummated their marriage circling around and around a darkened corner of the dance floor.

In sum, pseudo-events reinforce a sense of mechanical consciousness by which we narrow and ultimately destroy our experience. We substitute counterfeit for authentic experience. In place of the spontaneous happening, pseudo-events are contrived to offer the illusion of real experience without involving the authentic actor; it is living "second hand" by indirection. We become fixated by the familiar and, at the same time, are fascinated by the trivial and the novel.

Literary and cinematic portrayal of walkathon shows reveals how pseudo-events, bogus and counterfeit entertainment, fooled Americans into believing that illusion was reality, evidence that the absurd was ever present in modern American culture as elsewhere. Of all literary and cinematic accounts of the walkathon show, McCoy's novel captures the sense of the absurd most acutely. According to Stuart, "the enduring radicalism of McCoy's novel resides in no political program or ethical system, but from a passionate desire to affirm the human sense of life, despite the voids and vicissitudes, in a word, the absurdity, of our age" (Sturak 268-269).

Part
IV

The
Innocent Jail

Chapter Ten
Dance of the Automatons

But we must now raise the question in an ultimate form: among contemporary men will there come to prevail, or even to flourish, what may be called, The Cheerful Robot?

(Mills 189)

Show promoters boasted that walkathons were a Poor Man's Night Club. Understandably, they never referred to Gingrich's second allusion to the walkathon show, The Innocent Jail. Eells's observation of professional contestants adds credibility to this latter allusion. He notes: "I think there was a strong personality type that was attracted to this kind of thing. I think they would've adjusted as well to being in jail or being in the army...they probably would've made very good fascists because they were the kind of people who took orders (Martin, Interview with G. Eells).

Writers who describe the dance endurance contest in novels, plays, short stories and films were more in tune with Gingrich's second figure of speech than with his first allusion. McCoy refers to "shooting" in the title of his play; Wilson refers to "loneliness" in his short story; Ames refers to "madness" and "death" in her novel. I suggest that the most compelling simile for this mass culture amusement is "automaton." The dance endurance contestant was "The Dance of the Automatons."

The connection between the dance endurance contest and the automaton must have been in Charlie Chaplin's mind ever since he became an avid fan of walkathon shows. As reported earlier, Chaplin was the first director in Hollywood to purchase the screen rights to McCoy's novel. He released his film satire *Modern Times* in 1936, one year after McCoy's novel was published. In *Modern Times*, Chaplin plays the role of a factory worker, the hapless victim of the assembly line which succeeds in transforming him, by the end of the day, into an automaton, an extension of the factory machine. Though Chaplin never made the movie of McCoy's novel (for reasons he alone would know), my hunch is that if he had made a movie of the dance endurance contest, his purpose would have been to show how in play, as in work, we have become captivated by the machine.

The dance endurance contest reinvigorated the myth of the automaton (in modern times, the robot). The myth of the automaton, like all living myths, crystalizes significant societal values and needs and also identifies the dominant aspirations and assumptions in American culture. The dance endurance contest, in enlivening the myth of the automaton in the 1920s and 1930s, pointed to a clash of American values and needs, to a conflict in American aspirations and assumptions related to Americans' love affair with the machine. Eminent

147

anthropologist Ruth Benedict has contributed to our understanding of culture by differentiating between those cultures whose values and needs are more Apollonian or Dionysian. If Benedict's schema is applied not to an entire culture but to one institution within the culture—in this instance, one form of show business—the male-oriented, male-dominated world of the walkathons can be identified with Apollonian values and needs. But, as noted earlier, the Apollonian spirit present at walkathon shows was not that of a mature, wise god but of a puerile, opportunistic god. This less than admirable Apollonian world view came into strong conflict with Dionysian values and needs which were unacknowledged and repressed in this show business enterprise.

The myth of the automaton was the guiding theme behind the dance endurance contest, and paternalistic authoritarian Apollonian values and needs were the powering force. The three interpretations of the walkathon show: as "family-protection racket," as "the journey of the failed hero and heroine," and as a "danse macabre" point up how myth and value operated in this mass entertainment. Here are summaries of the three interpretations of the dance endurance contest as projected in literary and cinematic accounts.

The psychoanalytic interpretation of the dance endurance contest, the Dance of the Godfathers, exposed the walkathon show as "a family protection racket." From the view of psychoanalytic literary criticism, this show business enterprise was operated by authoritarian show promoter/emcees, men afflicted with a godfather complex. Colluding in this shady business operation are staff and hired professional contestants. The walkathon organization, under the control of a paternalistic father figure, shares many of the attributes of a dysfunctional family made up of parental figures who live in a symbiotic, dependency relationship with their siblings. The mode of interacting in the dysfunctional family, to alternately play the role of Top Dog and Under Dog, sadist and masochist, victim and victimizer, was how people in walkathon shows interacted. To a greater or lesser degree, contestants and show personnel in walkathon shows felt castrated and dehumanized.

The mythic interpretation of the dance endurance contest, the Glory Walk, unmasks show personnel and contestants as "failed heroes and heroines" who suffer defeat in their quest for fame and fortune. Show promoter/emcees and other males in authority personify the archetype of the Great Father in his destructive aspects as tyrant and villain. Female figures connected with walkathon shows embody the archetypal Great Mother in her dark aspect as mother/virgin devourer. In this mythic interpretation of the walkathon contest, male show personnel and contestants identify with the traits and values of the god Apollo, but with a self-aggrandizing, adolescent, self-centered Apollo. Walkathon personnel who mirrored this immature Apollonian stance in their consciousness and behavior had to reckon with Apollo's brother, Dionysus. Disenfranchised and devalued by Apollo, Dionysus undermined the success of walkathon shows.

The existential interpretation of the dance endurance contest, the Danse Macabre, reveals the walkathon show as absurd. For the duration of the show, contestants are transformed into automatons, mechanical men and mechanical women. From this perspective, walkathon shows are an aberration, a showcase for the alienated person who is estranged from nature, from himself and from others. In this charade of entertainment, contestants and show personnel play the role of Sisyphus destined to repeat his futile actions without hope, without meaning and without significance. In the walkathon parody of play, human beings labor under the compulsion of habit rather than from the stance of the authentic person. There is little in the sterile atmosphere of the dance endurance contest to give those who participate in these pseudo events a sense of dignity and worth.

The myth of the automaton came alive in the actions and events at the walkathon show where women and men moved around and around the dance floor as if they were wind-up toys. One contestant remembers how, in a state of half consciousness, he automatically changed directions on the dance floor when his feet hit the sideboard of the dance arena (like the conveyor-belt figures in an amusement-park shooting gallery which reverse their direction when the marksman hits the target).

Walkathon spectators, too, resembled automatons in their conditioned responses, now screaming and stamping, now laughing and crying, at the melodramas enacted by contestants and the floor judge in their rehearsed routines. In the walking act, fans anguished as their favorite team sank closer and closer to the ground, even though they knew, "secretly," that their team would recover just in time to avoid disqualification as they had done a hundred times before. In the sprint and derby races, the actions were also predictable; the Sweetheart Couple usually triumphed in the end despite the foul tactics of the Trouble-Making Couple. Contestants and audience seemed wired to the walkathon amusement machine operated by the show promoter/emcee, much as movie fans were wired to the Hollywood Dream Machine.

The spirit of the automaton hovered over dance endurance shows. Periodically, due to the lack of sufficient sleep and sustained time to dream, contestants went "squirrely" and hallucinated. At this point, they fit the full definition of the automaton: "a living being acting in a mechanical or involuntary manner; especially a person who follows a routine without active intelligence" (Webster). The dance endurance contest, reinvigorting the myth of the automaton, echoes a number of ancient and near modern texts.

Among the ancient texts is the story of Prometheus, a friend to mankind, who stole fire from heaven and gave it to men so that they might have the power of creation held by the gods. Zeus punished Prometheus for this act of hubris, a warning to all who would attempt to usurp the role of the gods. Mankind did use the god-like power of fire to create civilization through technology. However, the progress people made using the power of fire did not come without a price; the cost was in legions of people becoming automatons in the work place. Walkathon promoters may have unconsciously fancied themselves modern Prometheans with the power to create automatons in the play arena.

A more modern text exploring this theme of the automaton is Mary Shelley's gothic novel *Frankenstein*. Dr. Frankenstein creates a machine-like man, a tragic act in light of its consequences. Parenthetically, in walkathon contests floor judges were referred to as Frankenstein. The floor judges were the overseers and enforcers of the walkathon show; their role was to see that rules and regulations were obeyed. These latter Dr. Frankensteins created automatons out of contestants by keeping their creations in continuous motion all day and all night.

Perhaps the most striking precursor of the walkathon show was E.T.A. Hoffman's *The Sandman*, a short novel which Freud cited as a masterpiece of psychology, a work in which many of the insights he later discovered in clinical practice were implicit. Hoffman's novel is as fascinating as it is frightening, the story of how a somnambulant, a mechanical bride created by an alchemist gone mad, brings about the destruction of the hero. In this novel, Nathaniel, Hoffman's hero, is bewitched by Olympia, a female automaton, the creation of Coppelius and two other patriarchal authoritarian figures. Nathaniel dances with Olympia at a ball. Her movements are those of a mechanical doll, precise and measured; her expression is lifeless. Hoffman's depiction of Olympia might well have been a description of contestants at walkathon shows. At the climax, Nathaniel is driven to his death by Coppelius, the "Sandman," who had earlier traumatized Nathaniel by threats of castration. Literary and cinematic accounts of the relationship between show promoter and contestants mirror the relationship between the fearful Coppelius and his victim Nathaniel.

In recreating the archetypal myth of the automaton, Hoffman's story elicits primal anxiety, the response to the realization that persons can be transformed into mechanical creatures. Such primal anxiety evokes a sense of the uncanny, the experience of dread which comes from the feeling of homelessness, the sense that we are aliens in the world, strangers to ourselves and to our fellow man.

During the 1920s, the theme of the automaton continued to be prominent. The contorted postures and limp human bodies in walkathon shows were prefigured in *The Hollow Men* by T.S. Eliot:

> We are the hollow men
> We are the stuffed men
> Leaning together
> Headpiece filled with straw. Alas
> Shape without form, shade without colour
> Paralyzed force, gesture without motion.

In another prophetic poem, *The Waste Land*, Eliot evokes images redolent of the dance endurance contest, phantasms out of the dark unconscious. Madame Sosostria, the famous clairvoyant in this poem, sees crowds of people "walking around in a ring," always in meaningless motion, a literal description of the behavior of couples in the walkathon.

In 1921, two years before the advent of the dance endurance contest, Karel Capek premiered his play *R.U.R.*, initials which refer to Rossum's Universal Robots. Harkins notes that Capek coined the word robot from the Czech robota, meaning "forced labor" and "servitude." In Capek's play, robots, human-like machines manufactured at the Rossum factory, revolt and displace their creators. There is a resemblance between Capek's workers and contestants in dance endurance contests. For the duration of the show, contestants were transformed into zombie-like creatures, in servitude, inmates of The Innocent Jail. If this comparison between factory automatons and dance contestants seems far-fetched, remember that one of the standard events at walkathon shows was appropriately called the Zombie Treadmills. In this act, contestants were blindfolded, bound together with dog chains and forced to wander about in the darkened arena to the monotonous beat of a jungle tom-tom, like souls damned in hell. A danse macabre!

The robot for Capek is a complex symbol. The robot as machine has the power to free us of toil; that is the cure. At the same time, the machine can dehumanize us; that is the curse. The robot reflects our anxieties about modern technology. "From a technical point of view," Harkins writes, "man is an inefficient instrument, whose emotional and spiritual life only impede the drive of modern technology...either he must give way to the machine or he himself must become a machine" (85).

The ambivalence we feel toward the machine is the reason for repression; we deny our fears of the inanimate taking control of our lives. Though we use defense mechanisms like denial to repress this ambivalence, we know from Freud that, in one form or another, that which is repressed will come out. The walkathon contest, a modern medium to create robots out of people, triggered the irruption of dark unconscious forces through the medium of play. Capek's concern is primarily with the destructive force of the machine on human personality, and how it saps initiative and creativity. The robot machine, designed to eliminate labor, ultimately eliminates people; the human becomes extinct leaving a sterile substitute in its wake, an artifact without a soul.

Harkins identifies a corollary theme in Capek's play. The machine which destroys the relationship of man to the natural ecological environment is the product of selfish, industrial barons who promote their own profits, who promote war. For Capek, the machine and paternalistic, autocratic capitalism go hand-in-hand (Harkins 85). This image of the industrial baron reemerged in the behavior and consciousness of the autocratic moguls of the walkathon shows and in the "Fly-By-Night" operators who were out for themselves, to gain their own ends. Unlike the reports of walkathons shows in trade journals, in scrapbooks and face-to-face interviews, literary and cinematic accounts reveal the seamy side of the dance endurance contest. In exposing the exploitation and opportunism which were common practices in walkathon shows, these writers expose the covert American culture.

American Studies Professor Leo Marx defines the covert culture as "those unacknowledged, unaccepted, ignored, repressed American traits (and values) driven underground because of their serious inconsistency with the overt culture" (Bowron, Marx and Rose 92). In his seminal book *The Machine in the Garden*, Marx illustrates how writers project the covert culture through imagery and metaphor (27). He cites as one example Lansman's reference to the locomotive as an "Iron Monster." Through this symbolic reference, Marx sees this early American writer giving voice to unacknowledged traits of doubt, fear and hostility related to the impact of the machine in the settlement of the West. This allusion to the railroad as some kind of archetypal daemon has both sexual and aggressive overtones. The railroad, "an Iron Monster," ravished the garden, "the Virgin Land" of the West.

The literature of the dance endurance contest, like these ancient and modern texts to which it is related through the myth of the automaton, reflects, as in a mirror darkly, the covert American culture. The traits and values which were unacknowledged, ignored and repressed because of their serious inconsistency with the overt American culture were the traits and values of the automaton conspicuously identifiable in the dance endurance contest. Literary and cinematic accounts brought to the surface traits of doubt, fear and hostility related to the idea of being transformed into an automaton. Walkathon audiences were both fascinated and appalled by this prospect.

Critics who judged walkathon shows harshly for alleged immoral practices might better have reserved their criticism for more serious concerns. Instead of touting the dance marathon contest as "The Home of Romance," had walkathon emcees announced in the spirit of the carnival barker at a freak sideshow: "Ladies an gentlemen: I give you the Sweetheart Couple, Our Mechanical Bride and Groom, The Cheerful Robots," audiences, no doubt, would have been dismayed. Apparently, however, walkathon fans were not overly concerned that in going to walkathon shows, they lent support to a form of entertainment built on the real and simulated sufferings of fellow human beings.

Walkathon shows were fascinating in large measure because audiences were encouraged to view fellow creatures reduced to regressed levels of behavior, to the levels of automatons. Could it be that in seeing others so transformed, fans could assuage their own feelings of anxiety about leading the life of an automaton? In any event, those who participated in walkathon shows, whether as actors or spectators, may not have reckoned with the price to be paid for their involvement in this amusement. What was lost was human dignity, one of the "priceless unessentials" of life.

Chapter Eleven
The Dance of Death

The dance endurance contest, in giving life to the myth of the automaton, symbolized a twentieth-century dance of death. Walter Sorell, dance historian and critic, associates the dance marathons with the symbol of the dance of death in the following passage: "In the 14th century the plague killed about half the population of Europe. That the people should have been forced into dancing mania during these years is understandable. But cases of dance hysteria were recorded long before the black pestilence haunted Europe—and long afterwards. The Maenads were gripped by the same *enthousisimos* in celebration of Dionysius as the people in their dance marathons of the 1920s and 1930s. Then people danced for days and weeks, keeping awake through all kinds of tricks. These were the same symptoms of a similar malaise, even though at Madison Square Garden people competed for a prize. This irresistible urge to dance, which has its historic roots in the trance dances of earlier societies, has little to do with true ecstatic feelings and everything to do with a diseased, depraved and desperate mind" (18).

Remember that the idea of the dance of death took hold of the western imagination during the fourteenth century when the bubonic plague, a catastrophe of nature, decimated half the European population (Huizinga 189-1907). This plague brought in its wake an outbreak of St. Vitus Dance, an affliction of a diseased body. Six centuries later, World War I, a man-made catastrophe which claimed the lives of ten million people, brought in its train of destruction the dance marathon mania. Differences notwithstanding, the psychological climate of the fourteenth and twentieth centuries had this in common: both were times when mendacity, disillusionment and loss of faith were endemic. The responses to both plagues are appropriately symbolized as the dance of death since in both instances human beings in a state of crisis attempt to cope with the irrational in their nature and in their culture. The walkathon contest virtually featured the St. Vitus Dance, an affliction of a "diseased" spirit. Elliot speculates about what motivated audiences who came to walkathon shows. "Now, people came to see 'em suffer, and to see when they were going to fall down" (Martin, Interview with G. Elliot).

The symbol of the dance of death itself can be traced to two archetypal symbols which Jung identified in his study of the collective unconscious: the symbol of the physical hearth and the symbol of the sacred fire (Armens 26, 32). Locating both archetypal symbols in the imagery and metaphors of the dance endurance contest deepens our understanding of this modern expression of play by giving us a base in the collective unconscious which Jung uncovered in the human psyche. The walkathon arena as a symbol of the physical hearth is the domain of the archetypal Great Mother, the female aspect of the human psyche. The literature of the dance marathons depicts the physical setting where walkathon shows were held as a confining, restrictive and hostile environment. The walkathon arena is variously compared to a jail, a courtroom, a labyrinth, a treadmill, and the belly of the whale, all fitting environments to house automatons. Common to all these references to the archetypal Great Mother is the feeling of being enclosed and suffocated in a womb-tomb. In the journey of the walkathon hero and heroines, the frontier is closed (Simonson 120).

Similarly, the symbol of the sacred fire, identified with the archetypal Great Father, the male aspect of the human psyche, is projected in essentially dehumanizing images. Contestants are compared to the work horse, to cattle ready to be slaughtered, to a lonesome pioneer, to an immigrant shepherd who returns home to die, to a former college athlete accused of taking a bribe. Common to all these references to the archetypal Great Father is the sense of human beings reduced to elemental levels of existence, to a mode of existence where human power is devitalized and unactualized, the level and mode of the automaton.

Both symbols, the physical hearth and the sacred fire, when identified in the imagery of the dance endurance contest, reflect the regressive function of the symbol. Like a dream-turned-nightmare, images associated with the dance endurance contest express unconscious, repressed, archaic urges, longings and dreads (May 45). Participants described in the walkathon literature are depicted as failed heroes and heroines, victims of both the archetypal Great Mother, who suffocates, brings depression, sickness and death, and the archetypal Great Father, who is manipulative and castrating, who ultimately defeats the hero and heroine.

The symbol of the sacred fire identified with the figure of the archetypal Great Father, when associated with the male walkathon promoter/emcee and with professional male contestants, links the myth of the automaton and the symbol of the dance of death. Show promoter/emcees as authoritarian father figures manipulated contestants to become automatons performing a dance of death. The choreographers of this danse macabre were largely males with authoritarian personalities who were true believers in the Darwinian principle of the survival of the fittest, a vestige of the nineteenth-century robber-baron mentality.

Beyond probing the dance endurance form of play through dark recesses of the unconscious in the company of the depth psychologist, we also gain understanding of this medium of entertainment through the perspective of the social scientist. Sociologist Lewis Yablonsky acknowledges the virulence of the myth of the automaton in modern times in his concept of the robopathic personality. Yablonsky attributes the emergence of the robopathic personality to the destructive effects of the machine on human consciousness and behavior. The disease of modern times, for Yablonsky, is robopathology. This disease was reflected in the operation of the walkathon contest where the characteristics Yablonsky attributes to the robopath were also found in the behavior and consciousness of those who participated in walkathon shows.

The robopath is ritualistic. Ritualism was built into the format and operation of the dance endurance contest. The walkathon wedding was a glaring example of debasing a sacred ritual to ensure a sell-out crowd. Another ritual, the disqualification ceremony, was also trivialized by reducing it into a maudlin melodrama. The ritual of the disqualification ceremony was debased when, unbeknownst to show patrons, a professional contestant had been told to "take a fall," to let some local team win the contest and so please the audience.

The robopath is a conformist. Walkathon shows reinforced this characteristic by requiring that contestants follow an exacting list of rules and regulations under pain of disqualification. Contestants, full-fledged robopaths, obeyed.

The robopath lives in the past. Show emcees lauded the never-say-die courage and perseverance of walkathon teams, comparing their spirit to the pioneers of the American West. Wilson exploits this theme in his short story *The Lone Pioneer* in which a walkathon contestant dresses as a Western pioneer.

The robopath is concerned with image involvement. Show personnel in walkathon contests sought to differentiate themselves from others in their choice of stage names; professional contestants sought the same goal through specialty acts and by acting a particular role, for example, The Sweetheart Couple, or the Trouble Makers. The motivation behind these attempts by professional contestants to establish a recognizable persona is voiced by Rex, the show emcee, when he comments that all contestants "want to be big shots...and he's got their number" (Eells, Act 1, Scene 1).

The robopath resorts to aggressive acts in the interest of winning. Havoc in her play *Marathon 33* describes the professional jealousy which exists among contestants as they seek to undermine the position of their opponents. Under the appearance of friendly bantering, gossip has a more serious intent—to undermine a competitor's self confidence and/or create dissension between partners. At times, this jealousy takes more lethal forms than word play; some professionals resorted to slipping a potent laxative into an opponent's drink.

The robopath is self-righteous. Show promoters were highly individualistic and were quick to defend their tawdry practices in running walkathon contests. Though there was an attempt made by a group of leading promoters to adopt a code of ethics to reduce the stiffening opposition to walkathon shows, this attempt met with little success because promoters thought first of themselves, and second of the walkathon as a legitimate show business enterprise.

The robopath is acompassionate. In the film adaptation of McCoy's novel, Rocky attempts to justify his behavior when he deliberately confiscates the makeup-kit and dress of a female contestant, an act precipitating her psychotic breakdown. His rationalization is: "For the good of the show...that's what we're all interested in, isn't it? They [the audience] don't care whether you win or lose...they want to see a little misery out there so they can feel a little better maybe...they're entitled to that" (248).

The potency of the myth of the automaton as a guiding principle in the dance endurance contest, symbolized as a dance of death, was unmistakable. This thesis is further confirmed by regarding the dance endurance contest as a confidence game. Walkathon promoters typically regarded their business enterprise as a game, a win-lose game. The uppermost idea in the walkathon game was never to be a loser. Scientist Robert DeRopp distinguishes between win-lose "object games" and "meta games" (81). Object games have three characteristics: "hog in the trough," whose aim is wealth; "cock on the dunghill," whose goal is fame; and "the molock game," whose prize is glory or victory.

The dance endurance contest was played, in the main, as an object game. Walkathon promoters ran a "family-protection racket" to ensure being winners in the dance endurance games. Show personnel, including professional contestants, identified with an Apollonian, paternalistic, authoritarian consciousness, played all three forms of object games. Wealth, fame and glory, in some measure, were compelling motives in the dance endurance game. Object games and win-lose games, are games played between automatons.

Among the major achievements of the human race is foregoing an accidental advantage in a game or sport. Spectators rightly cheer this act and the contestant who, even in defeat, can smile and congratulate his vanquisher. In the walkathon show, when an adversary helped his opponent during a hotly contested Sprint or Derby foot race, more often than not it was an example of working heat, part of an object game. These staged performances in walkathon shows did not reflect a major achievement for the human race.

The walkathon expression of play had few, if any, characteristics DeRopp identifies with meta games: the master game which has as its aim awakening; the religious game which has as its goal salvation; and the art game which has as its prize beauty (13). The dance endurance contest was the product of a time appropriately referred to by social critics as "An Age of Contrived Play." Walkathon contests featured pseudo-events which were dramatic, which required careful preparation, cost money, were well advertised and which spawned other pseudo events. The walkathon show was a showcase for the celebrity contestant who imitated but never equalled the true artist performer. In substituting fake for authentic experience, walkathon contests reinforced the judgment that this form of entertainment was a Dance of Death.

As one expression of American amusement, dance marathon endurance contest offered escapist entertainment. This amusement had much the same appeal as the radio soap opera and the Saturday matinee movie serial. Unlike the passive, indirect act of identifying with a voice over the radio, or with an image on the movie screen, walkathon fans could relate to flesh-and-blood people who were within arm's reach.

The dance endurance contest viewed from the perspective of the automaton myth and as a symbol of a dance of death has revealed how a range of irrational unconscious needs were met through the walkathon expression of play. Huizinga's characterization of the play element in contemporary civilization as "Puerilism," play which blends adolescence and barbarity, is an accurate depiction of the dance endurance contest as modern play (205). The walkathon contest was directed at the American predisposition toward sensationalism, passivity, money-mindedness and crowd-mindedness, play which appeals to the lowest common denominator.

The awareness that the dance marathon was an aberration precisely because it reflected machine mentality went largely unnoticed by social commentators who judged this form of amusement on moralistic rather than on ethical grounds. Paradoxically, although dance marathons continue to be regarded a freak in the annals of American entertainment, "as Depression entertainment," they were an intrinsic part of American culture, albeit the covert dark side. The dance endurance contest blatantly exposed the condition of the modern age which Yablonksy named robopathology. Making human beings dance to the rhythm of the machine, the underlying message of the dance endurance contest, brands this show business amusement a twentieth-century dance of death.

Part V

✧

Dance of the Daemons

Chapter Twelve
The Manic Twenties

The Jazz Age, The Roaring Twenties, The Age of Wonderful Nonsense, The Age of Confusion, The Prohibition Era, The Golden Twenties and The Lawless Decade. Common to these metaphors of the volatile decade of the 1920s are attributes unmistakably Dionysian: rowdiness, irreverence, rebellion, lawlessness; in a word, excess.

Historian Frederick Lewis Allen describes the 1920s as a time when Americans had "a very general desire...to shake off the restraints of puritanism, to upset the long-standing conventions of decorum" (133-134). Part of this rebellion took the form of embracing what Allen refers to as "tremendous trivia." The dance endurance craze would have fit this description. Allen points to the essential feature of the 1920s, its curious transitional character, a time in which old familiar certainties were dislodged before new ones took their place. It was a time of unprecedented social dislocation and of social reform, of trivial pursuits and artistic achievements, of regressive politics and imaginative leadership. Paradox, identified with Dionysus, was omnipresent.

Dionysian rebellion against an Apollonian nineteenth-century code of puritanical restraints was widely visible in the determination of the young in the twentieth century to startle their elders. There was an air of novelty, a restlessness that invited rowdiness and intoxication. A generation of "flaming youth" smoked, drank, drove to petting parties, bent on burning the candle at both ends. The means to gain admittance to the domain of Dionysus—the cabaret and speakeasy—was abandonment.

The Editors of *American Heritage* contrasted the manners and morals of the nineteenth century with those of the 1920s and found the difference so absolute that they were hard put to believe that they were dealing with one country, one people, and a difference of only one generation. One social critic quipped: "Surely the flapper was not the child of the Gibson Girl: she must have appeared from the sea like Aphrodite, perhaps floating to shore on a barrel of bootleg whiskey" (337). The Gibson girl was an Apollonian ideal; the irreverent flapper was more at home with Dionysus.

The Maenadic women, female followers and priestesses of Dionysus, reappeared with the "the flappers." The characteristic identified with this emerging woman was motion; her traits were intensity, energy, volatility, qualities opposite to Apollonian restraint. The flapper challenged the Apollonian idealism of Victorian sexual morality which had reinforced a double standard, giving liberties to men but stigmatizing the same behavior in women. "This new woman threatened not only traditional morality but made an assault on the prerogatives of traditional masculinity as well, the final section of the

159

modesty-chastity-morality masculinity equation" (Yellis 49).

Prior to the advent of the 1920s, one event triggered the internecine conflict between Apollo and Dionysus. That event was World War I. This first global struggle was an all-out war of machines; the tank, the machine gun, the submarine, and the airplane. The commanding officers of the French, German, English, and later, the American forces, fought this war with a machine mentality that had catastrophic consequences for both sides.

Trench warfare became an exercise in losing and gaining a few yards of terrain at the cost of hundreds of thousands of lives. Apollonian pride between authoritarian patriarchs resulted in the death of 53,413 American soldiers with an additional 204,002 wounded. The cost to those engaged on both sides of this titanic conflict was ten million dead and 338 billion dollars. The tragic epic of this first World War highlighted the commanding role of Apollonian consciousness suffused with conceit even as it signaled the daemonic presence of Dionysus in the number of dead and dying on the battle field.

Before the outbreak of hostilities, a more benign event had changed the consciousness of the American people. Almost 50 percent of the American population in 1900 lived on farms; by 1929, that percentage had been reduced by half. This shift in population from country to city had a marked psychological effect reflected in the lyrics of one popular song composed in the wake of World War: "How ya' gonna keep them down on the farm after they've seen Paree." Said another way, how to keep the young dedicated to an Apollonian inspired American Dream, after meeting an intoxicated Dionysus abroad?

The often acrimonious internal conflict between Apollonian and Dionysian consciousness can be inferred in the behavior of a number of important Americans, for example, in that of the legendary Henry Ford. Foremost industrialist during the 1920s, Ford was a preeminent emissary of Apollo, an American Dreamer with a different view from other men of what was possible and impossible. His dream creation, the Model T Ford, was a machine which caused a revolution in American consciousness.

First the facts: between 1900 and 1920, motor vehicle registration increased from 8,000 to 8,000,000, a spectacular increase. During the 1920s, registration tripled again. Behind these statistics was the industrial giant Henry Ford. His creation of the machine affected not only the American economy but American courtship habits and family life. Ford, a Puritan at heart, denounced the intoxicating excesses of Dionysus: smoking, drinking and marital irregularities. Ironically, his machine creation, the Model T, was soon to become identified with a Dionysian instrument of pleasure; one wag described the automobile as "a bedroom on wheels." But we are ahead of our story.

Historian Allan Nevins describes Henry Ford as a complex man. Ford's reliance on intuition was responsible for his genius. His technological talent and astonishing feats as an organizer made his Highland Park Factory an inspiring showcase of American industrial know-how. Nevins records how Ford wove together new technological elements including precise standardization of parts, the multiplication and perfection of machine tools, separation of the job into minutely specialized functions, quantity manufacture, continuous motion and time motion studies to create mass production that could furnish Americans with millions of cheap vehicles.

Nevins observed that there was a peculiar sympathy between Ford and the machine. By his labors in bringing mass production to birth, by his gospel of high production, low prices, and large consumption, Ford became the key figure in a far-reaching revolution. City workers were able to move out into the country; farmers became less isolated. Americans could now explore far away places and do new things. More than the flag or the eagle, the Ford Model T became the concrete symbol of American freedom and independence. Paradoxically, the automobile, turned out in mass production on the assembly line, transformed workers into extensions of the machine, enslaving them in the work place as it freed them in play.

Ford's heavy reliance on intuition at the cost of reason in matters outside factory walls also accounted for a broad vein of ignorance, prejudice and suspicion. This lamentable aspect of his personality, his predisposition to identify with the less admirable sides of Apollonian consciousness, was manifested in a shortsighted harshness toward labor organizations and a posture of anti-Semitism. According to Nevins, Ford had the artist's desire to remake the world after his own pattern. Perhaps his most poignant failure to shape man to his measure was his attempt to make his son, Edsel, in the image of the father.

A hard worker, Ford tempered this drive in later years with a well advertised hobby, square dancing. He mounted a crusade to convince Americans, old and young alike, that the traditional dances, the Virginia Reel, Schottische, Varsovienne, Gavotte, and the Minuet were a more wholesome Apollonian form of recreation than the Dionysian Charleston about which more will be said shortly. Ford championed the patterned rhythm of the country fiddler (he purchased a $75,000 Stradivarius to play "Turkey in the Straw") to the spontaneous, syncopated beat of the urban jazz saxophonist. Tenacious in work as in play, Ford continued to evangelize his hobby of old-fashioned dancing and fiddling long after 1926 when it had lost its popularity.

Nevins characterized Ford as possessing "temperamental mutability...a mixture of warring elements" (581). In his pioneering thrust and reactionary conservatism, generosity and selfishness, Nevins saw Ford as holding up a mirror to the modern American character during the 1920s, an era reflecting our adolescent American civilization. In Nevins view, Ford's personality was something of a Jekyll and Hyde, "all cheeriness, kindness and idealism and...full of suspicion, candor and restlessness" (581). Cast in the matrix of myth and archetype, Ford exemplified the best and worst qualities of his mentor, Apollo. When he acted out the role of authoritarian patriarch, Ford invited the wrath of Dionysus who undermined an early idealism and converted it into a hardened cynicism in later years.

In his passion to create mass production, Ford embraced Frederick W. Taylor's program of industrial management based on time and motion studies. Hailed as a secular Great Awakening, Taylor's system reinforced the idea of man as machine. The factory became a macrocosm; the machine was to be the model for man in the workplace. The relationship between workers and management was defined by a technology based on a highly developed sense of mechanical consciousness. Taylor's factory was to be one big machine run by men with special training. They were to see that all the tasks were organized so that the gears of the machine would mesh smoothly.

On an individual level, Taylor's system saw the efficient person as an effective person, one who had turned away from feeling toward discipline, away from sympathy equated with femininity toward masculinity. When applied to the communal level, to workers in the factory, Taylor's system was geared to mechanical efficiency through scientific management. He popularized the technological method in the workplace by promoting standardization, by determining the "one best way" of working, and by attending to the controls to maintain these standards. Emulating the natural science method, efficiency was to be expressed in measurable, quantifiable terms. Technology and behavioral science were wedded in an effective relationship. Taylor's scientific management approach was to be completely free of value judgment. He hoped to discover that the laws of management, like the laws of nature, would be impartial and unprejudiced.

Nelson, in tracing Taylor's career, found that he also reinforced a view promoted during the early days of industrial capitalism in which employers treated the working man as no more than a beast of burden, "a man of the type of the ox" (x). Taylor made additional reference to workers as race horses and dray horses, to songbirds and sparrows. The title of McCoy's novel, *They Shoot Horses, Don't They?*, implies much the same idea though the reference is to the sphere of play. The underlying message in Taylor's approach was the message of Darwin—the survival of the fittest. Equating man to machine and to animal meant that the criteria to measure man were efficiency and usefulness. A dysfunctional machine and a crippled animal no longer had utility—and were expendable. McCoy's implied message is similar to Taylor's: a work horse which has broken its leg, and a human being who has been broken in spirit, have lost their efficiency and are no longer useful in the marketplace.

Nelson found Taylor's career filled with paradox, the sign of Dionysus intruding into the life story of a modern day Apollo. Taylor was extremely sensitive in his relations among his peers; on the other hand, with workers, he was often indifferent and frequently ruthless. Taylor's mother had a profound influence on his early upbringing. Nelson describes Emily Taylor as a woman with strong convictions about how to bring up children. Ascetic and use-minded in temperament, she sought to replicate the mechanization of the factory in the nursery. The child's upbringing had to be ruled and regulated.

Like his mother, Taylor demanded much of himself. He was a likeable and obedient but rigid son. Nelson reports a friend's recollections of Taylor's quarrels with childhood friends. These arguments arose from his insistence that their games follow strict and elaborate rules; even then, Taylor approached play as he approached work. Plagued with recurrent sleeplessness and indigestion, which he related to sleeping on his back, Taylor rigged up a number of "nightmare-fighting machines" to force him to sleep in a sitting position. Once again, in attacking Dionysus in his own domain—play and the underworld of sleep—Taylor, as a combatant in Apollo's cause, lost many battles.

Zaleznik, one of several biographers, speculates that Taylor experienced marked ambivalence toward his father which resulted in polar feelings about expressing his own authority (x). Work became a battleground for Taylor to resolve, if not solve, the conflict between father and son polarized as management and labor. Paradoxically, although he apparently did not want to replicate the authoritarian posture of his father, Taylor unconsciously "acted out" this rigid posture in relating to himself and to underlings.

Taylor was a reformer; he called for the services of experts and the elite to run a democracy. Scientific management applied to government reinforced the idea of social control, national guidance and the end of laissez faire. Like Ford, Taylor became obsessed with the idea of the myth of the machine and with the mythic figure of a Frankenstein creator.

Had Taylor been drawn to social dance, it is likely that he would have followed the footsteps of Ford and not the gyrations of young Americans in the 1920s. The younger generation was attracted to a rash of fast-paced dances including the Two Step, the Foxtrot, the Black Bottom, the Peabody, and most characteristic of the 1920s, the Charleston. This latter dance with its jaunty arm and leg movements was an exercise for the gymnast and not easily managed by everyman. Dionysian license was particularly evident in the spate of "animal dances," the Grizzly Bear, the Turkey Trot, the Lame Duck and the Bunny Hop. Surely, Dionysus, the god of intoxication, was the dance master in the cabaret and ballroom.

The passionate side of Dionysus became associated with one particular dance, the Argentine Tango. Originating in the brothels of Buenos Aires, this dance was performed by that torrid lover of the silent movies, Rudolf Valentino, a modern incarnation of Eros. His rendition of the tango in the film *Blood and Sand* aroused the ardor of American women movie-goers. These modern Maenads were in the majority at the overflowing crowd attending Valentino's funeral after his untimely death from an attack of appendicitis.

Ford and Taylor were part of a milieu which boasted such Promethean figures of the business world as supersalesman Bruce Barton and that "prince of promoters," Wilson Mizner. Barton's best seller, *The Man Nobody Knows*, published in 1928, portrayed Jesus as the greatest salesman of all time, the man who formed an unbeatable organization with worldwide power. Mizner eschewed the old gospel of nineteenth-century capitalism, "Work Hard & Buy On Margin." Composer Irving Berlin created words and music that proclaimed with narcissistic pride America's rising stature as a world power.

In the American community, Apollo (and his sometime companions, Prometheus, Narcissus and Hermes), were found in cults of high priests celebrating semi-sacred rituals at weekly business meetings. These services, attended by boosters of Apollo, were held by the Elks, the Rotary, the Kiwanis, the Lions and the Chamber of Commerce. Though they went by different names, these benevolent organizations were one with "pop" psychologist Emile

Coue in praising Apollo by chanting "Everyday and in every way, I am getting better and better."

The popularity of Coue's pop psychology was only one manifestation of American interest in psychology. During the 1920s, two schools dominated psychology—behaviorism and psychoanalysis. Psychology's brashness in explaining why and how people act had an immediate appeal in the university and marketplace. Behaviorists debated such topics as classical and operant conditioning, positive and negative reinforcement, stimulus generalization and extinction. The more exotic vocabulary of psychoanalysis, Oedipus complexes, Freudian slips, fixations, inferiority complexes, extroverts-introverts, neuroses, manias, fetishes, inhibitions, archetypes and the collective unconscious spiced cocktail party conversation.

It was during the early days of the dance endurance contest that psychology came in vogue in America, and the two phenomena are not unrelated. The dance endurance contest was linked to psychology in several ways. Show promoter/emcees saw themselves as seat-of-the-pants psychologists who intuitively knew how to use behavioral techniques to "make friends and influence people." But there was a more intrinsic connection. The dance endurance contest and the field of psychology based their mode of operation on a mechanistic model of reality; the myth of the automaton had vitality in both domains. Behind the mechanistic model and behind the myth of the automaton was the figure of the paternalistic authoritarian who played a powerful role in both domains, science and play.

In the domain of science, behaviorism early allied itself with the mechanistic orientation of the natural science, in particular, with physics, biology and physiology. The father of behaviorism, John B. Watson, an American, distinguished himself as an experimental psychologist at Johns Hopkins University. Watson regarded the major concern of psychology to be the prediction and control of behavior (Fancher). The behaviorists supported the belief that through the scientific method in psychology untold potentialities would be released in man. The *New York Times*, in 1924, lent weight to this hypothesis by proclaiming that behaviorism marked a new epoch in the intellectual history of man. Watson's immediate predecessor was the eminent Russian physiologist Ivan Pavlov, whose pioneer study in classically conditioning a dog to salivate was to set the direction for the emerging field of behavioral psychology. The theories and experimental findings of Pavlov, Watson and his successor, B.F. Skinner, give us insight into the domain of play, into the rationale and operation of the dance endurance contest.

Watson's doctoral study, *Animal Education: The Psychical Development of the White Rat*, was a landmark in experimental psychology. This experiment also illuminates events at walkathon shows. Watson's doctoral experiment was simple in conception but profound in consequences. Albert, an 11-month-old child, was presented with a white rat that he cheerfully played with for a period of time. Following this period of habituation, a conditioning stimulus was introduced, a loud noise made by striking an iron bar. The repeated presentation of the noise elicited a fear response; when the rat appeared, the response to the noise was associated with the rat. Albert persisted in showing a fear reaction even when the conditioning stimulus, the white rat, was no longer present. Furthermore, Albert came to fear white furry objects other than the rat, for example, his grandfather's white beard. Albert had been conditioned to fear an object formerly associated with pleasure, and his fear was then generalized to associated objects which resembled the original stimulus.

B.F. Skinner, Watson's successor and the father of operant conditioning, would have acknowledged the dance endurance contest as an excellent illustration of his theory of operant conditioning. He might well have regarded the walkathon arena as a giant "Skinner Box" in which contestants behaved like rats and pigeons in a laboratory experiment. Incidentally, walkathon promoters were referred to as "operators"; they functioned in some respects as behavioral scientists when they attempted to control and predict the behavior of contestants. A walkathon contest had other characteristics in common with a laboratory experiment: the emphasis on measurement and quantification ("How long can they last?"); the primacy given to prediction and control ("Who will be the next to go?"); the focus on physiology ("These boys and girls actually put on weight"); etc. Positive reinforcement was prize money and audience applause; contestants scrambling to retrieve coins strewn on the floor imitated the behavior of laboratory animals scurrying after pellets of food. Parenthetically, the positive reinforcement of a nickel, dime, or quarter became a negative reinforcement when a practical joker, a hoodlum in the audience, made a coin red hot before tossing it on the floor.

Back to Watson. A scandal triggered a series of events that led him to apply knowledge gained in the laboratory to the marketplace. In 1920, Watson had an extra-marital affair with a female student 20 years his junior. Later he would divorce his wife and marry her. The scandal resulted in his losing his professorial post. But leaving the academic world had its compensations. Watson was employed by the J. Walter Thompson Advertising Agency, one of the largest advertising firms in the country. In four years, he became one of the vice presidents at a salary of $70,000. Watson adeptly converted laboratory findings into marketing strategies.

In one campaign, he made pragmatic use of his experimental results with Little Albert, using a negative stimulus to elicit a fear response. David Cohen, in his biography of Watson, reports an advertising campaign which Watson orchestrated. The advertisement shows an operating room in which a surgeon is peering at this patient. The headline reads" "And the trouble began with harsh toilet tissue." The ad goes on to say that surgical treatment for rectal trouble is an everyday occurrence in hundreds of hospitals. Cohen notes that the message to the consumer was this: "if only the poor patient had had the sense to use Scots instead of some pebble-dashed toilet paper, he would have not been in this mess." Cohen adds wryly, "In a hypochondriac culture, it appealed" (188-189). Watson also used positive reinforcement to sell products. In the Maxwell House Coffee campaign, the canny industrial psychologist conditioned housewives by suggesting, through words and pictures, that if they served Maxwell House Coffee, they could project themselves into a world of superb elegance and gorgeous glamour in which their living room would be peopled by dashing officers and stunning women.

Watson had a marked impact on the field of American advertising. He instructed businessmen that potential buyers, if provided with an effective reinforcing stimulus, would automatically reach into their pockets like reflexive automatons. People, according to the gospel of this apostle of behaviorism, were pretty much alike. They could be conditioned to buy products, not for their intrinsic value, but for the images associated with them. Watson's image for Johnson and Johnson was purity; a mother who did not use Johnson products was a bad mother. Similarly, his image for Lux Toilet Soap was a woman arousing desire in men through her fresh odor. Watson took the position that good copy had to play on the three emotions of love, fear and rage, and these emotions had to be linked with food, shelter and sex. Walkathon emcees were advised by the show promoter to make sure that women in the audience were given the opportunity to vent their emotions, principally these three basic responses. Show personnel colluded with professional contestants to elicit these emotions by working heat.

After leaving the university, Watson continued to write articles—simplistic, occasionally unscholarly propaganda. Some titles were "Feed Me On Facts," "The Weakness of Women," and "Are Parents Necessary?" An autocratic paternalism was manifested most clearly in his spartan manual on child care. He cautioned mothers to control early masturbatory activity, recommending that the hands of younger children be put outside the bed covers. Watson urged parents to heed the following behavioral guidelines with their children:

Let your behavior always be objective and kindly firm. Never hug and kiss them, never let them sit on your lap. If you must kiss them, kiss once on the forehead when they say good night. Shake hands when they say goodbye. Shake hands with them in the morning. Give them a pat on the head if they had made an extraordinary good job of a difficult task. (81-82)

Watson's message sounds like that of an Apollonian sun god turned frigid and rigid. Still, many Americans heard his message as hopeful, which accounts for the enormous influence behavioral psychology has had on psychology to the present day. According to Watson, the scientist, by manipulating external behavior, could create people in whatever image he wished. Watson acknowledged the primacy of nurture over nature in his now famous challenge:

Give me a dozen healthy infants, well-formed, and my own specified world to bring them up in and I'll guarantee to take any one at random and train him to become any type of specialist I might select—doctor, lawyer, artist, merchant-chief and yes, even beggar-man and thief, regardless of his talents, penchants, tendencies, abilities, vocations, and race of his ancestors. (104)

Walkathon show emcees and show promoters were skillful practitioners of behaviorism in employing both positive and negative reinforcement to influence the behavior of contestants and the audience. Again and again and again, at the end of a specialty act, the appeal of the show emcee to the audience was "to reach down into your pockets...." Audiences came to respond automatically to the appeal. Parenthetically, in the mammoth dance marathon contest held in Madison Square Garden, in 1928, promoted by Milton J. Crandall, The *New York Times* referred to contestant Charlie McMillan as "the disciple of John B. Watson" who adapted the principles of Watsonian behaviorism to undermine the confidence of his fellow competitors. The imaginative if diabolical McMillan rolled coins along the floor with the hope that his groggy peers, convinced that they were hallucinating and had gone insane, would bolt from the building.

Freud, the psychoanalyst, like Watson, the behaviorist, was identified with the mechanistic orientation of the natural sciences. Freud was trained as a physician and embraced the Cartesian view of the body as a machine. Unlike Watson, Freud's legacy to science is ambiguous. On the one hand, Freud was committed to a positivistic rationalist medical tradition which gave central importance to genetics and physiology as the cause of behavior. For example, Freud, the materialist, regarded the ultimate explanation of the dream to lie in the psychophysiology of sleep. In this view, the dream allows us to keep sleeping; its ultimate source is the somatic stimuli of sexual tension. Thus, Freud reduced the interpretation of dreams to biology.

On the other hand, Freud viewed dreams as the royal road to the unconscious. From this perspective, Freud, the romantic, saw dreams as containing a personal message, an encoded letter from the "far country" to be decoded. The actions in the dreams were to be understood as an expression of hidden fantasies and wishes which the analyst tries to decipher in order to uncover the latent meaning. Dreams, in brief, allow us to go privately crazy each night as a vehicle by which we can express irrational needs and drives.

At every walkathon show one or more contestant went "squirrely," they hallucinated and exhibited childish and aggressive behavior. These episodes may well have resulted from the fragmented and interrupted pattern of sleep and dreaming to which contestants were subjected. Dement has demonstrated in his sleep laboratory that dreaming normally occurs during 22 percent of sleeping time; we dream about one and a half to two hours each night (Faraday 31-32). Sleepers who are denied REM sleep, the stage of sleeping in which dreams occur, manifest personality and behavioral changes resembling those of contestants who went squirrelly. Apparently "going squirrely" compensated in some way for the lack of dream time.

Dement also observed that sleepers denied sufficient REM sleep attempted to make up for lost dreaming by increasing their dream activity when they returned to normal sleep patterns. In creating this form of amusement, walkathon operators had tampered with nature's rhythm; a vital function of the psyche had been affected. It would appear that one way to create human automatons is to interfere with the natural rhythms of existence.

Psychology had critics as well as boosters. O'Brien and a chorus of other dissenters accused both behaviorism and psychoanalysis of being "half-baked." He asserted that America was rapidly turning into a vast psychological laboratory in which a minority of experimentalists vivisected the majority. O'Brien noted that both psychoanalysis and behaviorism had decided limitations: "psychoanalysis, in America, as a laboratory for studying the defective minority...while behaviorism is a laboratory designed to experiment upon the elementary and undifferentiated minority" (218).

If psychology had a single patron god among the deities of the Greek Pantheon, it would have been Apollo. The natural science approach in behavioral and psychoanalytic psychology was based on rationalism, one of Apollo's defining characteristics. But Apollo's spirit and those of his companion gods hovered in many other institutions besides science during the 1920s. Along with Hermes, god of records, Apollo officiated at stadiums and sports arenas boasting Million Dollar Gates with the appearance of Promethean sports figures such as Babe Ruth, "The Home Run King," and Jack Dempsey, "The Manassa Mauler." In the mass culture of the 1920s, as consumption rivaled production in importance, Americans idolized heroic producers of sport records like Ruth and Dempsey and hungered for the extraordinary, bigger than life personality.

Apollonian sublimity, however, was lacking in other respects during the 1920s. In place of enlightened communication, the accomplishment of a transcendent Apollo, there flourished "yellow journalism," the tabloidism of the publicity machine that had its beginnings in the late nineteenth century. Press agentry reached a low level in the sensational, insensitive reporting of the funeral of Rudolf Valentino, the mysterious disappearance of evangelist Aimee Semple McPherson, and the electrocution of Ruth Gray at Sing Sing.

Apollonian blind hope lay behind the ineffectual efforts of President Harding, in 1921, to return America to normalcy, a program undermined by the Teapot Dome Scandal. Harding's actions were grounded on the credo that government should not obstruct big business. His successor, Calvin Coolidge, the "President Yankee Squire," followed the same self-serving creed. Herbert Hoover, the self-made millionaire who followed Coolidge, also refrained from intervening in the affairs of big business during the early years of the depression.

Despite the new prosperity following World War I, half the country still lived in poverty. A 10-hour day with wages at 25 cents an hour was typical compensation for those who could find work. Apollonian exploitation by patriarchal authoritarian factory owners resulted in lack of jobs and labor unrest. The strikes that resulted from economic exploitation were blamed on radicals, usually on immigrants. Government reaction to the "red scare" took the unprecedented form of rounding up 3,000 allegedly disruptive aliens for deportation. To this day, serious questions are raised over the legality of the judgment of the court judge whose high-handed Apollonian stance sent two Italian radicals, Nicola Sacco and Bartolomeo Vanzetti, to the electric chair for murder and armed robbery.

Apollonian hubris reached shameful proportions in the paranoia of the Ku

Klux Klan which swelled to one million members in 1921. This group of self-proclaimed Aryan "supermen" preached the supremacy of the white race over the black. In Indiana, a state in which they controlled the elections, they boasted of lynching 281 black people. Apollonian conceit found an outlet in the cult of panacea-seekers, men like politician William Jennings Bryan and anti-communist, anti-Semitic Reverend Charles E. Coughlin. Bryan's evangelism during the Scopes court trial promised salvation to true believers of the Christian doctrine and eternal damnation to heretics.

More lethal in impact than these messianic messengers who sought to bring enlightenment to the American masses were the machinations of big-city bosses, Promethean Narcissistic figures who controlled major American cities as feudal barons. These authoritarian autocrats included Huey Long in Louisiana, Bill Thompson in Chicago, Frank Hague in Jersey City, Tom Pendergast in Kansas City, and Jim Curley in Boston. Ed Crump, prototype of the authoritarian patriarch, controlled Memphis, Tennessee with autocratic impunity. Crump ran his political machine by dispensing patronage, deploying his ward leaders in state and national politics and using "pork barrelling" to solidify his position of power.

One event more than any other act expressed the deep antagonism of Apollonian forces toward Dionysus, the god of the vine. That event was the passage of the Eighteenth Amendment, on January 16, 1920, making liquor, beer, and wine illegal. As a spokesman for the Apollonian way, President Herbert Hoover called the Eighteenth Amendment and the National Prohibition Act that enforced it, a great social and economic experiment, noble in motive. Hoover's voice was the voice of Apollo, the god of Enlightenment, expressing the virtues of purification, atonement and sublimity. However, the American people favored Dionysus over Apollo and flagrantly violated the Amendment crafted out of a misguided sense of civic virtue.

In an era given to Apollonian superlatives, two very different men of high aspirations became legends in their times: Charles Lindbergh and Al Capone. Lindbergh identified himself with the positive aspect of Prometheus by using the power of the flying machine to conquer the sky; his daring trans-Atlantic flight to Europe earned him a ticker-tape parade that inundated the streets of downtown New York. Capone, an outlaw celebrity, identified with the negative side of Prometheus, used the fire power of the Thompson sub-machine gun to hold vast control in Chicago, a city of 10,000 speakeasies.

Ironically, it was that exemplar of a lawless Prometheus "Big Al Capone," the most powerful godfather of the era, arch enemy of Apollonian law enforcement agencies, who profited most by the legislation making liquor illegal. Capone personified the promoter type, the autocratic patriarch, and wielded enormous lethal power. When likeable Capone appeared with his henchmen at a ball park or at the walkathon shows he frequented, he was roundly applauded by the crowds. Under an affable exterior was a man to be feared—but respected.

Noble "Kid" Chissell remembers the following event of 1931 when he was doubling as a bouncer in a walkathon held in Miami: "...a drunk in the audience started heckling the dancers. I rushed over to give him the heave when a dozen guys stood in front of me. I could see "Chicago" written all over them. Then a guy I recognized as Al Capone got up and told his boys to sit down. He took the drunk outside, slapped him around and shoved him into a limousine. Capone turned to me and said there wouldn't be any more trouble because he wanted to stay cool in Miami. There wasn't"(Interview).

Capone, an immigrant's child, slum-born, whom Fred Pasley referred to as "the Horatio Alger lad of Prohibition," possessed the characteristics found in the Apollonian world of business: daring, enterprise, determination and ruthlessness (Pasley 355). In his description of the gangster in the Prohibition Era, Alsop notes that Capone had followed the archetypal American norm codified by Max Lerner as "the success system" and its components: prestige, money, power and security" (xvii). Erick Mottram recounts the following episode which speaks to this archetypal American norm. Capone was interviewed in prison by a young member of the wealthy Vanderbilt family who had obtained a reporting job on a Hearst newspaper. Capone's advice to the young capitalist reporter was short and to the point. He said, "Us fellas gotta stick together." According to Mottram, this sage advice (which later became the title of Hugo Gellert's mural) "neatly encapsulates the Hearst-gangsterdom axis since the center of corruption, then as now, in America, was the interlocking of business and crime" (267). Mottram adds wryly, "Naturally, President Hoover, Henry Ford, J.P. Morgan and J.D. Rockefeller found Gellert's exhibition offensive since they were the 'fellas' in the mural with Capone" (267).

Capone, with a gangland army of seven hundred men, controlled bootlegging, gambling, prostitution, and dance halls in the Chicago area. Capone's business methods to maintain a monopoly included extortion and violence (or imposing the fear of violence) and the offer of substantial bribes to police and civic officials to collude in a Mafia family protection racket. Alsop, in an incisive analysis of this American crime celebrity, dismisses the idea that Capone had founded a syndicate of evil. "That is a lot of horsewoggle," notes Alsop. He continues: "This city [Chicago] was syndicated by the Anglo Saxons who founded it, by the first guy who sold a bottle of whisky to an Indian" (348).

Capone, one might fantasize, lived out the myth of Prometheus and suffered a fate similar to this Olympian god. It was Prometheus's cunning and fraud in stealing fire from heaven which brought the wrath of Zeus. As supreme ruler among the pantheon of Greek gods, Zeus, who fathered both Apollo and Dionysus, ordered Hermes to punish Prometheus by chaining the guilty god to a rock on Mount Caucasus. Nor did his punishment stop there; daily, a vulture devoured the liver of this daring god; each day, the liver grew and was subsequently consumed. This scenario was repeated daily for 30 years. Prometheus was finally freed by Heracles.

It was Zeus in the guise of the Treasury Department who indicted Capone for income-tax evasion and chained him to another rock, Alcatraz, where the vulture of syphilis, a curse from a modern Maenad, fed on his brain for eight years. Capone, unlike Prometheus who was admitted as a god to Mount Olympus, was finally freed in 1947 to die in a Miami Beach estate, his earthly paradise. One can only speculate that Capone, born into the Catholic faith, was not accorded the honor given Prometheus but found his final resting place in a torrid clime.

Capone, celebrity of "The Lawless Era, "was only one of a number of underworld figures who played the deadly game of cops and robbers in the 1920s. Posing as an Apollonian champion, J. Edgar Hoover was relentless in his pursuit, not only of Capone but of a whole band of criminals with descriptive names like "Robin Hood folk hero," John Dillinger, "Baby Face" Nelson, "Machine Gun" Kelly, "Pretty Boy" Floyd, "Ma" Barker and her boys. Not to be overlooked in this rogue's gallery were the most sadistic of the lot, Bonnie Parker and Clyde Barrow.

A decade later, in movies like "The Roaring Twenties" and "Little Caesar," the deadly struggle between Apollo and Dionysus was pictured as a contest between good and evil with the good guys ultimately prevailing over the bad. Film producers and directors in charge of creating Apollonian illusion through the Hollywood "Dream Machine" made Dionysus the bad guy. If truth be told, the role of a high-handed Apollo was as much behind the mayhem of the 1920s as that of his brother god, Dionysus, who received much of the blame.

Clearly Dionysus and his unruly followers contributed to this mayhem. Perhaps the most celebrated example of the "Maenadic woman" in the Dionysian camp was Texas Guinan whose name became synonymous with the "Night Club Era." A modern Circe, Guinan, who owned several nightclubs, was both promoter, emcee and clown. June Havoc, as a teen-age contestant in several walkathon shows, remembers the enticement of $1,000 which Guinan offered her to quit the contest and join her entourage of girls. Havoc declined this tempting offer from Guinan, whom she regarded as a fraud.

Guinan's most cherished possession was the bronze medal presented to her by Field Marshal Joffre in recognition of her heroic services entertaining service men under fire at Verdun in World War I. Ironically, the flamboyant performer, an avowed Catholic who went to early mass each Sunday and whose six uncles were priests, was identified more with the shadowy underworld of Dionysus than the celestial world of Apollo. On stage, at 1:00 a.m., in one of Texas Guinan's five nightclubs, patrons could watch a nude female dancer perform an exotic act with a sleepy, eight-foot boa constrictor. Audiences responded with enthusiasm to the wild, hectic, abandoned gaiety of a Dioynsian evening in a Guinan nightclub. There, the hostess might play leap-frog with out-of-town buyers if it moved her, or hammer a socially prominent matron over the head with a clapper. Seated atop a piano, she rendered her tribute to the "butter-and-egg man" by making him an object of universal love. In spirit, she was like her predecessor, J.P.Barnum; Guinan greeted audiences with her exuberant signature: "Hello Suckers." Patrons loved it (225).

Nietzsche identified Attic tragedy as the highpoint of ancient Greek drama. The conjunction of the two dialectical principles underlying creative equilibrium, surging Dionysian vitality and rational Apollonian order, was rare in the figures who paraded across the stage during the 1920s. One couple who came closer to this ideal was that supreme ballroom team, Vernon and Irene

Castle. Frederich Lewis Allen, noted historian of the 1920s, observed that the Castles "sublimated the dance craze." The Castles, according to Erenberg, had an important influence in helping to make dancing a mass leisure activity by communicating through their dance three important values: personal freedom, refined eroticism and social duty (15).

The Castles associated social dancing with aristocratic Apollonian imagery by performing in expensive and luxuriously decorated cabarets. They projected grace in their dance rather than fiery passion; their appeal was visual rather than sensual. They sought to eliminate the excesses of the new styles of dances which included a variety of "animal dances" by transforming dangerous impulses into healthful exercise. The Castles maintained that their Tango had European not vulgar Latin origins; Parisian not Argentinian style. Like others of their decade, the Castles favored Apollo and made Dionysus a step-child of the times. Social dance as performed by the Castles was prophetic. However commendable their attempt to blend Apollonian form and Dionysian vitality, the Castles, in their artful ballroom dancing, honored Apollo more than his more earthy brother.

Such was the broad American Scene during the 1920s. The patriarchal authoritarian personalities in positions of power in America, men who embraced the myth of the automaton by giving ascendance to the machine over man, men with ambition and hubris, brought the era to a close with the tragic Wall Street Crash. Had Dionysus not been devalued and disenfranchised through arrogance and fear, the catastrophic events of the decade to follow might have been averted.

Chapter 13
The Depressive Thirties

The frenetic acts of the 1920s culminating in the Wall Street Crash propelled Americans into the 1930s with a vengeance. Apollonian sins of the father were visited on the children and Dionysian retribution took full measure. The irrepressible spirit and manic presence of Dionysus in the 1920s brought little distress; everyone was supposed to be having a good time.

All of this changed in the decade to follow. This time, Dionysus called his brother Apollo to account by nagging Americans with the sense of something gone wrong, even though they didn't know exactly who or what to blame. In place of mania, Dionysus brought depression; the dark night of the soul had begun for the American people. The 1930s signaled the release of repressed forces in the unconscious which took the form of fear, frustration and anger. The first three years of the Depression brought the deepest economic crisis in American history. Buried were the Apollonian paper dreams and paper profits of the preceding era. One fourth of the labor force was out of work, production was down 40 percent, and foreign trade had come to a standstill.

The collective effect of this catastrophe was for many Americans a nightmare never before experienced on such a large scale for so long a duration. Images now associated with the Depression were shocking when first they appeared and are still shocking: men, solitary and desperate, scrounging for food in garbage dumps, sleeping on park benches; women on bread lines, their homes threatened with foreclosure; youth, on hold, waiting to get an education, waiting to get a job, waiting to get married. Bankruptcies, factory shutdowns and farm and home mortgage foreclosures were at an all-time high. The fact that the effects of the Great Depression were felt world-wide, due to the collapse of the market economy established in the nineteenth century, did little to soften the impact on the American people.

Variety the trade journal of show business, acknowledged the role of an Apollonian industrial elite who were behind the stock market crash of 1929 with the wry headlines: WALL STREET LAYS AN EGG. Many Americans believed, with characteristic Apollonian gullibility meant to mask a strong materialistic bent, that Senator Everett Dirksen was right: the cause of the economic disaster lay not with a sick society, but with one that had been mismanaged.

Preceding this economic catastrophe, Americans, content with the prosperity of the early 1920s, elected Herbert Hoover president. A mining engineer by profession, Hoover approached politics as a socially minded efficiency expert caught up in the myth of the automaton. Saddled with poor planning in the Coolidge administration and surprised by the impact of over speculation, Hoover spoke with Apollonian optimism during the throes and in the aftermath of the stock market crash. Along with others in government office, Hoover denied the severity of a Dionysian plague by attempting to create the Apollonian illusion that the depression was a passing storm, not a tidal wave that had engulfed the entire nation.

Humanitarian at heart, Hoover was the prisoner of fixed ideas. Like Henry Ford, who supported his political stand, Hoover held to an outdated economic theory of laissez-faire and refused to try anything new or bold, the flaw in the Apollonian character. On December 7, 1931, Hoover declined to see the first "hunger marchers" who had come to Washington to demand jobs. The next year, on July 28, after General Douglas MacArthur, aided by General George Patton and Major Dwight Eisenhower, routed an unarmed "bonus army" of jobless veterans from a squatters' encampment near the Capitol, Hoover thanked God that Americans still had a government that knew how to deal with a mob. Capitalist paternalism suited the President even if it did not suit the times.

A small minority of Americans felt that the capitalist system was in default and had to be changed. They questioned the Apollonian dream that everybody could "make it big" in America. Ironically, it was the logic of Apollonian reasoning which unmasked the flaw in the Apollonian Dream; if one man makes $1 million, he can do so only because 1,000 men are making 3 thousand. The reasoning seems logical, the moral clear; the message was irrefutable. Money is nearly always acquired at someone else's expense. The corollary to this proposition was also clear. The ethics of private profit had primacy over the well-being of the community. Apollonian individualism took precedence over Dionysian community.

Among the minority groups disenchanted with the American business ethic were writers who blamed the system of capitalism which they regarded as opportunistic and anarchic. Attracted by the myth of a stainless Soviet state which was to combine an intransigent idealism and a pragmatic realism, these proletarian writers overlooked the resemblance of the Soviet system to the American. In both political systems during the 1920s and 1930s the real power rested in the hands of the few rather than the many.

There were other American writers, John Dos Passos, James Agee and Clifford Odets, who did not share the view of the proletariat writers. They attempted to convey the despair and hopes of the American people searching not for political panaceas but for a social identity, a meaningful life through bonds with the community. Swados noted that common to all major writers in the 1930s was "the passion of their response along with a determination to bring to imaginative life the terror and glory of countrymen struggling to cope with economic and social darkness" (xxxiv). These writers sought to focus on the twin evils: Apollonian over idealism, with its temptation to make-believe, and Dionysian retribution, with its rush to abandonment and dissolution.

One such writer chose the vehicle of the Twenty-Third Psalm to expose those he felt were responsible for the Great Depression. Donald Whisenhunt reports one version of this sacred text entitled, "The Bard in the Depression":

Depression is my shepherd; I am in want.

He maketh me to lie down on park benches;

He leadeth me beside still factories.

He restoreth the bread lines;

He leadeth me in the paths of destruction for his Party's sake.

Yea, though I walk through the Valley of Unemployment, fear every evil;

For thou are with me; the Politicians and Profiteers they frighten me.

Thou preparest a reduction in mine salary before me in the presence of my creditors;

Thou anointest mine income with taxes; my expenses runneth over mine income.

Surely unemployment and poverty will follow me all the days of the Republican administration;

And I shall dwell in a mortgaged house forever. (375-76)

The struggle between two forms of consciousness, the "cheap happiness" of Apollonian optimism and the "exalted suffering" of Dionysian pessimism, polarities which Dostoevsky identified in his *Notes From Underground* were reflected in the titles of popular songs. Apollonian Dreamers crooned: "Life Is Just A Bowl of Cherries," "Happy Days Are Here Again," and "Wrap Up Your Troubles in Dreams." Dionysian Cynics sang the blues: "Brother Can You Spare a Dime?" "Shanty in Old Shanty Town," and "Time On My Hands."

The Depression, though it carried shock waves across the American nation, did not affect everyone the same way. Reactions varied with family background, social status and individual character. If one could identify a common response among the American people, it was the preoccupation with money. Studs Terkel in *Hard Times* highlighted this preoccupation in identifying the repeated theme of fear and greed in many of his interviews with a cross-section of American people. Fear is symptomatic of Dionysian hysteria, a response to the Apollonian sin of greed.

What Americans feared most was that, as parents, they would not be able to feed their children. Apollonian blind hope reinforced the belief that money was the most important thing in the world since it would allay this paralyzing fear. Beyond fear as a response to the Great Depression, there was a gamut of emotions which included a sense of disillusionment and resentment. Americans felt bitter when they read of the corrupt practice of large companies who, it was alleged, poured milk in the gutter to keep prices up while children suffered from malnutrition.

Despite a sense of deep fear, the response of Americans to the Depression was not unilateral despair. This catastrophe did have a marked effect on many Americans. Thousands of families were broken up, devastated by the economic blight and torn apart by illness and desertion. Contributing to the breakup of families was the foreclosing of 1,000 homes each month. Families in the drought-ridden plains of Oklahoma and Arkansas were particularly affected by the Depression. Homesteaders, forced to become migratory workers, headed toward California following the Apollonian dream of finding the proverbial land of "milk and honey." What they found was a territory overrun with others of their kind who were being shamelessly exploited by owners of fruit orchards. John Steinbeck depicted the plight of these outcasts of the Depression in his searing novel *The Grapes of Wrath*.

Though families responded differently to the crisis of the Great Depression, it was the middle class family and, more particularly, the American male breadwinner and conventional head of the family, who became most dispirited. As main if not sole support of the family, these men felt guilty because of their inability to cope. They attributed their condition to delinquency or lack of talent on their part. Many men came to feel useless and questioned their identity as men since they were unable to provide for their wives and children. They blamed themselves and not the system for their unemployment. As a consequence, they saw their plight as due to personal failure. Their confessions were not a sign of Apollonian atonement as a means of purification; rather, the voice which spoke came out of Dionysian despair, the feeling that they were reduced to the elemental level of survival.

Women were early victims of the economic crisis. They were laid off first and were also the first to have their working hours and pay reduced. Rather than respond to such patriarchal authoritarian practices with bitterness and vengeance as the Maenadic Women had done in Euripidean drama, most women turned their energies to firming up the weakened family structure; they remained steadfast as their husbands became more and more despondent. These "Furies" turned "Gentle Ones" swallowed their pride and accepted whatever public and private assistance to keep the family solvent.

The 1930s, a time of anguish and insecurity, brought prominence to a number of patriarchal figures, each of whose personality combined the traits of Prometheus and Narcissus. Among political leaders there was the aristocrat patriarch, Franklin D. Roosevelt, the 32nd president of the United States, who was hailed, by many, as an Apollonian healer. Roosevelt, unlike his conservative predecessor, did not hesitate to introduce bold and innovative programs into the American economy. He prescribed a number of cures whose names read like a recipe for alphabet chicken soup: the N.R.A., the C.C.C., the W.P.A. and the P.W.A. Another Promethean patriarch was labor leader John L. Lewis, who, like a biblical David, challenged the Goliaths of American industry, General Motors and U.S. Steel and their squads of strikebreakers, the Pinkerton guards.

The image of the authoritarian patriarch which cast its shadow over the American continent loomed even larger and more ominously in Europe and the Far East. Demagoguery reached a new high in Europe when an Austrian corporal, Adolf Hitler, a man with a consuming Promethean-Narcissistic Complex, elevated himself to the position of dictator of Germany. By the year 1933, Hitler issued a decree which forbade all criticism of himself. In a reign of terror to follow his ascendance to power, Hitler used his Nazi military machine to suppress all opposition in Germany and to intimidate the rest of the world. Touting Germans as "The Master Race," it was a bitter pill for Hitler and his squad of "Supermen" to swallow when two black American athletes challenged this Nazi doctrine. First, Jesse Owens outran the fleetest track stars of the white Aryan master race at the Berlin Olympics; then, Joe Louis, in a rematch, floored Max Schmeling in the opening minutes of the prize fight.

Hitler's counterpart in Italy, Il Duce, Benito Mussolini, used tanks against Abyssinian natives on horseback to conquer that country. Hitler and Mussolini lent their support to fellow dictator, General Francisco Franco, who tested the arsenal of weapons of his allies against his own countrymen, the Loyalists. In Russia, Joseph Stalin initiated an extensive series of purges against dissenters which victimized millions. Japan, condemned as an aggressor for its Manchurian activities and its attacks on China, walked out of the League of Nations, thereby undermining still further an organization dedicated to keeping world peace. This dreary account of events in both the domestic and world arena should not suggest that Apollonian consciousness cast a pall on American culture that was everywhere present during the decade of the 1930s. Two World's Fairs, one in Chicago, in 1933, and on an even grander scale, a second in New York, in 1936, proudly exhibited "A Century of Progress."

To complete this brief excursion of the Depression Years, let us look at some of the ways Americans sought to amuse themselves during these bleak times. Three forms of entertainment which were (or had been) highly popular among Americans and which directly influenced walkathon shows were vaudeville, the radio and the movies. Vaudeville had long passed its heyday when dance endurance contests began as a fad. Radio and the movies, however, were enormously popular forms of entertainment during the 1920s and 1930s. What all three media had in common (true of dance marathons as well) is that these forms of entertainment were owned and operated by patriarchal autocrats who ran their business enterprises to suit their purpose and whim. We learn much about dance endurance contests as an expression of American entertainment by probing behind the scenes of each of these forms of amusement.

Vaudeville: The Two-A-Days

Walkathon shows drew upon classic vaudeville comedy and melodrama as "filler" between the repetitive walking acts and the frenetic athletic events. A staff of walkathon comics and clowns amused audiences with a continual round of slapstick, pratfalls, comic make-up, wheezy jokes, and risqué playlets, staples of vaudeville and burlesque shows. Contestants who had some talent, however modest, were called to the bandstand to perform their specialty act, usually a song or dance or a comedy routine. Vaudevillians like June Havoc were periodically hired to supplement this in-house entertainment.

In the 50 years that it flourished, from 1880 to the early 1930s, modern vaudeville provided Americans relief from the dreary impact of the rise in technology and the relatively new industrial complex. Vaudeville, for the most part, created entertainment that was neither complex nor profound but readily comprehended; its unpretentiousness appealed to walkathon audiences as well. As a predecessor to walkathon shows and the movies, vaudeville established practices which were later adopted by other forms of show business. The major vaudeville circuits were manipuated by a few all-powerful moguls while the affiliated minor circuits cooperated through central booking offices and through a protective association of vaudeville managers. A few theaters were run locally, much like independent merchants who operated outside the great store chains.

Vaudeville promoters who dominated the metropolitan houses and major circuits varied in their attitudes toward performers and the public; some were austere, others were expansive; some were genial, still others were vindictive. There was skullduggery, fraud, good faith and betrayal. Most managers, according to Sobel, made box office receipts their prime consideration. Their attitude toward actors depended upon how useful they considered them to be. This purely mercenary motive was present to the extreme in the walkathon circuit among the "Fly-By-Night" dance promoters.

In its heyday from 1905 to 1913, vaudeville was largely controlled by two tycoons, Benjamin Franklin Keith and his strong-arm partner Edward Albee. In a backstage drama of show business, they sought without scruples to win control over such rivals as William Morris and William Hamerstein. Keith built an immense organization run like a machine. Albee ruled the United Booking Office which had a practical monopoly on booking all acts for all theatres. According to Sobel, Albee acquired a black reputation for cutting actors down to size, slicing salaries, restricting freedom of movement and blacklisting on impulse. He made his own rules and, "if he didn't like the material in an act, it was out, for he had a contract which gave him the authority to censor any word, line, business or costume which violated his idea of decency" (66).

Performers referred sardonically to the small-time circuits with names like "The Death Trail" and "The Aching Heart" in recognition of the tribulations they experienced with heartless managers, uninspired beaneries and miserable hotel accommodations. But not all patriarchs of vaudeville ruled as despots. Beck paid big salaries to concert musicians and ballet dancers, for he felt that many people enjoyed good music. F.F. Proctor was one of the first managers to provide decent dressing rooms, modern heating and ventilating systems. Unlike Albee, one of the robber barons who "sold out and retired wealthy to nurse his bruised pride or angry spleen," Proctor, although he seldom went backstage, left $1 million to the Actor's Fund at his death in 1928 (65).

The autocratic stance of Albee and others of his kind, by throttling competition and by consolidating through fraud and betrayal, hurried the decline of vaudeville. In 1920, when Albee forsook the two-a-day show for a five-a-day presentation at the expense of his performers who were forced to rely on stale jokes and old routines, he delivered the coup de grâce. The demise of vaudeville was attributed to causes not unlike those which brought about the decline of walkathon shows: greedy managers, disillusioned performers and changing times with new found sources of amusements.

Radio: The Voice in the Box

The radio reached more people in more far distant locations than had any medium of amusement prior to the invention of this machine. During the 1930s,

E.B. White observed that the radio had a pervasive and somewhat godlike presence which had come into the lives and homes of the American people. Of all the various types of programs, none had more interest than the afternoon soap operas which carried the spirit of the walkathon contest. James Thurber, inimitable chronicler of female-male relationships in the 1930s, reported his impressions of the soap opera genre in an extended series of articles for *The New Yorker* magazine entitled, "Onward and Upward With The Arts." In one article, he rendered this pithy description of the inhabitants of "Soapland":

A soap opera is a kind of sandwich, whose recipe is simple enough, although it took years to compound. Between thick slices of advertising, spread twelve minutes of dialogue, add predicament, villainy, and female suffering in equal measure, throw in a dash of nobility, sprinkle with tears, season with organ music, cover with a rich announcer sauce and serve five times a week. (34)

In Thurber's view, the characters depicted in the radio soap operas were not authentic human beings but flawless projections of the housewife as ideal woman. He speculated that audiences for this type of entertainment identified themselves with the characters who were most put-upon, most noble, most righteous, and most dehumanized. Such a syndrome of personality characteristics would seem to reinforce the view of one of soap opera's strongest critics, psychiatrist Dr. Louis Berg. In his opinion, "these serials furnish the same release for the emotionally distorted that is supplied to those who derive satisfaction from a lynching bee, who lick their lips at the salacious scandals of a crime passionnel, who in the unregretted past cried out in ecstasy at a witch burning" (The New Yorker 63).

One event celebrated over the radio as well at the walkathon arena that had an irresistible appeal for female audiences was a wedding. When Dr. John Wayne married the heroine of "Big Sister," a radio soap opera which enjoyed perennial success, truckloads of wedding presents arrived at the radio studio. A similar response occurred with the announcement of a forthcoming walkathon wedding. That both events were grounded in Apollonain illusion—the radio actors did not marry each other nor did the "Sweetheart Couple" at the walkathon show—did not lessen the appeal of this time-honored ritual.

In ways other than staging mock weddings, radio programs and walkathon shows were similar in exploiting human interest stories. John J. Anthony invited listeners to publicly reveal their emotional plight to which Anthony, "The Voice of Experience," would respond with some nostrum. Walkathon emcees mixed fact and fiction in describing the plight of contestants in dance endurance contests.

Another form of exploitation, practiced to a greater or lesser degree in radio, was the amateur hour. One of the most popular programs of this genre was promoted by Major Bowes. By the year 1935 Bowes had grossed $1 million through his various show business enterprises. His backers were enthusiastic about the show as a proving ground for the discovery of new talent. His critics accused him of mild deceit for reinforcing the idea that contestants with some talent would automatically gain fame and fortune, a possibility which rarely materialized. Similar criticism was directed at walkathon show promoters.

Bowes opened his show with the lines, "Round and round she goes and where she stops nobody knows." This introduction was accompanied by the sound of spinning a "Wheel of Fortune." Walkathon emcees opening the evening show echoed a similar refrain: "Welcome to the CHAMPIONSHIP DANCE ENDURANCE CONTEST OF THE CENTURY, Ladies and Gentlemen. Around and around and around they go and who will win nobody knows. This dance of Destiny...."

Movies: The Dream Machine

The motion picture industry was a gargantuan business during the 1920s and 1930s, the nation's newest and largest medium of mass entertainment. While the rest of the country was in the throes of the Great Depression, Hollywood, The Tinsel Town, was flourishing. References made to the men who controlled the Hollywood studios included the terms "mogul," "absolute monarch," "tycoon" and "dictator." These men ran the movie industry with absolute power over everyone involved. (Though walkathon promoters were less imaginatively identified, these appellations were more or less accurate.)

There was Louis B. Mayer at M.G.M., Jack Warner at Warner Brothers, and Harry Cohn at Columbia. Also in this illustrious pantheon of Hollywood gods were men of Promethean stature— Adolf Zukor, Samuel Goldwyn, David O. Selznick and Darryl F. Zanuck. Cecil B. De Mille, who became famous for producing biblical epics on the screen, wrote: "Mr. Zukor enjoys power...he would put his two clenched fists together and, slowly separating them say to me, 'Cecil, I can break you like that' " (Haskell 57). Zanuck had an office about the size of the room in which Mussolini received his ministers; he sat at an enormous desk at the far end of the room from his underlings, who sat at a respectful distance in giving their reports. These founding fathers ran the movie industry and had absolute power over everyone working in it.

With the exception of Zanuck, what these show promoters shared besides an autocratic personality was a common background. They were Jews, mostly immigrants, the sons of fathers who were failures. Competitive risk-takers, they soon established their empires among the gentile establishment.Before their meteoric rise, these ambitious men had married refined, generally German Jewish women whom they later found to be albatrosses around their necks. As fathers, they were regarded by their college-educated sons with fear or contempt; father and son lived in estrangement from one another. Gabler points out the irony that the actual families of these show business moguls became a kind of studio; the studio became a kind of surrogate family.

Farber and Green note the discrepancy between the family life of these movie giants and the depiction of family life in their movies. The families projected in the films they produced, *Meet Me In Saint Louis* and *Mrs. Minever*, are not consistent with the fact that Jack Warner, Mayer, Selznick, Goldwyn and Cohn divorced their Jewish wives and married women of other faiths. In their yearning to assimilate, these larger-than-life figures sought to project an image still grander.

Heads of Hollywood dynasties, these mortal men did, nonetheless, identify with the ancient Greek gods. An exemplar of this type of man-god was Samuel Goldwyn. This Apollonian inspired producer wanted to make great motion pictures, Goldwyn epics. Alva Johnson notes that movie making, in Goldwyn's Promethean conceit, was man's only legitimate interest. Moreover, pictures to be pictures had to be Goldwyn Pictures. Willing to experiment and take chances, the "Goldwyn Touch" was manifested, not in brilliance or sensationalism, but in honest workmanship in which the intelligence of the audience was never to be insulted (Johnson 16).

Apollonian inspired, with the Promethean aspiration of an absolute monarch, Goldwyn was captive to a Narcissistic Complex. He loved being met by impressive turnouts on his arrival from New York to Europe. When he had problems, he saw them, automatically, as world concerns; he assumed the rest of the universe revolved around him. Adopting the psychology of the autocrat, Goldwyn could not stand an equal or superior in authority; he demanded unflinching loyalty from his faithful vassals. He owned 100 percent of his company and was unwilling to let anyone encroach on his sovereignty. Goldwyn quit the Hayes organization and withdrew from the Central Casting Agency because he wanted to choose his own actors, even for the smallest parts.

Goldwyn paid fabulous salaries to obtain "Big Names," particularly the services of well known writers. Although notorious for tirelessly exploiting the imagination of talented authors like F. Scott Fitzgerald, his approach to subordinates did little to endear him to these gifted writers.

Goldwyn's chief trait according to Johnson was a love of battle, a quality the producer said he learned from Theodore Roosevelt. A man who loved to fight, Goldwyn had boundless courage and was at his best when the chips were down. Goldywyn was heard to say about the movie industry: "This business is dog eat dog, and nobody is going to eat me" (Johnson 76).

Although identified with a proud Apollo, the dynamic movie producer was a prisoner of Dionysus. Always in a frenzy to turn out good pictures, he exploded with great rages and fury at subordinates. With his peers, Goldwyn could play on human weaknesses using histrionically rendered execrations and heartbroken cries to bring his adversaries around to his side. Incessancy was one of his leading characteristics. According to Johnson, Goldwyn could switch in an instant from the wrath of a Genghis Kahn to the charm of a Mr. Pickwick (74).

As Hollywood metamorphosed rapidly from small to large scale industry, producers established a code of ethics with loose boundaries. Directors, writers, and screen players, as a condition of employment, were required to sign contracts binding them to a studio for seven years; the studio's commitment, however, was for no more than six months. Talented actors and actresses in disfavor were forced to take nondescript movie roles; refusal to do so meant dismissal.

Stars were a producer's chattel. They were his property and were never sold. Either he fired them or leased them out in contract. The "farming out" or lending of stars became the quintessence of the manipulation game. Loaning out his stars was one way to minimize the practice of stealing such valuable property by a competitor. In their dealings with show personnel, the Hollywood moguls often treated their employees and their peers as if they were cogs in a gigantic machine with themselves at the controls. Their guiding myth was that of the automaton which brought more productivity than art.

The Central Casting Corporation, created in 1926, had exclusive rights to furnish extras to the big studios. One consequence of this regulation was that few actresses and actors could make a living as Hollywood extras; more poignantly, the path to stardom for the multitude of aspiring hopefuls was all but closed. McCoy's novel, *They Shoot Horses, Don't They?*, depicts the plight of the Hollywood extra who enters a walkathon contest as a last desperate attempt to crash the gates of the Hollywood bastion.

Hollywood was in the business of creating illusion; hence its patron saint was Apollo. Anthropologist Dr. Hortense Powermaker makes this connection clear in the title of her study of the movies, *Hollywood: The Dream Factory*. The metaphor of the dream factory applied to Hollywood is rich in resonance and will be explored more fully later in this chapter.

Here, it is sufficient to note that dreams, nature's way of creating illusion, a form of tension release, were artificially produced in Hollywood on a mass scale. The movies during the 1930s made a deliberate and enormously successful attempt to provide escape. In filling this need, the movies also had a marked impact on the psyche of the American people. Eighty-five million Americans each week paid an entrance fee of 25 cents to lose themselves in a land of make-believe where romance and adventure were within reach of everyone. Woody Allen's film, *The Purple Rose of Cairo*, is a recent reminder of how American movie fans, particularly women, used the movies as a source of refreshment from the dullness and routine of daily existence.

Going to a movie meant that, for a brief space of time, mortal men and women could identify with their favorite gods and goddesses in the Hollywood pantheon. Many of the chief archetypal motifs and figures of myth were presented on the large movie screen to satisfy everyone's needs: lovers, like Jeannette McDonald and Nelson Eddy; child star Shirley Temple; fearless cowboy Tom Mix; jungle hero Tarzan; spacemen Flash Gordon and Buck Rogers; and Jack Armstrong, "The All American Boy." The movies during the years of the Great Depression gave Americans a chance to substitute sunny daydreams for dark nocturnal nightmares.

If the Depression had depleted financial resources, the movies attempted to fill up this void with an abundance of entertainment. Melodramas abounded: the shadowy exploits of gangsters in such films as *Little Caesar, Public Enemy* and *Scarface*, and the potboilers, the Saturday afternoon serials. There were travelogues and newsreels which transported moviegoers to exotic far-away locations and to places close to home. The *Pathe News* recapped beauty contests, prize fights and football games. If the movie fare was largely escapist, there were moments of sheer delight in the matchless dancing of Fred Astaire and Ginger Rogers. In addition to standard fare, movie houses featured a number of attractions such as Bank Night and Prosperity Night; spinning the "Wheel of Fortune" offered patrons a chance to feel lucky when it seemed that luck had run out. Walkathon shows followed the same practice.

The movies fostered the star system which served the needs of the Hollywood producer and the Hollywood consumer. The star system was created through collusion between the movie producers manipulating the stars as transcendent symbols and movie fans dissatisfied with anonymous idols. Star-struck moviegoers wanted models with whom they could identify. By about 1920, the star system was well established; high salaries became news which, in turn, reinforced the system. Mary Pickford, "America's Sweetheart," was among the first stars shifting the emphasis from the star film to the film star. She was "the embodiment of the nation's sexual and spiritual childhood...it has been said truly that a major turning point in national history was reached on the day when Mary Pickford cut her curls" (Suckow 192-193).

Parker Tyler, a movie critic who drew heavily on Freud and mythologist Frazier in analyzing Hollywood and the movies, compared the star system to the Greek pantheon; actors and actresses were deities continually experiencing death and transfiguration, characteristics of Dionysus. In one Columbia epic, the heroine dies in one film but is mysteriously reunited with her hero in a subsequent movie. It would seem that all things were possible among the gods of ancient myth and the stars of Hollywood. Tyler characterized Hollywood as "a superlatively equipped factory prepared to transfrom anything according to a flexible method of manufacture" (84).

The star system was skillfully promoted by the fan magazine which nurtured the myth of the Cinderella fairytale. Suckow traces the Apollonian myth which these publications reinforced, "the myth of the overnight rise to fame and material wealth, to social opulence, with Sex and Beauty in headline type, and all turned out in mass quantities with great technical smoothness and ingenuity by machinery" (189). Hollywood exploited a parallel myth, one of the world's oldest folk tales: Boy Meets Girl; Boy Loses Girl; Boy Gets Girl. In the film version of McCoy's novel, emcee Rocky Gravo repeats this script verbatim adding with chauvinistic bravado, "...and isn't that the American way!"

In Hollywood's "stellar liturgy," the fan club fostered a cult of true believers. The letters sent to the stars expressed this adoration. Movie magazines with their multiple glamorous photographs nourished the fantasies of worshipful fans. On a much reduced scale, walkathon contestants received fan mail from young admirers.

Joan Crawford, one of a select group of Hollywood stars, personified the female Narcissus. Identified as the prototype of the flapper, her performance of the Charleston in *Our Dancing Daughters* gained her a host of worshiping admirers. The Joan Crawford Fan Club was one of the best organized in Hollywood. Her story before she became a super star in Hollywood is dramatized, if not fictionalized, in Edward Field's narrative poem entitled, "The Life of Joan Crawford." Part of Field's poem is excerpted below:

She got a job as a dance-hall hostess, dime-a dance, six months pregnant, but with a brave smile as the customers stepped on her toes. They found her a good joe and a willing ear as they told her their troubles while rubbing off against her to a slow foxtrot. One of her customers, impressed by her dancing, got her to enter a dance marathon with him for prize money—she needed that dough for the little stranger—but the strain was too much for her, marathon-dancing in her seventh month! She came to on a hospital bed with no makeup on and a white cloth over her forehead like a nun to see her griddle-faced father looking down on her, his mouth boozy as ever, but in his heart vowing to go on the wagon if God would spare her life: "Come home with me, Joanie, I'll take care of you." "And baby too, papa?" "Didn't they tell you Joanie? The baby..." "Oh no..." And tears of mourning still in her eyes she went back home to the Hollow and kept house for her father. (192-93)

Field, by describing his heroine as working as a dance-hall hostess and later as a contestant in a dance marathon before becoming a Hollywood star, brings the world of the movies and the walkathons together. The dreams of the walkathon contestant were not qualitatively different from the aspiring extra on the Hollywood lot hoping to be discovered and catapulted to instant fame. Some of the themes dramatized in the movies were staple fare for walkathon melodramas. The triangle of the "big cop," the "large woman," and the "little man," which created a nightmare for the child, portrayed in the movies by Edward G. Robinson with his grotesque infant-face, and by Buster Keaton with his big-eyed baby-face, was re-enacted in walkathon shows.

The Trouble-Makers in walkathon shows were teams frequently composed of a large woman and her smaller partner, both subject to the dictates of a big menacing floor judge. The "little boy-man" at the walkathon show was the victim of both his cruel mother in the form of a henpecking partner and a menacing father in the person of the floor judge. In contrast, the Sweetheart Couple of every walkathon show was modeled upon the enormously popular movie team Janet Gaynor and Charlie Farrell. Movie and walkathon fans sought to maintain the Apollonian illusion that this movie team was the model for real life.

The power of the myth of the automaton perpetrated by the Apollonian movie mogul surfaced in a number of forms in the Hollywood motion picture. Two examples make the point: "The Ziegfield Girl" personified the somnambulant myth in her strictly standardized gait. The dehumanized brilliance of the Apollonian-ordered Busby Berkeley dance-routine were, in Eric Motran's view, extravaganzas which "used large abstract patterns of light and dark with human lavishness" (275).

The conflict between Apollo and Dionysus was thematic material for the "Hollywood novel." In this genre, none had a more biting impact than Nathaniel West's novel, *The Day of the Locust*. West's apocalyptic description of a Hollywood premier portrays the dire struggle between Apollo and Dionysus. One reviewer referred to West's depiction of the Hollywood premier as "Nietzschean revenge of Dionysian frenzy against a fraudulent Apollonian dream" (Wilson 339-340).

Hollywood signifies for West a microcosm of the whole American society. Hollywood, and by extension America, is viewed as an enclosed and seedy place. West focuses on the devastating impact upon masses of people who come to Hollywood, as to Eden, in search of a Paradise on earth. What these masses discover is that the promises of "The Golden West" turn into the reality of "A Valley of Ashes."

One of the most complex and potent metaphors of American culture to arise out of the 1930s is the symbol of Hollywood as the Dream Machine. Johnson associates Hollywood with glamour, money, success and retribution. Hollywood during the 1920s and 1930s is variously regarded as "a graveyard of broken dreams" and a "Sargasso of the imagination" (1). For John Dos Passos, Hollywood was synonymous with capitalism, hypocrisy, perversion and deceit. As a symbol, Hollywood came to stand for a place as well as a state of mind in which the distinction between reality and illusion was blurred.

West describes Hollywood, a locale of movie sets, assorted architecture, strange religious sects and local worship of glamour as "a dream dump" (Simonson 120). He views the Hollywood of the 1920s and 1930s as the most terrifying town in America, a place filled with marginal personalities, a domain of opportunists and confidence men, of people desperately on the make. The somnambulists who walk this terrain are like zombies who, as an antidote to boredom and ennui, devour newspaper and fan magazines to heighten excitement by reading about scandals and crimes.

The characters in West's *The Day of the Locust* are grotesque, dishonest, artificial, self-deceptive and frustrated people, living in a commercialized society that arouses, cheapens and ultimately thwarts their dreams. As a model of the migrant to Hollywood, West's Homer Simpson seeks escape from a life that lacks variety or excitement. Homer is like the character in Elmer Rice's play, *The Adding Machine*. His life is given to totalling figures and making entries. Homer is seduced by Faye Greener, West's tough, promiscuous heroine, who reduces him to a condition of servitude in the crazy, violent half-world of Hollywood.

Tod Hackett, a young painter, reflects West's stance in his novel. Hackett adopts a peculiar combination of detachment and obsession toward his characters who include Homer, Faye, her father and a band of "outlaw" friends. Tod's ambition is to paint "The Burning of Los Angeles," a picture which will stand as an indictment if not prediction of the future for those who live empty lives of illusion and pretense.

Tod's painting brings him a shock of recognition; nothing less than a total conflagration will awaken the masses to the illusion and denial in their lives. There is a more profound shock awaiting Tod when he realizes that truth, itself, is destruction. In a macabre ending, described as "a ceremonial dance riot," Tod is caught in a surging mob of movie fans made up of lower middle-class citizens who act out through this Hollywood spectacle their bitterness, frustration and repressed sexuality as an antidote to their lives as somnambulists. Whipped to a state of frenzy by radio announcers who describe the arrival of celebrities to a Hollywood premier at Kahn's Persian Palace, the unruly mass of spectators react with violence as they become part of a mob. West's radio commentator performs the same orchestrating function as the master of ceremonies Rocky Gravo in McCoy's novel, with much the same effect.

West describes the fate of the Los Angeles migrants in the crowd:

All their lives they had slaved away at some kind of dull, heavy labor...saving their pennies and dreaming of the leisure that would be theirs when they had enough. Finally that day came...once there, they discover that sunshine isn't enough:...Their boredom becomes more and more terrible. (411)

Existential panic from living empty lives and paralyzing boredom gives the surging crowds at the Hollywood premier an outlet to vent their frustation. Having discovered that the American dream is fraudulent, they suffer "a deeper sickness than boredom...not only do they feel cheated, but, more importantly, they feel lost" (Simonson 123-124). The hordes, according to critic Simonson, do not see Hollywood for "the dream dump it is ...that the Golden West promised—the sex-dream, the Christ-dream, the million-dollar dream—all tried and untrue, must now make way for the paradise dream" (Simonson 123-124).

West's depiction of the Hollywood premier is surrealistic and nightmarish. At a high-point of frenzy in the riot, West describes what happens to Tod as he is caught up by the surging mob:

He was carried through the exit to the back street and lifted into a police car. The siren began to scream and at first he thought he was making the noise himself. He felt his lips with his hands. They were clamped tight. He knew then it was the siren. For some reason this made him laugh and he began to imitate the siren as loud as he could. (421)

This action parallels the experience of Robert Syverten, the hero in McCoy's novel, who cannot differentiate between his own screams and the siren of the police van taking him to jail after he has killed his partner. West and McCoy make the same irrefutable point: society, in frustrating its citizens, unleashes forces that are directed both outward, toward others, as well as inward, toward the self. Dionysian retribution is relentless once it is aroused. Sturak notes that the enduring radicalism of McCoy's novel (true of the novels of Nathaniel West) resides in no political program or ethical system, but from a passionate desire to affirm the human sense of life, despite the voids and vicissitudes of our age. The implied message of these two writers is perhaps best summed up in Clifford Odet's plea, "Life should have some dignity" (Sturak 268-269).

In the world of the movies, one figure, perhaps better than anyone else, illuminated the ongoing struggle and uncertain resolution between Apollo and Dionysus—Charlie Chaplin. As imaginative film director, Chaplin sought Apollonian perfection, taking and retaking the same scene hundreds of times; as inimitable actor and clown, Chaplin created "The Little Tramp," the apotheosis of Pan and Dionysus. Chaplin's keen sensitivity to the play of these two gods is evident in both his silent and talking films.

As noted earlier and worth remembering, Chaplin went to see walkathon shows held in an amusement park on the outskirts of Hollywood. He was the first to purchase the film rights to McCoy's novel *They Shoot Horses, Don't They?* A good hunch is that Chaplin's interest in filming McCoy's novel was related to the theme which appeared in his classic movie *Modern Times*—how human beings have been transformed into extensions of the machine.

Modern Times begins as a social satire on machine-age mores. Chaplin appears in this film as a member of the working class employed in a factory on the assembly line. His job is to twist bolts on a conveyor belt. Chaplin is hard put to keep up with the pace of the moving belt with its line of machine bolts. The message of the plant manager like that of the floor judge at a walkathon contest is "Keep moving!"

Apollonian insult is added to injury when the automatic feeding machine with Chaplin as experimental guinea pig goes haywire. Initially, the robot machine pushes small squares of food into Chaplin's mouth; following the consumption of these morsels of food, an automatic arm, with an absorbent roller, wipes his mouth. Midway through this demonstration, the feeding machine begins to malfunction; bolts dislodged from the machine are shoveled into Chaplin's mouth and the moving napkin becomes a battering ram directed at his face. Apollonian inguenuity has created a diabolical machine whose effect is dehumanizing.

When Chaplin returns to the assembly line after his encounter with the feeding apparatus, he becomes the victim of still another machine which sucks him into its revolving wheels. As he goes round and round the cogwheel, his body momentarily appearing and disappearing in the revolving gears, his movements are accompanied by the music of a carousel. Chaplin's actions symbolically replicate the repetitive movements of walkathon contestants as they traveled round and round the dance arena to the music of a live jazz band.

After a day of twisting bolts, Chaplin is turned into a hapless extension of the machine. As he leaves the factory building, he wobbles down the street, his arms and hands twitching all the while, simulating the repetitive movements on the assembly line. His attention is drawn to an attractive female walking toward him. Like a deranged Pan, the only Pan the twentieth century can know, he pursues her, mistaking the buttons on her dress, placed in front and rear in unmistakable erogenous zones, for the bolts he has been turning hour after hour on the assembly line.

Chaplin rescues a female gamin from the clutches of Apollonian do-gooders who seek to arrest her for vagrancy. As a picaresque finale to his film, the rootless pair travel down the open road toward an open horizon; the injunction from the local authorities is to "Keep Moving!" The same injunction was repeated ad nauseam by the floor judge to contestants at the walkathon contest.

The 1930s ended as it began, in crisis. A second World War threatened. Apollonian and Dionysian consciousness continued to be polarized with devastating consequences. One crisis was to follow another throughout the twentieth century. Leonard Bernstein in his Charles Elliot Norton Lectures, given at Harvard in 1973, paused in the middle of one of his talks, and with deep concern summarized the events of the twentieth century as follows:

"The twentieth century," Bernstein began, "has been a badly written drama from the beginning.

Act I: Greed and hypocrisy leading to genocidal World War; postwar injustice and hysteria; a boom, a crash; totalitarianism.

Act II: Greed and hypocrisy leading to genocidal World War; postwar injustice and hysteria; a boom, a crash, totalitarianism.

Act III: Greed and hypocrisy leading to...I don't dare continue." (314)

Americans were quick to welcome the dance endurance contest during the early 1920s and continued to support this form of amusement during the 1930s. As entertainment, the dance endurance contest mirrored the rapidly changing milieu in America during these two fateful decades. What has been uncovered in this indepth examination of one form of American amusement, the dance endurance contest is the prevailing power of patriarchal autocrats who controlled and dominated the amusement industry. But there was also another discovery: that men and women living in America were willing to collude with these show business moguls to gain their own ends. The dance endurance contest continues to be regarded by social critics (and by the man on the street) as a freak event in the annals of American history. It was not.

Part VI

◇

The Dance Marathon Craze

Chapter Fourteen
The Great American Sham

The dance endurance contest was bogus show business and indelibly stamped "Made in America." Earlier referred to as pageants of fatigue, dance endurance contests evolved into a novel form of show business, an amusement which blended vaudeville, burlesque, night-club and sport. What began as a craze, one of many fads which surfaced during the 1920s, soon was adapted into a money-making venture defined by guile and collusion.

A "Poor Man's Night Club," walkathon shows entertained audiences with skits, comic routines and song and dance exhibitions. Featured at these shows were fast-paced sprint and derby foot races choreographed for maximum melodramatic impact. Preceding and following these highlighted events, somnambulant couples milled round and round the dance floor, each team appearing on the verge of collapse. Add to this adulterated mixture of show business entertainment and sport, a nominal entrance fee, 24-hour access, specialty nights, door prizes and free gifts, and there is no mystery about the popularity and longevity of the dance endurance contest. These shows appealed to the same simple and uncomplicated tastes of people who enjoyed vaudeville, burlesque, the night club and sports.

But behind the facade of the walkathon show, there was sham. Show promoters and professional contestants colluded in running this business venture as a "family protection racket." In the walkathon family, paternalistic, often authoritarian, promoters/emcees manipulated their underlings by taking the stance of top dog and under dog, sadist and masochist, victimizer and victim. Professional (and amateur) contestants used the vehicle of the walkathon to travel "The Glory Walk." The counterfeit mode of operation of walkathon shows—most, if not all, contests were fixed—made this show business venture for those who participated, "The Grandiose Road" (Bly).

Dance endurance shows became the target of middle-class critics, state and country wide. Vocal and vociferous, these watchdogs of public morality denounced dance endurance contests as immoral...and un-American. However merited the first criticism, walkathon shows were unmistakably American. Defining the format and operation of walkathon shows were many traits which historian Lee Coleman identifies with being American: predilection for display, the love of action and incessant activity, competitiveness, achievement and success, efficiency, chance taking, opportunity, love of size and bigness, bragging and boasting, the star celebrity system, evangelism, gregariousness, equality for all, friendliness and sociability, sympathy for the underdog, and glorification of the common man (McGiffert 28-29). Hovering in spirit over every walkathon show was P.T.Barnum, the imaginative show promoter who unashamedly exploited the American passion for humbug.

Walkathon shows projected traits and values with which Americans openly identify, and, paradoxically, walkathon shows projected traits and values which Americans often profess not to esteem. Among these "less acknowledged, even repressed" traits and values which were part of the fabric of dance endurance contests are the following: dominance of the machine, uniformity, conformity, monotony, commercialism, national conceit, gambling and materialism. One prized American value that was tampered with was freedom. How does one understand the popularity of an amusement with traits and values which Americans profess both to prize and to abhor? In attempting to answer this question, we gain some insight into the social climate and character of Americans living during the tempestuous eras of the 1920s and 1930s.

One way to approach this seeming paradox in value orientation is through the work of anthropologist Clifford Geertz. In his exemplary study of the Balinese cockfight, Geertz gives us a close reading of the cockfight as one text in Balinese culture (412-453). Viewed much as a literary text, Geertz was able to penetrate different levels of meaning of the cockfight. Geertz observed that through this expression of play, the Balinese mirror themselves and their social order. Furthermore, they give expression to deep-seated needs and drives. The cockfight resonates with such themes as animal savagery, male narcissism, opponent gambling, status rivalry, mass excitement and blood sacrifice (449).

In the cockfight, the Balinese are bound into a set of rules that allows them to contain rage and, at the same time, permit them to play. Through this symbolic function of play, the Balinese can, over and over again, intelligibly experience the reality of inner afflictions. Geertz sees this expression as one way Balinese men (they are the only ones permitted to participate in cockfights) have the opportunity to exorcise their inner daemons related to status concern, masculinity, pride, loss and death (443).

But the Balinese culture is Apollonian at heart: the Balinese value poise and balance, harmony, detachment and coolness. The cockfight brings to imaginative realization dimensions of Balinese experience which go against the grain of Balinese values manifested in other texts of Balinese culture, for example, the ceremony consecrating a Brahmana priest (452). Geertz is aware that while the cockfight is not the master key to Balinese life, what this play reveals about the soul of the Balinese is important. The cockfight apparently reflects the shadow side of Balinese character, the covert Balinese culture.

Adapting Geertz's approach, we can identify the following themes surfacing in the dance endurance contest: mechanical consciousness, commercialism, display and communal conformity. Overarching these four motifs is the seminal theme of the automaton. The dance endurance contest fascinated and captivated American audiences because it exhibited the mechanical man, what Americans unconsciously feared most becoming and had become. The dance endurance contest reinforced those values and needs giving primacy to the dominance of the machine and mechanical consciousness: contestants lived by the clock; events were serialized and fragmented; emphasis was on continuous motion and effort; there was a sense of impermanence and interchangeability; and conformity and uniformity were expected within the regimented environment of the dance endurance contest.

Walkathon shows were, first and last, commercial ventures; making money was the primary goal; witness the walkathon wedding where precedence was given to the secular over the sacred. Gambling, speculation and chance-taking were part of every dance endurance contest. The importance given friendliness and sociability by the show promoter/emcee had more to do with running a smooth business operation than concern for providing a setting for genuine friendships to develop. Further, national self-consciousness and conceit were exploited at walkathon shows by touting the values of American materialism.

As display, the walkathon show was a caricature of the movies cranked out by the Hollywood "Dream Machine." Contestants were glorified as show celebrities but also as "the average man," the underdog. Variety, diversity and contrasts were important features of every successful show: bigger was better. Bragging, boasting and humbug were part of the everyday rhetoric of those who promoted and operated this show business enterprise.

The rhetoric of the walkathon contests trumpeted the great American value of individualism. Show emcees congratulated the self-made man behind a string of American clichés: every man a king; rags to riches; reach high; local boy makes good; look out for Number One! Despite glorifying individualism, walkathon shows run as a "family protection racket" reinforced the values of communal conformity as a means of optimizing profits for walkathon show promoters and professional contestants. In sum, the American character reflected through the walkathon contest was one in which mechanical values had ascendance over human values; materialism over humanism, display over play, and conformity over individuality.

But the dance endurance contest did not begin as a sham. Like other crazes and fads, dance marathons began innocently enough. The idea was to prove that one American could do something longer if not better than any other American. The challenge was simple: to remain upright longer than anyone else while simulating dancing to music. This challenge, which could be met by anyone with sound feet, much determination and a measure of conceit, attracted scores of Americans and immigrants who set out to prove that they were, indeed, special.

The advent of the dance marathons and the walkathon contest—the change from fad to show business—tainted this form of entertainment. Guile replaced innocence; opportunism and collusion seeped into the fabric of the walkathon show and, over time, ultimately ruined it as a business enterprise. Literary and cinematic accounts, along with newspaper and magazine reports, pointed to the counterfeit practices endemic in this show business venture. It is what was behind the facade of walkathon contests and what lay below the surface of this brash form of show business, its sham practices, that is of most compelling interest.

The premise of the walkathon contest, the show format and mode of operation, evoked a sense of the uncanny, an eerie feeling that there was something not quite right about this genre of show business. There was something not quite right about an amusement in which human beings walk in their sleep and act like automatons propelled by hidden forces over which they have little control. There was something not quite right about subjecting contestants to successively more arduous trials of strength as they became progressively weaker from lack of sustained periods of rest and sleep. There was something not quite right about operating a show business venture as "a family protection racket" in which staff and contestants collude. Not least, there was something not quite right about running a form of show business in which profit, not public service, is the primary goal.

Overall, there was something not quite right about this form of amusement because it was a sham. Show personnel and professional contestants duped audiences into believing that walkathon contests were run fairly, that they were on "the up and up." In fact, most if not all walkathon contests were fixed. Though walkathon audiences might suspect that there was more to this form of amusement than met the eye, they were, nonetheless, beguiled by the pseudo-events featured at walkathon shows, more spectacle than genuine article.

Audiences, show personnel and contestants chose to repress what was not quite right about this form of public amusement: turning people into automatons. Were it true that "what you don't know (or acknowledge) can't hurt you," then there would be little psychological value in probing further into the role unconscious forces in the collective American psyche played in this communal play. But Freud was on target in observing that what is unacknowledged and repressed will come out...in one way or another. During the 1920s and 1930s, one way in which part of what was repressed in the American psyche surfaced in the dance endurance craze. Hence, the story of this expression of play gives us a unique opportunity to probe deep below the surface of American culture to covert hidden levels, there to uncover the shadow side of the collective American psyche.

This depth exploration of the dance endurance contest reveals that all was not well in American culture during 1920s and 1930s, two decades exhibiting some symptoms of manic-depression. The dis-ease in American culture during these two decades is reflected in the outpourings of artists and social scientists who sought to bring some order to the confused times. One expression of this dis-ease was the dance endurance contest. Literary and film critics of walkathon shows exposed this amusement as bogus entertainment.

Walkathon shows were a sham in the guise of play. Nature's rhythms were disrupted; sleep and rest patterns were radically altered. Every hour, on the hour, day and night, contestants had to be on their feet, and in motion, for 45-minute periods leaving 15 minutes to perform all other functions including sleeping in a bed. This daily requirement affected not only behavior but consciousness as well. Outcomes of tampering with nature's rhythms were the periodic episodes when contestants were "squirrelly." Contestants hallucinated, mimicking psychosis. During these temporary but recurring bouts of abnormality, contestants directed their aggressive drives toward their partners, unwitting victims. During these acts, when unconscious forces take over as they do in the nocturnal dream, contestants performed ludicrous acts causing later embarrassment. "Going squirrelly" was one of many reminders that in tampering with nature, contestants lost some degree of rational control, of human dignity.

"Going squirrelly" was dehumanizing. But other aspects of walkathon shows did little to enhance a sense of self worth. Contestants lived in a hothouse climate where men and women were segregated into two separate, large, open rooms where they slept on cots and lived out of their suitcases. They were further restricted by being prohibited from leaving the building for the duration of the show. When not in rest quarters, contestants had even less privacy since they were required to be on display, on the dance floor, always in view of the audience. On Cot Night, the small degree of privacy afforded by rest quarters during the eleven minute break was taken away; during this act, contestants were exhibited in full view of the audience as a stunt to stimulate the voyeuristic needs of walkathon audiences.

The physical environment was not the only element that made the atmosphere of the walkathon show toxic. Walkathon shows, it was earlier noted, were often run as a family protection racket under the rule of a patriarchal show promoter; at best, he was paternalistic; at worst, unconscionable. Whatever prompted show personnel and contestants to act out behavior found in dysfunctional families, to be top dog and underdog, sadist and masochist, victimizer and victim, was reinforced in walkathon shows. All in all, walkathon shows were not a hospitable environment to enhance a sense of well being.

Like the Balinese cockfight, the dance endurance contest did give contestants and spectators an opportunity to vent repressed narcissistic and aggressive drives unexpressed in everyday living. Professional contestants (and amateurs, as well) could prove that they were as good, or better, than their peers, that they were "somebody." Spectators were able to sublimate their narcissistic needs by identifying with contestants who were the celebrities of the show. In the act of satisfying their inflated ego needs, contestants and spectators were also able to ventilate their aggressive drives. In traveling the Glory Road, contestants were willing to use any tactic, fair and foul, to undermine their competitors. Audiences channeled their aggressive drive by shouting and yelling and booing the Trouble Making couple.

The dance endurance contest exposed values, needs and drives which Americans want not to acknowledge, but to repress. Perhaps this is why walkathon audiences were both fascinated and captivated by what they witnessed at walkathon shows: fascinated because they saw human beings reduced to the level of automaton, and captivated because, unconsciously, they sensed that their lives were not very much different from those of the contestants they were observing.

What happens when we adhere, simultaneously, to logically incompatible values, in this instance, values related to the machine and to the love of the machine and to the fear of the machine? Freud sheds light on this question as well. He notes that when we have ambivalent feelings, we experience anxiety and fear; and when we are anxious and fearful, we repress. At core, what had to be repressed by contestants and audience was the realization that the walkathon contest was an exercise in reductionism, a form of play transforming the person into an automaton.

The dance endurance contest as an expression of the covert American culture gives us insight into the shadow side of American culture. On one hand, the dance endurance contest presented to the American imagination and sensibility the tragic life lived as an automaton. On the other hand, the dance endurance contest enabled Americans an opportunity to exorcise, to some degree, their inner daemons associated with living a partial life, the life of an automaton.

The dance endurance contest was an aberration precisely because it reinforced a form of consciousness and behavior associated with the automaton.

Contestants lived an existence in which the traits and values linked with the machine were reinforced. The rules and regulations of this show business enterprise stressed punctuality and regularity, the standardization of performance and product, contraction of time and space and collective interdependence. These characteristics are part of the ideal of mechanical regularity and mechanical perfection which Mumford identifies in the ideology of Western culture from the eighteenth century on (430).

Walkathon show promoter/emcees manipulated the behavior and consciousness of contestants and show personnel so that their existence came to resemble the lives of assembly-line factory workers with this difference: at the end of the day, factory workers left the workspace and could resume normal living; their weekends were free. Walkathon contestants had neither of these options. In the walkathon, the technological mentality was pervasive and perverted play as earlier it had perverted work. The structured mechanical routine contestants were forced to follow, day and night, in the walkathon show read like a curriculum for the robopath. But there were other facets of walkathon show which made this form of show business a school for turning out robot-like creatures.

Walkathons featured a variety of sports. Jacques Ellul links sport to the technological society. He writes, "In sport, the citizen of the technical society finds the same spirit, criteria, morality, actions, and objective—in short, all the technical laws and customs—which he encounters in the office or factory" (384). Ellul notes that mechanization of action in sport, the exact measurement of time with stop watches and starting machines, the precision training of muscular action, and the principle of the "record," all repeat the essential elements of industrial life.

Ellul would have found the walkathon contest an excellent example of sport as an expression of the technological mentality. Walkathon audiences were reminded hourly of the passage of time and its wear and tear on the human body: posted daily were the number of days and hours that had elapsed since the beginning of the contest, the number of contestants and the last contestants disqualified. Other aspects of the walkathon contest expressed the technological mentality. Walkathon contestants lived by the clock: they had two minutes to leave the floor at the conclusion of the 45-minute walking act; they had 11 minutes for rest and recreation. When contestants' internal clock mechanisms wound down and no longer worked efficiently, their owners were disqualified.

At evening shows, although the repetitive hourly routine was momentarily suspended, the emphasis on measurement continued in the featured athletic events: the number of turns around the dance floor in the lap races was carefully recorded; each Dynamite Sprint was accurately timed. In the Zombie Treadmills, partners were hooked together by dog chains so that, like two cogs of a machine, the parts would not fly apart. Spectators, caught up in this spectacle of human beings turned automatons, became themselves automatons by returning compulsively, night after night, to witness the grinding down of the machine-like contestants.

Ellul observes, further, that as human beings become an extension of the machine, and as mechanical techniques of interaction become prized, the values of improvisation and spontaneity are lost in the pursuit of efficiency, records and strict rules. In his incisive analysis of the technological society, Ellul points to the paradox of mass culture in which "...the average man is inevitably conscious of the obvious crashing absurdity of life in a technical world...and must therefore becloud his consciousness at any cost...then he is in essential accord with the needs of a technical society" (383). The walkathon show highlighted this paradox of mass culture; contestants were lauded for being "the average man" to distract them from the realization that they had been reduced to mechanical objects.

But the invidious effect of the machine on American behavior and consciousness did not only erupt in the dance endurance contest. The traits and values which surfaced in this form of amusement were present in other institutions of American culture during the 1920s and 1930s. Henry Ford and Frederick Taylor, during the 1920s, championed the idea of a technological society made up of automated machines and automated factory systems. John B. Watson, aping his Russian counterpart, Ivan Pavlov, evangelized a theory of psychology in which conditioning techniques were to be the key to adjust Americans to living in a technological society. Al Capone, prototype of the godfather promoter, proved the effectiveness of the mechanistic mentality by using the machine gun and an army of automaton thugs to rule an American city.

During the 1930s, the myth of the automaton maintained its power to capture the imagination of the American people. Film producers and directors in charge of the Hollywood "Dream Machine," the Warner Brothers, Mayer, Selznick, Cohn and Goldwyn, operated their own brand of family protection racket to create automatons out of their underlings, which is to say everybody else. Not unlike walkathon promoters, these show business moguls ruled with near impunity. Samuel Goldwyn was a model of this breed of show business autocrat to the point of caricature. Nathaniel West exposed the sham side of the movie industry, a show business operation in which the authoritarian mechanistic mind held sway. The Hollywood "Dream Machine" manufactured

Apollonian fantasies and illusions to help Americans escape the hollow life of the automaton. Happily, it also created classic films of worth.

Despite the sham attendant in running walkathon shows, this entertainment medium did have redeeming features. Professional walkathon contestants, like today's disadvantaged citizens who use athletics and show business to gain access to the good life in America, had an opportunity to earn a livelihood and gain some degree of recognition as celebrities through this show business enterprise. Such opportunities were rare to come by, then and now, for men and women with limited work skill and education, for those whose only assets were athletic prowess and show business brass. But for a few genuinely talented women and men, walkathon shows were a stepping stone to more prestigious and legitimate forms of show business. Even amateur contestants, the cannon fodder of walkathon shows, did not come away from participating in walkathon shows much the worse for wear. Moreover, the dance endurance contest provided jobs for show business specialists and workers with only rudimentary work skills. Communities, though often inhospitable, profited from the income generated by walkathon shows.

It is left to the historian to make a final judgment about the worth, value and impact of this one craze on American culture. Insofar as those who participated in these events are concerned, George Eells's observation is worth noting. He conjectured that the longer people participated, the more likely inherently destructive aspects would rub off and lessen the stature of the individual. Furthermore, while many professional contestants and show personnel did not relish everything connected with working in this show business venture, particularly being exploited (not uncommon in all show business enterprises), they felt, nevertheless, that there were worse ways of making a living and receiving recognition than being part of the world of walkathon show business. In the final analysis, American audiences willing to support dance endurance shows contributed as much to this lamentable form of amusement as the show personnel only too happy to satisfy largely escapist needs and desires of Americans living in unsettled times.

Chapter Fifteen
Dance Endurance Contest

> I believe that a man's growth is a process of continuous birth, of continuous awakening. We are usually half asleep and only sufficiently awake to go about our business; but we are not awake enough to go about living, which is the only task that matters for a living being.
>
> "Credo" Erich Fromm (178)

First-time visitors to a walkathon contest must have been struck by what they saw, a mass of women and men, slumped over each other, milling around and around the dance floor as if they were sleepwalking. Often, this was literally true; as couples inched around the dance arena, one partner slept, the other acted as guide and support. Because they were deprived of normal sleep time, contestants had to try to sleep during the walking acts. But contestants in walkathon shows were sleepwalkers in more than a literal sense. They, and show personnel and audiences, exemplified what Fromm believed to be true of modern man: that we are usually half asleep, only sufficiently awake to go about our business, but not awake enough to go about living. Said another way, the format and operation of walkathon contests were like laboratories to condition the human animal to remain half asleep, to continue existence as an automaton. The mini-culture of the walkathon contest reinforced those aspects of behavior and consciousness which keep us only half awake, half alive, in a state of arrested development. The walkathon contest projected this disturbing message which resonates from the deep unconscious: our unspeakable daemon is our willingness to be conditioned to live the life of automatons.

Sleepwalking is nature's signal of psychological unrest. When Lady Macbeth walks in her sleep and gestures to rid herself of blood stains of the murdered Banquo, we guess what troubles her soul. When contestants walked in their sleep and became "squirrelly," we may guess that nature was signaling psychological unrest, the unrest attendant on being an automaton. In 1923, the year the dance endurance craze began in America, the poet William Carlos Williams wrote: "That's the trouble with us all. We're not half used up. And that unused portion drives us crazy" (Mottram 285). More recently, Dr. Frederick Perls, founder of Gestalt Therapy, writes: "I don't want to be saved, I want to be spent" (Leonard 30).

Despite the sham connected with walkathon shows where rules and regulations were circumvented as stratagems to "work heat," the restrictive and suppressive environment of walkathon show, The Innocent Jail, reinforced the repetitive, banal habits of the automaton, the robopath. Living the existence of the automaton might satisfy the security needs of contestants and hence dampen

198

the anxiety of meeting the challenges of living in modern times. Paradoxically, living the life of an automaton aroused existential anxiety as well, the anxiety which comes from living unfulfilled lives.

The world of the walkathon contest as dramatized in the film *They Shoot Horses, Don't They?* prompted some show critics to view McCoy's novel as an allegory: "Life is like a dance marathon." If life is a dance marathon, it is a sham. Life is a sham when we adopt the posture of the authoritarian personality, when we settle for the life of the celebrity in place of the hero, when we become partners in a danse macabre. Life is a fraud when we prefer repression, remaining unaware of how we are living the life of an automaton, to living with genuine spontaneous expression. Life is bogus when we choose pseudo-events as escape in place of genuine experience.

In *Civilization and its Discontents*, Freud describes the evolution of civilization as the struggle between Eros and Thanatos, the struggle between the instincts of life and the instincts of destruction. On the level of myth, these two forces are brought into play in the encounter between Apollo and Dionysus. When these brother gods covenant in the spirit of genuine play, they are models for human fulfillment; Eros triumphs. When these two forces are not in harmony, when Apollo takes a self-aggrandizing stance and Dionysus becomes his brother's nemesis, they are models for dehumanization; Thanatos triumphs. The dance endurance contest as an American amusement was more aligned with Thanatos than with Eros; as an expression of play, the dance endurance contest symbolized a Dance of Death rather than a Dance of Life.

The dance endurance contest was only one form of amusement to which Americans were drawn during the 1920s and 1930s. Certainly, all was not sham in the field of American show business. During the 1930s, one couple in their incomparable performance celebrated the human spirit through their exhibitions of ballroom dancing. To this day, both in America and abroad, Fred Astaire and Ginger Rogers are remembered for embodying in their dance style both Apollonian form and Dionysian vitality. Their inventiveness and creativity, combining "a breezy sophistication and a charming sexuality," enchanted movie audiences (Sonnenshein 500). Astaire and Rogers did restore to the popular imagination a sense of genuine playfulness through ballroom dancing. Partnered in dance, they symbolized the Dance of Life, the triumph of Eros over Thanatos.

Another instance in which Eros bested his arch rival Thanatos was in an event which took place in 1936, the year that the walkathon contest reached its zenith of popularity and notoriety (and began its slow decline). That event was the gala Harvest Moon Ball in Madison Square Garden, in New York City. In this exciting dance contest, with Ed Sullivan as emcee, a large array of ballroom teams, costumed in gowns and tuxedos, competed in American and Latin dances. Unlike the walkathon contest, dancing skill was valued in the Harvest Moon Hall. Judging was done by leading dance authorities and based on competence, on skillful and graceful performance. C.G. Jung would have viewed this apparent coincidence, the demise of the walkathon contest and the introduction of the Harvest Moon Ball, as an example of synchronicity, a sign that redemptive powers in the collective American psyche were at work.

Other examples of authentic play include the music of jazz innovators Louis Armstrong and Duke Ellington; dances such as the exciting Lindy Hop and the graceful Fox Trot; and the stage dramas, the powerful plays of Eugene O'Neill and Clifford Odet. Hollywood, at its best, could produce classic memorable films along with the preponderant dross. For example, the musical comedy came to full flower during the 1930s on stage and screen. In sports during the 1920s and 1930s, newspaper reporter Paul Gallico identified "The Golden People," American athletes like Babe Ruth, Jack Demsey, Babe Diedrickson, Big Bill Tilden and Bobby Jones, as genuine heroes, not mere celebrities, as women and men who would have graced the ancient Olympian games.

The dance endurance contest as it evolved into the walkathon show combined two forms of play: show business and sport. These two expressions continue to draw mammoth audiences attesting to the important role of play in modern times. Huizinga, in his classic study *Homo Ludens*, regards play as the basis of every culture (21). He defines play as a voluntary activity taking place within certain fixed limits of time and space according to rules freely accepted but absolutely binding. Play is not a means to an end but an end in itself. In playing, we experience feelings of tension and joy, a sense of flow. Importantly, play is freedom.

But the dance marathon as an expression of play did not meet the requirements Huizinga found essential to genuine play. By delimiting and compromising the spirit of freedom, the dance marathon contest was a travesty of play. In submitting to the regimentation of the walkathon contest, to a life of an automaton, contestants lost freedom and lost their souls.

Philosopher/theologian David Miller affirms, like Huizinga, that play defines meaning and significance in contemporary culture. As the root metaphor of the ancient Greeks was Logos, of the Jews, Covenant, and of the Chinese, the Tao, the root metaphor for modern man, according to Miller, is Play (136). Despite the importance of play in modern culture, the phenomenology of play remains a relatively uncharted territory. Play in American culture in general and American social dance in particular is yet to be explored in depth. Going back to early sources, my choice of guide to explore the hidden continent of play is Dionysus, the god of play and dance.

Dionysian consciousness continues to be misunderstood and mistrusted. It was Neitzsche in *The Gay Science* who announced the good news which Dionysus brings: life is worth living. In *Thus Spake Zarathustra*, Neitzsche's hero is a dancer who has learned to overcome gravity, the symbol of the spirit of the Devil weighing down the human will with all the burdens of life. Zarathustra is able to blend all opposites into a new unity; he exhibits no rancor; he is not a despiser of life, or of the body, or of the earth; he represents the dancing god, Dionysus, at his best. Literary critic Norman Brown notes that only Dionysian consciousness is strong enough to endure full life. In not observing limits, Dionysian consciousness overflows; it does not negate anymore (175).

The Dionysian spirit evoked by Neitzsche is found in more recent literature in Kazantzakis's novel *Zorba The Greek*. Zorba is a prototype of the dancer who lives life as play with Apollonian grace and Dionysian vitality. It is Zorba who best exemplifies the true dancer, the individual who knows how to play. Despite the terrors, horrors and burdens of existence that he has experienced, Zorba strives to be the lightest and most transcendent of beings, a dancer who attempts to overcome the laws of gravity. In joy, Zorba leaps from the ground with gaiety and exuberance; in sadness, Zorba works through his sorrow with the same spirit of abandon. Zorba dances in work and in play. He devotes the same passion when extracting coal from a mountain as he does when dancing the Slo Hasapiko, or playing his beloved instrument, the Santuri. In all he does, Zorba feels himself free. Zorba's dance is the Dance of Life. In contrast to Zorba's vital attitude toward life, walkathon show personnel lived, for the most part, an existence defined by repression and lack of genuine vitality.

Depth psychologist Otto Rank was closer to the truth than his mentor Freud in identifying man's basic drive, not as sex or aggression, but as the quest for immortality. In *The Denial of Death*, sociologist Ernest Becker cites Rank's work. According to Rank, human beings deny their humanness; we repress the knowledge that, one day, we will die. Becker identifies this repression as man's essential cowardice. Out of the anxiety that no one will remember us (and honor us), human beings seek to ensure our own immortality, through group identifications, through progeny, through creative work, and through accomplishment. In this way, we attempt to overcome the terror that, one day, we will die and be forgotten. The critical question for Rank and Becker is this: By what means and in what spirit do we seek to cheat death of final victory?

If Rank is right and our basic drive is for immortality, perhaps walkathon contestants (and walkathon fans who identified with them) may have been seeking a means, if not of becoming true heroes and heroines, at least celebrities, the object of public attention and admiration. Using the walkathon show as a way to travel the "Glory Walk" was one way to become "somebody" and may have assuaged the unconscious needs of show performers and fans in their quest for immortality.

The tragic element in the story of the dance endurance contest was that in seeking to become celebrities, those who participated in these events as contestants or audience ran the risk of regressing further as sleepwalkers. Walkathon shows reinforced the human predisposition to sleepwalk, to live in the past and the future, not in the present; to model our life on the automaton, preferring habit to change and growth; to inhabit the world of fantasy rather than reality. Sleepwalking is the mode of existence for inmates of "The Innocent Jail."

Sleepwalking, the occupation of walkathon contestants, may be the metaphor which best expresses the actions and experiences of human beings living in the twentieth century. During the 1920s and 1930s, it was sleepwalking masses who contributed to the rise of totalitarianism on a global scale, to the ascendance of the machine as a model of human consciousness and a weapon of mass destruction of man and nature. The option for modern citizens of the world is whether to continue sleepwalking or choose to awaken.

In his credo, Fromm identifies the great benefactors of humankind as those who, like Christ and the Buddha, seek to awaken us from being half asleep (178). In modern times, secular voices, writers and social scientists, voices as different as Charlie Chaplin, Nathanael West, Horace McCoy, Lewis Mumford, Jacques Ellul and Lewis Yablonsky, have alerted those who would listen to ways in which we choose to stay half asleep. One mode of being half awake is to escape through spurious play; during the 1920s and 1930s, the dance endurance contest offered just such an escape. Telling the story of the dance marathons, in exposing this mode of play as a sham, may serve a therapeutic purpose if it reminds us that we are, more often than not, only half awake. In this state of half slumber, we are closer to death than to life.

Notes

Introduction

[1] I am greatly indebted to George Eells for our several meetings and extended correspondence. Eells assisted me in contacting show personnel and professional contestants who were difficult to locate and, once found, evasive. Eells warned of the habit of professional contestants to "put people on" when inquiries were made about the operation of this form of show business. Despite the truth behind Eells's observation, a number of professional contestants who were interviewed were candid about their experiences. Most helpful were the following informants: Jimmy Priori, Johnny Makar, Louie Meredith and Noble "Kid" Chissell.

I am also indebted to Union College for several grants which enabled me to carry on this research.

[2] There is a dearth of available material on dance endurance contests. Valuable information was obtained from *The Billboard*, the leading weekly newspaper of show business. This publication began reporting news of dance endurance contests under the heading "Endurance Shows" on February 24, 1934. Don King was the first editor and was succeeded by Roger Littlefield and Bill Sacks. News of contests about to open and descriptions of events at ongoing shows were reported. Contestants used this source to keep in contact with former teammates and friends from walkathon shows. This publication was also used by show personnel to air problems related to the operation of walkathon shows and as a forum for ideas and useful practices. Within two years, notices began to dwindle. In the July 5, 1941 issue, the name was changed to "Derby Show News." The last reference to this show business enterprise appeared in the Dec. 25, 1943 issue.

Beyond this source, there is a spate of newspaper reports, often sensational accounts which exposed the collusive practices between some dance marathon operator and a local law enforcement agency. Periodically, on the front pages of yellow-journal newspapers, appeared the accounts of crusading, civic-minded women and clergy groups who demanded that dance marathons be banned due to allegedly immoral practices.

Several scrapbooks found in public and private collections containing photos and accounts of dance marathon shows proved of some use. Invaluable was Lawrence Mathews's *Scrapbook:* Dance Marathon Clippings, Tickets, Announcements, Business Cards and Correspondence 1929-1942. This document is available on microfilm at the Dance Research Library, Lincoln Center for the Performing Arts, New York Public Library.

Martin completed a doctoral dissertation *A History of the American Dance Marathon* in 1991. I found this valuable source after I had completed this manuscript.

[3] Literary and film documents consulted in this analysis of the endurance contest are the following sources: *They Shoot Horses, Don't They?*, a novel written by Horace McCoy; *They Shoot Horses, Don't They?* a film (the screenplay written by Robert E.

Thompson and directed by Sidney Pollock); *Marathon 33*; a play by June Havoc, excerpted from her autobiographical novel, *Early Havoc*; *The Glory Walk*, an unpublished play, by George Eells; *High Times, Hard Times*, an autobiography by Anita O'Day; *The Benefits of American Life*, a short story, by James Farrell, who also describes a dance marathon contest in the last book of his trilogy *Studs Lonigan*, in the volume entitled "Judgment Day"; *The Lone Pioneer*, a short story by William Wilson; *Marathon*, an unpublished play, by Isabel Dawn and Boyce DeGaw, and *The Dancing Madness*, a novel by Mildred Ames.

In addition to these sources, at least two films were released between 1931 and 1933, one entitled, *Marathon Dance*; the other film, *Hard To Handle*, in which a marathon dance was featured, starred James Cagney in the role of a dynamic publicity agent. In the opening sequence of *Hard to Handle*, one spectator among hundreds of persons watching two surviving couples at a marathon dance remarks that she regrets "having to wait a long time before someone drops dead!" See *New York Times Review*, 21:5 (1933): F2.

The reader is cautioned that each of the literary sources does not carry the same authoritative weight. McCoy, a seasoned reporter, was a bouncer in two walkathon shows which took place near the Hollywood area during the early 1930s. Havoc and O'Day were 14 years old when they participated in a number of walkathon contests over a two-year period during the mid-1930s. (Eells assisted June Havoc and Anita O'Day with their manuscripts). Farrell, Wilson and Ames were spectators at one or more dance endurance contests during the 1930s.

Sydney Pollock, who directed the filming of McCoy's novel, disclaimed that he was making a documentary of dance marathons. Nonetheless, Noble "Kid" Chissell, who acted as advising consultant, reported that Pollock was "a stickler for realism." Pollock put the cast (and himself) through strenuous paces by making "the whole cast go strictly heel and toe around the huge replica of the dance floor for ten times until he got the fatigued expression he wanted." See *Hollywood Independent*, 4 Sept. 1969. Parenthetically, both film director Sidney Pollock and McCoy pointed up the barbarism implicit in this form of entertainment though they underplayed the fact that walkathons were, first and foremost, show business.

⁴Wellek has identified three approaches to literary criticism as "non literary" techniques and bodies of knowledge which draw upon psychology as a primary source. See Wellek, Rene, *Yale Review*, Fall, 1961. See also Scott, Wilbur, *Five Approaches of Literary Criticism*, Macmillan Publ. Co., N.Y., 1962. These three approaches are summarized as follows:

Psychoanalytic literary criticism, originally based on Freud's theories, presents an image of man as a victim of biology in bondage to his libidinal compulsions. Man, in this view, is a victim of the environment and the repressions society forces upon him. The psychoanalytic critic seeks to uncover these sources of victimization and to search for the unconscious patterns which motivate a character. Importantly, in this study of play, attention is given to manifestations of the repressed unconscious which surface in symptoms, complexes and dreams.

Mythic literary criticism associated with the works of Frazer and Jung affirms the validity of myth as man's natural participation in the collective unconscious. The critic's aim is to decode the forgotten language of myth and the collective dream in order to identify the presence of archetypal motifs and figures and, hence, to discover basic cultural patterns which assume a mythic quality in their permanence within a particular society.

Existential literary criticism is a phenomenology, an attitude which attempts to reconstruct the author's intentionality, his relation to time and space, to nature and society. Schiller's goal of aesthetic education, "to recover the world by making us see it not as it is, but as if it had its source in human freedom," reflects the stance of the existential critic.

Works Cited

Allen, Frederich L. *The Big Change*. New York, 1952. "When America Learned to Dance," *Scribner's Magazine* 102, September 1937.

Allsop, Steward. *The Bootleggers and Their Era*. New York: Doubleday, 1961.

Ames, Mildred. *The Dancing Madness*. New York: Delacorte P, 1980.

Armens, Sven. *Archetypes of the Family in Literature*. Seattle: U of Washington P, 1966.

Becker, Ernest. *The Denial of Death*. New York: The Free P, 1973.

Berne, Eric. *Games People Play*. New York: Grove P, 1964.

Bernstein, Leonard. *The Unanswered Question: Six Talks at Harvard*. Cambridge: Harvard UP, 1976

The Billboard 26 April 1933.
        17 Feb. 1934.
        14 April 1934.
        26 April 1934.
        25 Aug.1934.
        29 Sept. 1934.
        20 Oct. 1934
        8 Dec.1934.
        29 Dec. 1934.
        2 Feb. 1935.
        17 March 1935.
        24 March 1935.
        8 June 1935.
        29 June 1935.
        31 Aug. 1935.
        28 Sept.1935
        12 Oct.1935
        19 Oct. 1935
        26 Oct.1935
        13 Nov. 1935.
        16 Nov. 1935.
        30 Nov. 1935.
        7 Dec. 1935.
        21 Dec. 1935.
        16 Jan. 1936.
        1 Feb. 1936.
        12 Feb. 1936.
        16 Feb. 1936.
        28 March 1936.
        15 Jan. 1938.

29 Jan. 1938.

27 March 1938.

23 July 1938.

24 Sept. 1938.

27 Jan. 1940

17 Feb. 1940.

16 March 1940.

10 May 1941.

7 June 1941.

2 May 1942.

23 May 1942.

26 Sept. 1942

18 Oct.1942.

5 June 1943.

Bird, Caroline *The Invisible Scar*. New York: David McKay Co., 1966.

Bly, Robert. Iron John: *A Book About Men*. New York: Addison-Wesley Pub. Co., 1990.

Bogardus, Emory. *Fundamentals of Social Psychology*. New York: Appleton-Century Co., 1942.

Boorstin, Daniel. *The Image: Or What Happened To The American Dream*. New York: Atheneum, 1962.

Bowron, Leo Marx and Arnold Ross. "Literature and Covert Culture." *Studies in American Culture*. Eds. J. Kwait and M. Turpie. Minneapolis: U of Minnesota P, 1960.

Broun, Heywood. "Waltz Me Around Again, Willie." *Vanity Fair*, Sept. 1928, Vol. 31.

Brown, Norman. *Life Against Death*. New York: Random House, 1959.

Buber, Martin. *I and Thou*. New York: Scribner's Sons, 1958. *Buffalo Evening News*, Jan. 20, 1933.

Cable, Mary. *American Manners and Morals: A Picture History of How We Behaved and Misbehaved*. New York: American Heritage Pub. Co. Inc., 1969.

Cable, Mary and The Editors of American Heritage. *American Manners and Morals*. New York: American Heritage Pub. Co. Inc., 1969.

Calabria, Frank. "The Dance Marathon Craze." *Journal of Popular Culture* X:1, 54-69.

Campbell, Joseph. *The Hero With A Thousand Faces*. New York: Pantheon Books, 1949.

Camus, Albert. *The Myth of Sisyphus and Other Essays*. Trans. Justin O'Brien. New York: Random House, 1959.

_____.*The Plague*. Trans. Stuart Gilbert. New York, The Modern Library, 1948.

Capek, Karel. *R.U.R.* New York: Doubleday, 1923.

Chaplin, Charles, dir. *Modern Times*. Film, 1936.

Chissell, Noble "Kid." Interviews in Hollywood, 1971.

Cohen, David. *J.B. Watson, The Founder of Behaviorism, A Biography*. London: Routledge & Kegan Paul, 1979.

Coleman, Lee. "What is American?" *The Character of Americans: A Book of Reading*., Ed. Michael McGiffort. Illinois: The Dorsey P, 1964.

Collier, 23, July, 1932.

Craven, Gerald and Richard Mosely. "Actors on the Canvas Stage: The Dramatic Conventions of Professional Wrestling." *Journal of Popular Culture* Fall, 1972,

6:2.

Davis, Maxine. *The Lost Generation: A Portrait of Youth Today*. New York: Macmillan Co., 1936.

Dawn, Isable & Boyce DeGaw. *Marathon*. Unpublished play. 1933.

Drama Research Public, Lincoln Center for the Performing Arts, New York Public Library.

Dement, William C. *Some Must Watch Wile Others Must Sleep*. San Francisco: W.H. Freeman and Company, 1972.

DeRopp, Robert. *The Master Game: Pathways to Higher Consciousness Beyond The Drug Experience*. New York: Delacorte P, 1968.

Eells, George. *The Glory Walk*. Unpublished Play. 1952. Drama Research Library, Public Library, Lincoln Center for the Performing Arts, New York Public Library.

_____.Letter, 12 Nov. 1970.

_____."Some 20,000 were in Marathon Dance Biz at Zenith of Craze." *Variety*, 7 Jan. 1970.

Elliot, T.S. "The Hollow Men." *Collected Poems 1909-1935*. New York: Harcourt, Brace and Company, Inc., 1936.

_____."The Waste Land." *Collected Poems 1909-1935*. New York: Harcourt, Brace and Company, Inc., 1936.

Ellul, Jacques. *The Technological Society*. New York: Alfred A. Knopf, 1964.

Erenberg, L. *Steppin' Out, New York Nightlife and the Transformation of American Culture, 1890-1930*. Chicago: The U of Chicago P, 1981.

Farber, Stephen and Marc Green. *Hollywood Dynasties*. New York: Deliah/Putnam Pub. Co., 1984.

Fancher, Raymond E. *Pioneers of Psychology*. New York: W.W. Norton, 1979.

Faraday, Ann. *Dream Power*. New York: Coward, McCann and Geoghegan Inc., 1972.

Farrell, James T. "The Benefits of American Life." *The Short Stories of James T. Farrell*. New York: Halcyon House, 1941.

_____.*Studs Lonigan, Judgement Day*. New York: The New American Library, 1958.

Field, Edward. "The Life of Joan Crawford." *Mirror of Man: Readings in Sociology and Literature*. Ed. Jane Dabaghaian. New York: Little, Brown & Co., 1970.

Freud, Sigmund. *Civilization and Its Discontents*. Trans. Jane Strachey. New York: W.W. Norton and Co., 1961.

Fromm, Erich. *Beyond The Chains of Illusion*. New York: Simon and Shuster, 1962.

Gabler, Neal. *An Empire Of Their Own*. New York: Crown Publishers, 1988.

Gallico, Paul. *The Golden People*. New York: Doubleday & Co., 1965.

Geertz, Clifford. "Deep Play: Notes on the Balinese Cockfight." *The Interpretation of Culture*. New York: Basic Books, 1973.

Gingrich, Arnold. "Poor Man's Night Club," *Esquire*. Autumn 1933.

Green, Abel and Joe Laurie, Jr. *Show Biz from Vaude to Video*. New York: Henry Holt & Co., 1951.

Haber, Samuel. *Efficiency and Uplift: Scientific Management in the Progressive Era 1890-1920*. Chicago: The U of Chicago P, 1964.

Havoc, June. "Marathon 33." New York: Dramatists Play Service Inc., 1969.

_____.*Early Havoc*. New York: Simon and Shuster, 1959.

Harkins, William E. *Karel Capek*. New York: Columbia UP, 1961.

Haskell, Molly. "Epic! Heroic! American!" *N.Y. Times Book Review*, 23 Oct. 1988.

Hillman, James. *Re-Visioning Psychology*. New York: Harper & Row, Pub., 1974.

Hoffman, E.T.A. "The Sandman." *The Best Tales of Hoffman*. New York: Dover Publications, Inc., 1967.

Hollywood Independent 28 Aug. 1969.

_____.4 Sept. 1969.

Hollywood Studio Magazine June 1970.

Huizinga, Johann. *Homo Ludens: A Study of the Play Element in Culture*. Boston: The Beacon P, 1950.

_____."Fascination with the Dance of Death," *The History of Popular Culture*, Ed. Norman Cantor and Michael Wertham. New York, Macmillan Co., 1968.

The Irish Echo, 30 April, 1932.

Johnson, Nora. "Novelists in the Dram Factory." *New York Times*, Section 7, 4 Nov. 1984.

Johnston, Alva. *The Great Goldwyn*. New York: Random House, 1937.

Journal of Social Hygiene, Forum, 20 March 1934.

Kaplan, Richard. "An Appeal to Reason." *The Billboard* 29 June 1935.

_____."Are Walkathons Lawful?" *The Billboard* 2 Feb. 1935.

Kazantzakis, Nikos. *Zorba The Greek*. Trans. Carl Wildman. New York: Simon and Shuster, Inc., 1963.

Keen, Sam. *To a Dancing God*. New York: Harper & Row, 1970.

King, Don. "Old Time Marathon Revived, Goes 107 Hours," *The Billboard* 31 August 1935.

Levi, Albert. "Existentialism and the Alienation of Man," *Phenomenology and Existentialism*. Eds. E. Lee and M. Mandelbaum. Baltimore: The Johns Hopkins UP, 1967.

Literary Digest. "Tripping The Long, Hard Fantastic For A Record." 5 May 1923.

Makar, Johnny. Personal Interview in California. 1971.

Martin, Carol. Interview with Betty Herndon Meyer. *New Observations*, 39:11-15, 1986.

_____.Interview with George Eells. *New Observations* 39, 1986.

_____.Interview with Richard Elliot. *New Observation* 4 April 1985.

_____."Dance Marathons 'For No Good Reason'," *The Drama Review* 31.1 (Spring 1987).

Martin, Carol Joyce. "A History of the American Dance Marathon." DAI 52 (1991): 9124744.

Marx, Leo. *The Machine in the Garden*. New York: Oxford UP, 1964.

Mathews, Lawrence. *Scrapbook: Dance Marathon Clippings, Tickets, Announcements, Business Cards and Correspondence, 1929-1942*.

_____.Patsy Salmon.

_____.Hal J. Ross Souvenir Farewell Program, 28 Feb. 1941.

_____.*New York Daily Mirror* 2 May 1932.

_____."5 Couples Dance 106 Days, Labor Law May Stop 'em." *The Evening World* 3 March 1930.

_____."Dance Contest Ends as Bishop Calls in Police." 28 May 1933.

_____.*Sunday Herald*. "Circus Hot Stuff: Title Lures Children into 'Naughty' Show; Free-For-All Hushed."

May, Rollo. *Symbolism in Religion and Literature*. New York: George Braziller, 1960.

McCoy, Horace. *They Shoot Horses, Don't They?* New York: Avon Books, 1969.

_____.*They Shoot Horses, Don't They?* Screenplay by Robert E. Thompson. New York: Avon Books, 1960.

Merloo, Joost A. *The Dance*. New York: Chilton Company,1960.

Miller, David. *Gods and Games: Toward a Theology of Play*. New York: The World Publishing Company, 1970.

Miller, Leslie. "Intervention For What? The Question of Paternalism." *Phenomenology and Pedagogy* 2.1.

Mills, C. Wright. *The Sociological Imagination*. New York: Pelican, 1970.

Mottram, Eric. "Living Mythically: The Thirties." *Journal of Popular Culture* 6, Dec. 1972.

_____."Living Mythically: The Thirties." *Journal of American Studies* 6, Dec. 1972.

Mumford, Lewis. *The Myth of the Machine: The Pentagon of Power*. New York: Harcourt, Brace, Jovanovich, Inc., 1964.

Nelson, Daniel. *Frederick W. Taylor and the Rose of Scientific Management*. London: The U of Wisconsin P, 1980.

Neumann, Erich. *The Great Mother*. New York: Pantheon Books, 1963.

Nevins, Allan with the collaboration of Frank Ernest Hill, *Ford*. New York: Scribner, 1954.

New York Times. "Girl Seeing Things as Dance Drag On." 20 June 1928.

_____." 'Mutiny' Quelled in Dance Marathon," 27 June 1928.

_____ "Harlem Derby opens under J. Lazarro," 13 June 1928.

_____.11 April, 1923.

_____.15 April 1923.

_____.6 May 1923.

_____.7 Aug. 1923.

Nietzsche, Friedrich. *Thus Spake Zarathustra*. Baltimore, Maryland: Penguin Books, 1961.

_____.*The Gay Science*. New York: Random House, 1974.

Nye, Russell. "Saturday Night At the Paradise Ballroom: or, Dance Halls in the Twenties," *Journal of Popular Culture* 6:1 (Summer 1974).

O'Brien, Edward J. *The Dance of the Machines*. New York: The Macaulay Co., 1929.

O'Day, Anita. *High Times, Hard Times*. New York: G.P. Putnam's Sons, 1981.

Pasley, Fred. *Al Capone: The Biography of a Self-Made Man*. New York: Ives Washburn Pub. Co., 1930.

Perlman, Everett and G.W. Nelson. *The Marathon Guide*. Unpublished booklet, 1929.

Pollock, Sydney. Forward to the Sceenplay *They Shoot Horses, Don't They?* New York: Avon Books, 1966.

Powermaker, Hortense. *Hollywood: The Dream Factory*. Boston: Little, Brown & Co., 1950.

Ripton, Ray."Singer Frankie Laine: He Could've Danced for Days and Did!" *Los Angeles Times* 29 Nov 1970.

Rogers, Agnes. *I Remember Distinctly*. New York: Harper, 1947.

Rorty, James. "Where Life Is Better: An Unsentimental Journey." *The American Writer and the Great Depression*, Ed. Harvey Swados. New York: Bobbs-Merrill Co.,

1966.

Sann, Paul. *Fads, Follies, and Delusions of the American People*. New York: Crown Publishers Inc., 1967.

Sartre, Jean-Paul. *Being and Nothingness*. Trans. Hazel E. Barnes, New York: Citadel P, 1965.

Schwartz, Teddy. Personal Interview in Manhattan, 1980.

Scott, Jimmy. "We Danced All Night—And All Day," *Ballroom Dance Magazine* July 1961.

Seligson, Marcia. *The Eternal Bliss Machine*. New York: William Morrow & Co., 1973.

Seltzer, Leo. "What future—Walkathons?" *The Billboard* 29 Dec 1934.

_____.Telephone conversation, 1974.

Shelley, Mary. *Frankenstein*. New York: Pyramid Books, 1957.

Simonson, Harold. *The Closed Frontier: Studies in American Literary Tragedy*. New York: Holt, Rinehart & Winston, 1970.

Sobel, Bernard. *A Pictorial History of Vaudeville*. New York: The Citadel P, 1961.

Sonnenshein, Richard. "Dance: Its Past and Its Promise on Film." *Journal of Popular Culture* 12.3 (1978).

Sorrell, Walter. *Dance In Its Time*. New York: Columbia UP, 1986.

Stearns, Marshall and Jean Stearns. *Jazz Dance, The Story of The American Vernacular Dance*. New York: The Macmillan Co., 1968.

Sturak, John T. *The Life and Writings of Horace McCoy: 1987-1955*. Diss., U of California, Los Angeles, 1975.

Suckow, Ruth. "Hollywood Gods and Goddesses," *Harpers* 173 (June-Nov., 1936).

Survey. "Dance Marathoners." 70 (Feb. 1934).

Swados, Harvey, ed. *The American Writer and the Great Depression*. Indianapolis: The Bobbs-Merrill Co., 1966.

Terkel, Studs. *Hard Times*. New York: Avon Books, 1971.

Thurber, James. "Onwards and Upwards with the Arts: Soapland." *The New Yorker*. Part 1 (15 May 1948).

_____.*The New Yorker*. Part 5 (24 July 1948).

Toll, Robert. *On With The Show*. New York: Oxford UP, 1976.

Tyler, Parker. *Magic and Myth of the Movies*. New York: Simon, 1947.

Watson, John B. *Behaviorism*. 2nd ed. New York: Norton, 1930

_____.*Psychological Care*. New York: Arno P, 1928.

Webster's New International Dictionary of the English Language, 2nd ed. Unabridged. Springfield Mass: G. & C. Merrian Co. Pub., 1940.

West, Nathanael. *The Complete Works of Nathanael West*. New York: Farrar, Straus and Cudahy, 1957.

Whisenhunt, D. "The Bard in the Depression: Texas Style." *Journal of Popular Culture* 2 (Winter 1968).

Wilson, William E. "Hollywood's Dance of Death," *New Republic*. 89 (26 July 1939).

_____."The Lone Pioneer," *Literary America* Feb. 1935.

Yablonsky, Lewis. *Robopaths: People as Machines*. Baltimore: Penguin Books Inc., 1972.

Yellis, Kenneth A. "Prosperity's Child: Some Thoughts on the Flapper." *American Quarterly* 12.1 (Spring 1969).

Zaleznik, Abraham. *Frederick Taylor, A Study in Personality and Innovation.* Cambridge: MIT P, 1970.

Index

1920s, 147, 150, 159, 160.
1930s, 18, 65, 66, 88, 124, 129, 173-176, 182.
Allen, Frederick Lewis, 19, 159, 172.
amateur and local contestants, 32, 57, 65.
American traits and values, 190-192.
Apollonian values in walkathons, 148; in culture, 160, 163, 166, 168, 169, 187.
appeal of shows, 52, 80, 179; power of purchase, 64; sado-machochism, 64, 128.
archetypal references in literature; anima, 131, 135; Great Father, 133, 148; Great Mother, 131, 133, 134, 148, 154; shadow, 130, 135.
Astaire, Fred & Ginger Rogers, 199.
athletic acts, as sport, 18, 21, 32, 52, 195; and lap races, 35, 80, 83; and sprint races, 37, 72, 80; and Zombie Treadmills, 151. See also programs.
audience, 22-25, 32, 54, 82, 88, 142, 147; "marathonitis," 34, 48, 72; sporting element, 142.
Ballroom Dance Marazine, 11.
Bernstein, Leonard, 187.
Billboard, 10, 17-20, 22, 24, 25, 28, 32, 34, 35, 38-41, 43-47, 49.
Bird, Caroline, 18, 24.
Bogardus, Emory, 1.
burlesque, 2, 24, 62, 177.
cabaret, 6, 31, 52.
Campbell, Joseph, 130.
Camus, Albert, 141.
celebrities at shows, 20, 27.
Chaplin, Charlie, 186, 187.
Clark, Earl, 25, 27, 47.
closing a show; grind period, 83; "non-stop," 36; positive elimination feature, 88; and victory ball, 33.
cock fight, 191, 194. See also Gertz.
Coleman, Lee, 190.
collusion and chicanery, 38, 56, 64, 123, 192; family protection racket, 123-125; "putting fans on," 81; salaries, 57; "taking a fall," 38; team effort, 71;

two-handed games, 123.
comedians, role of, 24, 61.
court decisions, 38, 41.
covert culture, 151.
cultural milieu; flappers, 1; hard times, 36, 37; psychology, 164-167; social dancing, 5, 6, 172. See also covert culture, radio, 1920s, 1930s.
dance marathons, 10, 48; and blacks, 16.
Dance Derby of the Century, 11, 15.
dances: Charleston, 1, 102; foxtrot, 12; lindy hop, 15, 16; tango, 21, 22, 172.
Day of the Locust, 184, 185.
depth psychology; role of collective unconscious, 131, 138, 153; oedipus complex, 126.
Dionysian values in walkathons, 148; in culture, 161, 173, 174, 175, 181, 184.
disqualification, 29; ceremony, 88.
drugs (called tea), 31, 70, 74.
Dunlap, "Pop," 35, 39, 49.
Eells, George, 2, 17, 27, 37-39, 47, 125, 130, 137, 155.
Elliot, Richard, 22.
Ellul, Jacques, 195, 196.
emcee, role of, 24, 39, 46, 61, 81, 122, 138.
endurance records; earliest in U.S.A., 5; in England, 6; as fad in U.S.A. (see Literary Digest) 8; as dance marathon, 15; as walkathon, without athletic features, 28; as solo in walkathon, 28.
eroticism, 73; and snake room, 74.
ethics of, 142, 157; and opportunism, 125.
fads and crazes, 5-7, 21; bunion derbies, 1; flag pole sitting, 1; roller derbies, 35, 49, 80.
floor judges, 25-27, 46, 63, 64, 77, 122; names for, 25, 149, 150.
Ford, Henry, 160, 161.
Freud, Sigmund, 126, 167, 193, 199.
Fromm, Erich, 198.
Geertz, Clifford, 191.
"going squirrely," 77.
Goldwyn, Samuel, 181.

213

CPSIA information can be obtained
at www.ICGtesting.com
Printed in the USA
FFOW04n1501081116
29082FF